THE BRASSERIE COOKBOOK

70 RECIPES TO EAT AND DRINK À LA FRANÇAISE

NOUVELLE GARDE

The BRASSERIE COOKBOOK

70 RECIPES TO DRINK AND EAT À LA FRANÇAISE

Photography by Pierre Lucet-Penato
Food Styling by Garlone Bardel

Hardie Grant
NORTH AMERICA

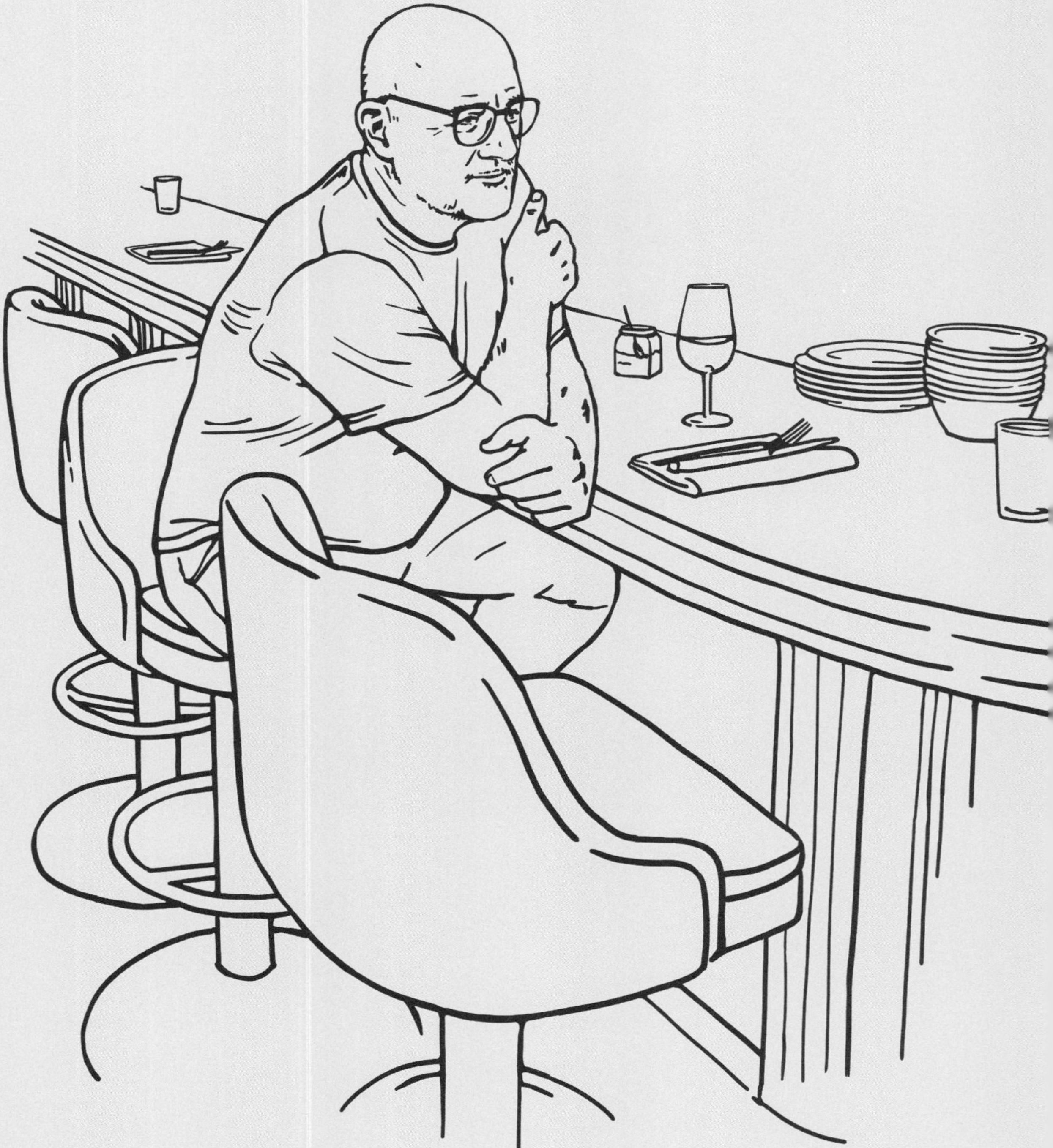

I watched this restaurant come to life daily as I passed by it on my commute to work. Each morning and evening, a bit more of its new interior décor and vibrantly colored façade was revealed. Finally, on April 24, 2019, Brasserie Bellanger opened its doors—the first of the Nouvelle Garde restaurant group's brasseries was officially in business.

On the day of the very first lunch service, I hesitantly pushed open the restaurant's doors. The staff greeted me warmly and invited me to choose my seat. Without much thought, I grabbed a stool and sat at the counter.

Once seated, I realized I was in for a treat. I was in the heart of the kitchen, facing the cooks and pastry chefs. The staff sprang into action, attentive as the chef shouted orders in a voice that was commanding and calm at the same time. The clang of the pots and pans and the aromas drifting from the kitchen stirred childhood memories of vacations at my grandmother's house, playing in the kitchen while she prepared meals.

Since that day, Brasserie Bellanger has become "my cantine," as I affectionately call it. I return every afternoon, eager to savor their dishes and soak in the brasserie's vibrant atmosphere. Here, the menu is simple, but simplicity is never dull.

The quality of each meal is a result of the dedication behind it—the commitment to using only the freshest produce and highest-quality products, and to sourcing these ingredients locally—and the pride taken in forging relationships with the farmers.

These values are reflected in every dish, from BB's famed croque monsieur (a signature dish that put the restaurant on the map) to the sausage and mash, the catch of the day, or the steak tartare. The *plat du jour* is always a welcome surprise, and the starters and desserts are not to be missed. From the sausage to the au jus, everything here is homemade.

My hope is that this cookbook inspires you to turn on the oven and share these dishes around a table filled with family or friends. Or to grab a table at Brasserie Bellanger, Brasserie Dubillot, or Brasserie Des Près and experience the work of these talented teams for yourself.

By Christophe,
Brasserie Bellanger's first "regular"

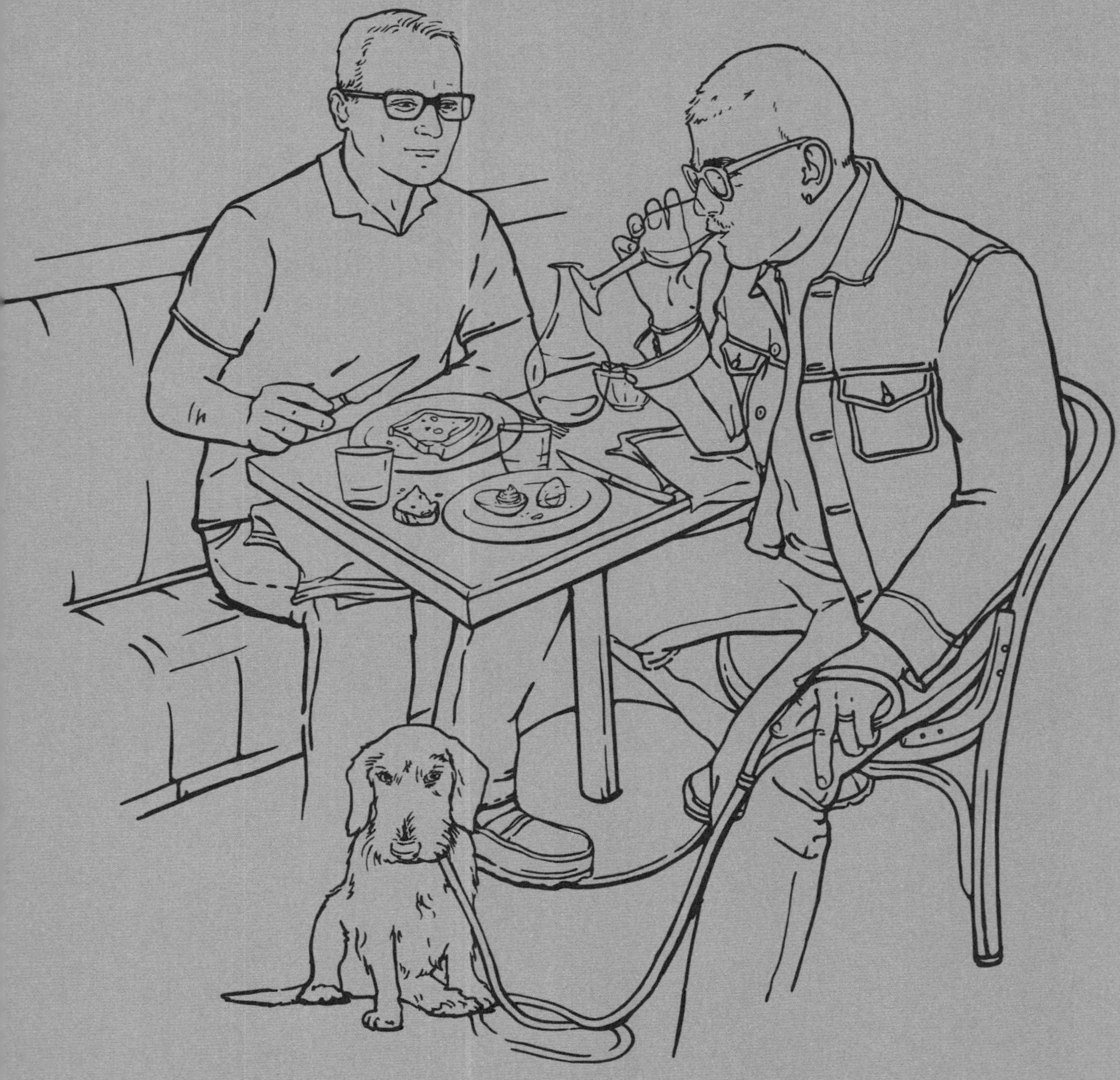

It all began with a plastic banner. That was our first encounter with La Nouvelle Garde restaurant group: a simple banner announcing the future opening of Brasserie Bellanger. Standing in front of this sign a few years ago, my husband and I looked at each other and said, "Finally, maybe we'll have a stylish restaurant in the neighborhood!" We took note of the opening date and made sure to return. The moment we stepped inside, we discovered a warm atmosphere, a welcoming crew, and two founders who cared for the brasserie as though it were their child. Young, charismatic, and a bit mischievous, they embarked on an adventure several years ago, and we have been following it ever since.

That first meal at Bellanger was quickly deemed a success. The entire team is wonderful—stressed to the max, but professional and always in good spirits. The sausage and mash transported us straight back to childhood and the Paris-Brest blew our minds. We were hooked, but the adventure was only beginning. We've enjoyed meals, each one better than the last, gained a few extra pounds, knocked back gin and tonics a little too quickly, and shared endless laughter each evening with Victor and Charly's teams.

We quickly became regular customers at the brasserie. We've brought our friend group here and it's become the place where we celebrate birthdays and raise our glasses to good wine, good food, and good friends. And as La Nouvelle Garde continues to open brasseries across the city, we continue to discover more places to gather, as a couple or with a group.

La Nouvelle Garde has become our neighborhood bar, and in a way, we have become the pillars of their counter.

A heartfelt thank-you to everyone with whom we have enjoyed—and continue to enjoy—sharing conversation, laughter, and drinks: Charles, Clément, Steven, Thibault, Peter, AD, Margaux, PA, Adrien, Victor, Charly, and all the others.

By Patrick, Renaud, and Ilang,
Regulars at all La Nouvelle Garde's brasseries

INTRO

The Parisian brasserie was born at the end of the 19th century, when innkeepers from Alsace-Lorraine fled to the city to escape German occupation. They brought with them traditions of beer and *choucroute* and quickly began erecting spectacular Parisian beer halls. These vibrant embassies of gastronomic culture gradually transformed into the establishments we know today, offering an incomparable ambiance, lively atmosphere, steaming plates, and spirited conviviality. These iconic brasseries popped up near clubs, theaters, and cabarets and became the first stop of the evening for Parisians looking to feast before a night out on the town.

Adorned with traditional wood-paneled walls, gilded chandeliers, ornate frescoes, gleaming brass bars, moleskin banquettes, and mirrored ceilings, the Belle Epoque was the golden age of the Parisian brasserie. They offered tableside service, traditional dishes, extended hours of operation, and an unparalleled atmosphere that was somewhere between a friendly celebration and an intellectual frenzy. Within the walls echoed the whispers of Guillaume Apollinaire, Joséphine Baker, Jacques Offenbach, Honoré de Balzac, and even Gustave Flaubert . . . these sanctuaries of socialization have surely collected more stories than any book could tell. More than one of these establishments and their restaurateurs have been recognized, like the Grand Colbert, classified as a French historical monument in 1974, or Louis Bignon, the first restaurateur to receive the Legion of Honor in 1868.

For us, traditional brasserie is the very embodiment of the French *art de vivre* and a true cornerstone of our cultural heritage. Over time, it has become a pillar of social and cultural life in Paris. And so, we wanted to keep the party going—but in our own way, preserving the soul of the traditional brasserie while also pushing the boundaries. We maintained its spirit, but we're breathing new life into it.

We began by opening up the kitchens and installing bars to accommodate more guests. We reimagined every detail, down to our cooks' uniforms, because we wanted to create a welcoming atmosphere. From the very beginning, we made a promise to maintain fair prices and to never serve a single bite that doesn't respect our mission: to source strictly French products and locally-raised seasonal produce, and to create all dishes using only the freshest produce. Yes, we're putting it all on the table—along with all the sacred classics of French cuisine.

We set out to create more than just restaurants, and our teams are the heart of everything we do. With an apprenticeship program and personal development opportunities, we are a place where ambitions thrive. We are a home to future generations of cooks, servers, and maybe even restaurateurs. With this vision in mind, we want to continue to enrich the Parisian dining scene while expanding across France and England so that everyone has a place to gather whenever the craving strikes.

NOUVELLE GARDE

TABLE OF CONTENTS

THE ART OF SETTING THE TABLE
17

MENU PLANNER
20

PANTRY STAPLES
22

STARTERS
27

MEAT
69

FISH
105

VEGGIE MAINS
129

SIDE DISHES
145

DESSERTS
167

BASE RECIPES
205

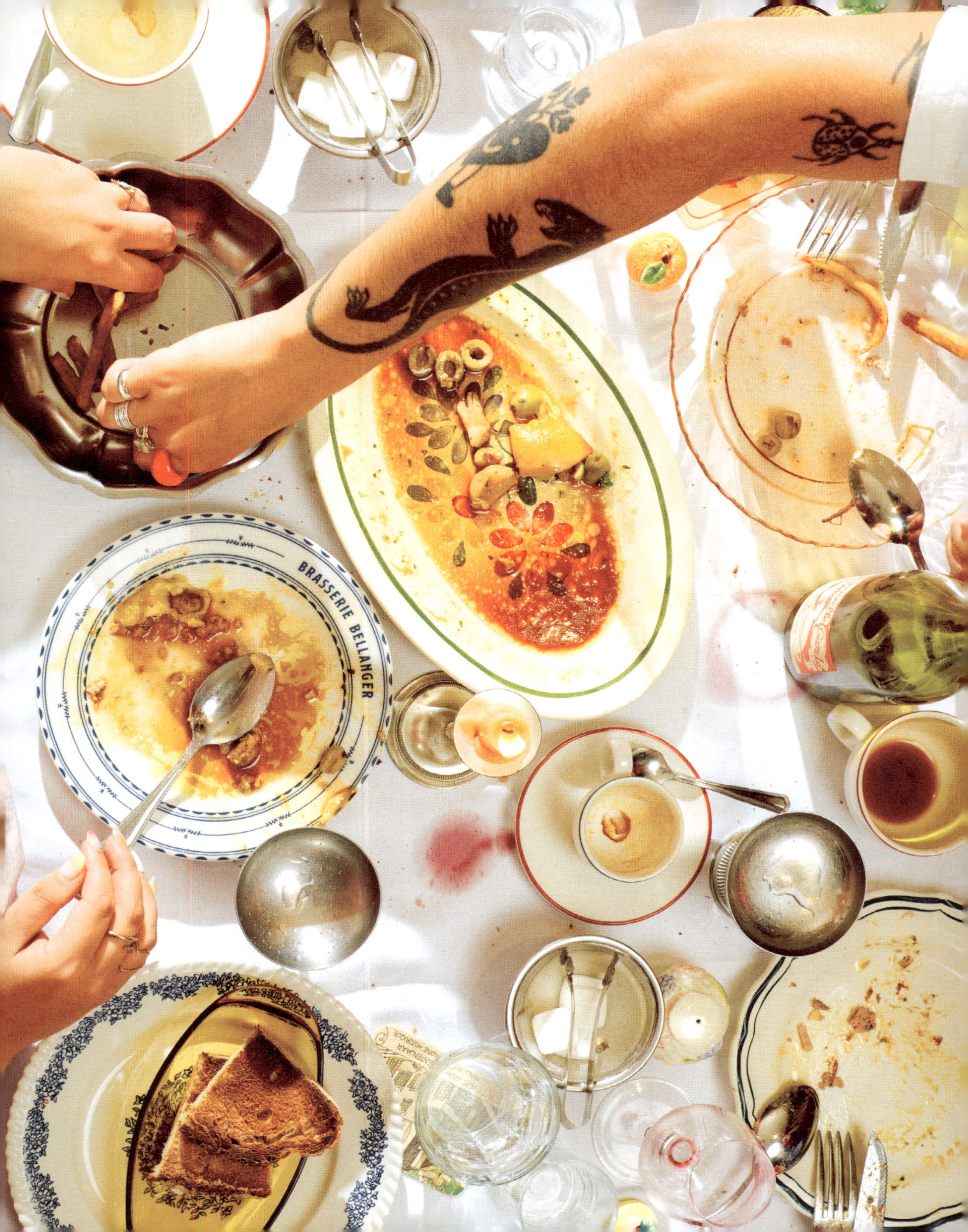
BRASSERIE BELLANGER

The Art of Setting the
TABLE

Whether your table is elegantly laid or simply set, draped in linen or bare, trendy or classic, quiet or loud... it doesn't matter, as long as you sit down and enjoy.

From antiquity to the present day, the opulent art of setting the table has elevated the traditional French meal. Today, the French gastronomic meal and its rituals are officially recognized as part of the intangible cultural heritage of humanity.

We have identified seven *petites madeleines* throughout history which demonstrate how our relationship with the table has gradually evolved beyond its original function of nourishment to become one of the cornerstones of our legendary French *art de vivre*.

— Mealtimes have captivated people since antiquity. Even though they were more like testosterone-filled feasts in those days, Plato and Xenophon each devoted entire books to the art of the banquet. Through these two Greek aesthetes, we learn that the "after-party" is far from a modern invention. At the time, banquets were held in two stages. The first was dedicated solely to the meal: chitchat was forbidden, and no thought was given to what was being eaten. The second was the symposium, which means "drinking together." As its name implies, the symposium was much less boring and much more social. Wine flowed freely, and the gathering transformed into a lively intellectual exchange with a series of learned discourse delivered by guests. The table became a stage for conversation, oration, and recollection.

— The dining table became theatrical during the Renaissance. Dancers, acrobats, and musicians performed, and the table transformed into a lively stage. Guests were seated on the same side of the table with a front row seat to the spectacle before them, accompanied by a lively soundtrack. The pirouettes eventually subsided, and perhaps the fanfare was a bit *too much* at times, but one thing remains certain: there is an underlying consensus that a meal should never be enjoyed without music.

— The concept of a dining room being a space dedicated to meals first emerged in the 17th century. At the time, this idea was motivated by the desire for intimacy, but it would take another century before the dining table claimed a permanent spot in the home. The 18th century marked the beginning of dedicated rooms for different activities, but the permanent dining table did not make its grand entrance until the reign of Louis XVI. Before that, mealtimes were dictated by hunger, and "setting the table" was as simple as placing a large wooden plank on trestles.

— In the second half of the 17th century, dining became an art form. Gourmet literature was born, paving the way for the elaborate new tableware designed to showcase the latest culinary creations. The medieval habit of drowning dishes in spices to mask the flavor of gamey meat was left behind. In its place, "modern" cuisine emerged, with more sophisticated and refined dishes. This cuisine showcases rich foods, harmonious flavors, the discovery of new foods, the importance of high-quality products, and unique new ways of presenting, serving, and enjoying dishes. Gastronomic literature took off and a myriad of culinary works with avant-garde concepts and elaborate recipes were published, including the bestseller of the time, *Cuisiner français* ("Cooking French") by François Pierre La Varenne, written in 1651.

— The table received a makeover in the 18th century. Dull pewter tableware was replaced with a dazzling array of faience and porcelain pieces, hand-painted in vibrant hues that breathed new life into mealtimes. Tableware became an art form, and a plethora of new items appeared on the table like centerpieces, gravy boats, and salt and pepper shakers. This aesthetic mission was matched by a revolution in table manners, dictated by the skillfully orchestrated service "à la française." The concept was simple. Five to six courses, on average. Impeccable decorum. No improvisation with the selection or placement of dishes—every soup had its tureen. Communal dishes were placed on the center of the table and guests (occasionally) served themselves. The result? It was a feast for the eyes ... but the food was cold.

— The Age of Enlightenment gave birth to the most beautiful traditions of all worlds: the restaurant, once known as a *maison de santé* or "health house." In 1765, Mathurin Roze de Chantoiseau opened the first modern restaurant in Paris, near the Louvre. In the beginning, restaurants were elegant and expensive. Nevertheless, they provided aristocrats the opportunity to dine in a way that had been previously reserved only for royals. It was not until the mid-19th century that blue-collar taverns like the raucous Flicoteaux, a refuge for artists and students in the Latin Quarter, began to emerge. The development of the restaurant gradually introduced the ritual of the meal as the delicious social practice that we know today. On the menu at these lively taverns? The legendary *Harlequin*, a terrine made from scraps salvaged from the larger restaurants bound with eggs, served sliced. Yum.

— The 19th century saw the emergence of service à la russe—the precursor to modern plated service—which would completely transform French dining during the Second Empire. Perfectly suited for restaurants, this style elevated headwaiters to celebrity status and solidified the crucial role of dining room staff. Initially, meats were carved in the kitchen before being presented to guests. A few years later, waiters took center stage with tableside service, offering carving, flambéing, and filleting as a captivating spectacle for diners. This development was thanks to Prince Alexander Kurakin, the Russian ambassador to France at the start of the century. He famously hosted grand Russian-style receptions, reminiscent of the Tsar's court, to create a lively atmosphere for all of Paris.

— We see the table as a sociological point of reference, impossible to put under a bell jar; it will continue to change as long as society evolves. No longer reserved for the privileged few, the table has become a place to gather, celebrate, and take pleasure.

Menu PLANNER

	MONDAY	**TUESDAY**	**WEDNESDAY**
LUNCH	**Quick and Easy** Frisée and Lardon Salad — 40 Salade Niçoise — 111 Grilled Cheese à la Française — 133 Rice Pudding — 197	**Lunch Break** Haricots Verts with Gribiche — 32 Veal Axoa — 99 Croque-Monsieur with Braised Gem Lettuces — 84 Pear and Almond Tart — 172	**Better Than Takeout** Celery Root Remoulade — 44 Leeks with Vinaigrette — 56 Cordon Bleu with Braised Peas — 102 Cassoulet — 79 Île Flottante — 168 Flan Parisien — 201
DINNER	**French Comfort Foods** French Onion Soup — 34 Beef Stew — 76 Gnocchi Parisienne — 130 Rum Raisin Ice Cream — 195	**Sauce is the Star** Steak with Peppercorn Sauce — 70 Veal Stew and Rice Pilaf — 96 Poached Eggs in Piperade — 139 Chocolate Mousse — 175	**Date Night Dishes** Mackerel Escabeche — 50 Braised Rabbit in Mustard Sauce — 90 Scallops with Celery Root Purée — 126 Lemon Meringue Tart — 176

THURSDAY	FRIDAY	SATURDAY	SUNDAY
Finger Foods Shrimp Croquettes 61 Stuffed Clams 43 Mussels with Poulette Sauce 122 Financiers 183	**Proust's Madeleine** Octopus and Tomato Pie 67 Endive and Ham Gratin 73 Stuffed Veal with Potato Purée 100 Crème Brûlée 178	**Brunch à la Française** Poached Eggs in Red Wine 46 Sausage in Brioche 28 Roast Chicken with Confit Lemon 82 Salt-Baked Sea Bass with Ratatouille 114 Paris-Brest 171	**Fresh from the Market** Chilled Tomato Soup 31 Asparagus with Mousseline Sauce 54 Sole Meunière 125 Onion Tarte Tatin 141 Fraisier Cake 185
Eat Hearty Before the Party Stuffed Mushrooms 62 Beef and Beer Stew with Fries 89 Skate Wing with Grenobloise Sauce 120 Tarte Tatin 189	**Recipes for Recovery** Oeuf Mayo 59 Veggie Quiche 134 Bouillabaisse 116 Cherry Clafoutis 187	**Fit for a King** Foie Gras 49 Braised Chicken with Morels and Vin Jaune 87 Vegetable Torte 143 Berry Pavlova 191	**For the Whole Family** Country Terrine 36 Stuffed Cabbage 75 Monkfish Stew 106 Braised Lamb Shoulder with White Bean Ragout 95 Crème Caramel 198

Pantry Staples

In the Pantry

- Fine salt and sea salt
- Olive oil
- Neutral oil (canola, sunflower)
- Wine vinegar, apple cider vinegar
- Onions and shallots
- Garlic
- Aromatic herbs
- Tomato paste
- Tomato sauce
- Honey
- Potatoes
- Tabasco
- Espelette pepper
- Nutmeg
- Cloves
- Cumin and coriander seeds
- Fennel
- Paprika
- White and red table wine
- All-purpose flour
- Sugar
- Pickled vegetables
- Chocolate
- Worcestershire sauce

In the Refrigerator

- Fresh herbs (chives, chervil, dill, mint, parsley . . .)
- Salted butter
- Whole milk
- Eggs
- Cheese
- Lemon
- Mustard
- Anchovies
- Cornichons
- Capers

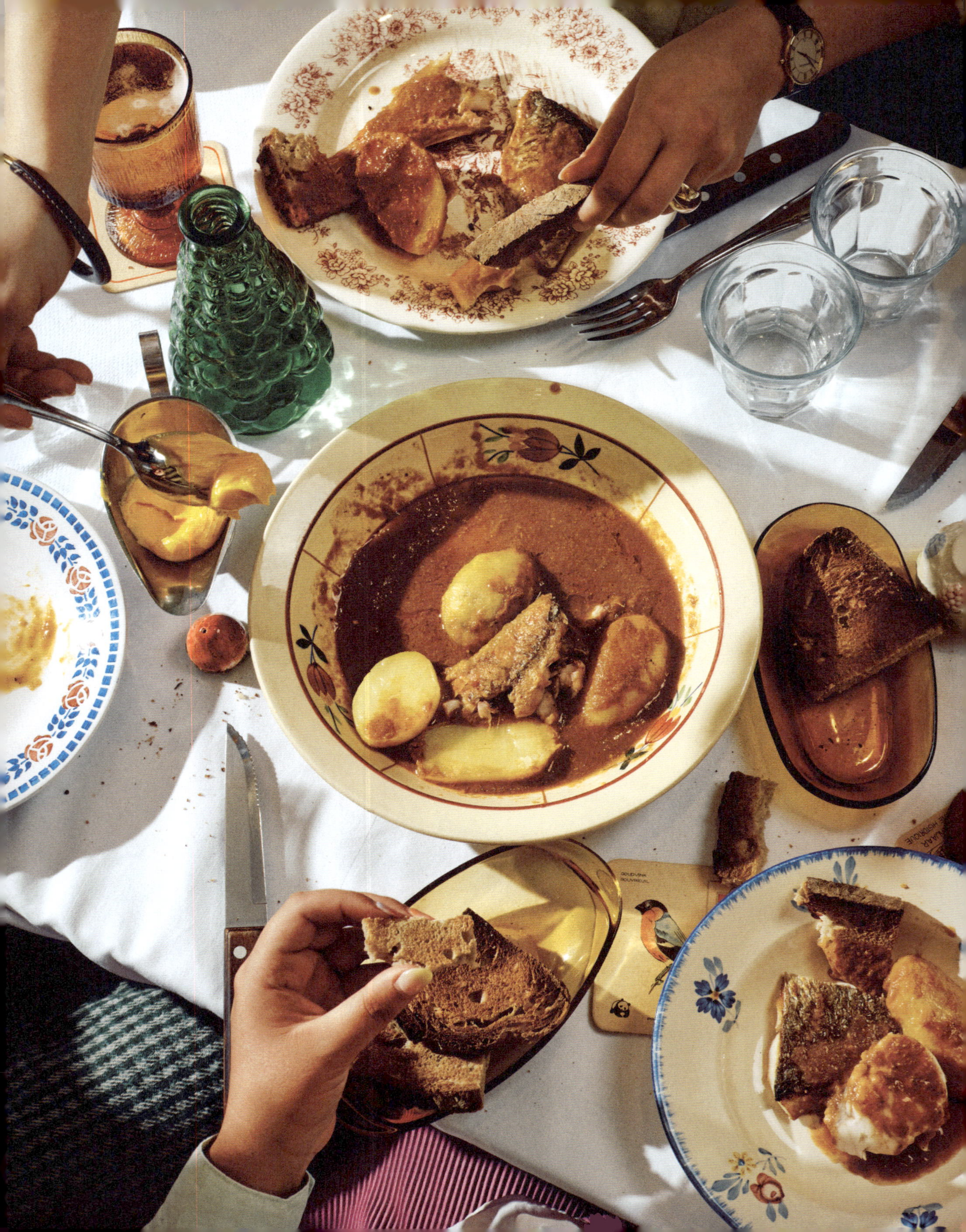

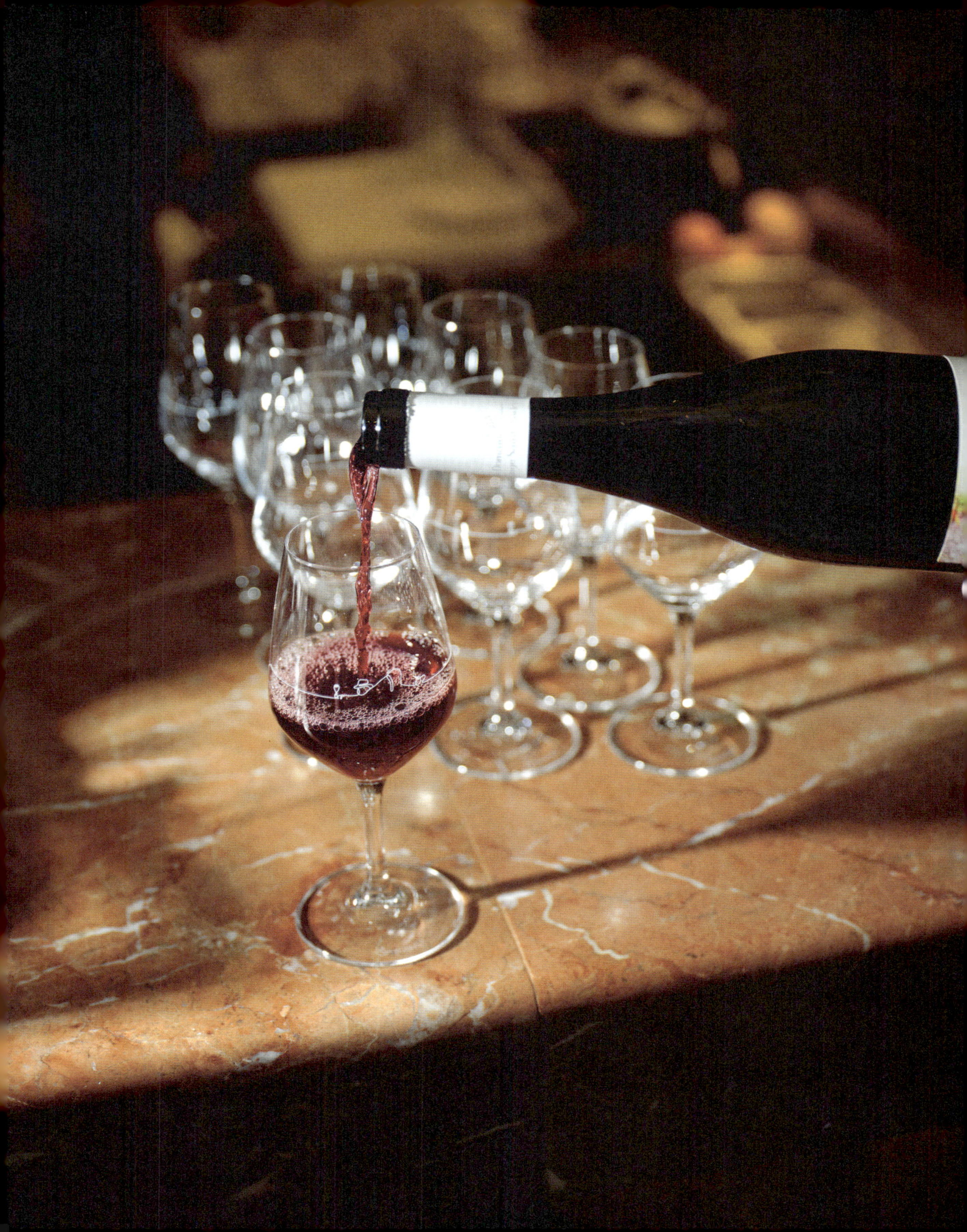

BRASSERIE BELLANGER

140 rue du Faubourg Poissonnière - Paris 10

BRASSERIE DE QUARTIER

STARTERS

STARTERS

Sausage in Brioche

SAUCISSON BRIOCHÉ

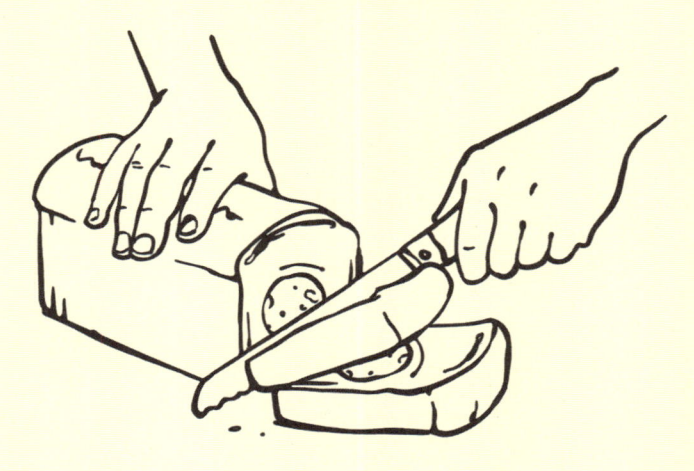

PREP TIME
45 MINUTES

COOK TIME
1 HOUR

REST TIME
3 HOURS
30 MINUTES

SERVES 6

For the brioche 1 teaspoon active dry yeast or 10 g fresh baker's yeast · 2 cups (250 g) flour + extra for kneading · 3½ teaspoons (15 g) sugar · 4 eggs · 1 pinch salt · 5 teaspoons (25 ml) milk · ⅔ cup (150 g) butter, melted **For the sausage** 1 sausage link with pistachios (the same length as your loaf pan), purchased from your butcher · 1 egg **For the charcutière sauce** 3 cornichons · 4 sprigs of parsley · ½ shallot · 3 tablespoons plus 1 teaspoon (50 ml) chicken stock · 1 teaspoon whole-grain mustard · a touch of Dijon mustard · 1 teaspoon red wine vinegar **To assemble and cook** butter · flour

THE BRIOCHE (PREPARE 2 HOURS 30 MINUTES IN ADVANCE) —— Mix the yeast with a little warm water to activate. Combine the flour, sugar, eggs, salt, milk, melted butter, and yeast mixture. Dust your hands with flour so the dough doesn't stick to your fingers, then knead until the texture is smooth, even, and elastic. Cover the ball tightly in plastic wrap and rest for 30 minutes at room temperature. Punch down the dough, then cover once again with plastic wrap. Chill for at least 2 hours.

THE SAUSAGE —— Add the sausage to a large pot of boiling water. Reduce the heat to a simmer and cook for about 30 minutes. Remove the casing while the sausage is still hot, then let the sausage cool. Crack the egg into a bowl and lightly whisk it with a fork.

THE CHARCUTIÈRE SAUCE —— Dice the cornichons and finely chop the parsley and shallot. Mix together with the remaining ingredients in a small bowl.

TO ASSEMBLE AND BAKE —— Generously butter and flour a loaf pan or terrine. Dredge the sausage in flour, shake off the excess, then dip in the beaten egg. Roll out the dough to about ½-inch (1.5 cm) thick. Dip a pastry brush in water and moisten the dough slightly, then place the sausage at one end of the dough and roll it up in the dough, wrapping the dough around the sausage as tightly as possible. Place the dough in the pan with the seam at the bottom and brush the top generously with the beaten egg. Let rise for 1 hour.

Bake at 325°F (160°C) for 30 minutes. Let the brioche cool for 5 minutes outside of the oven before removing it from the pan. Serve with the charcutière sauce and a small salad.

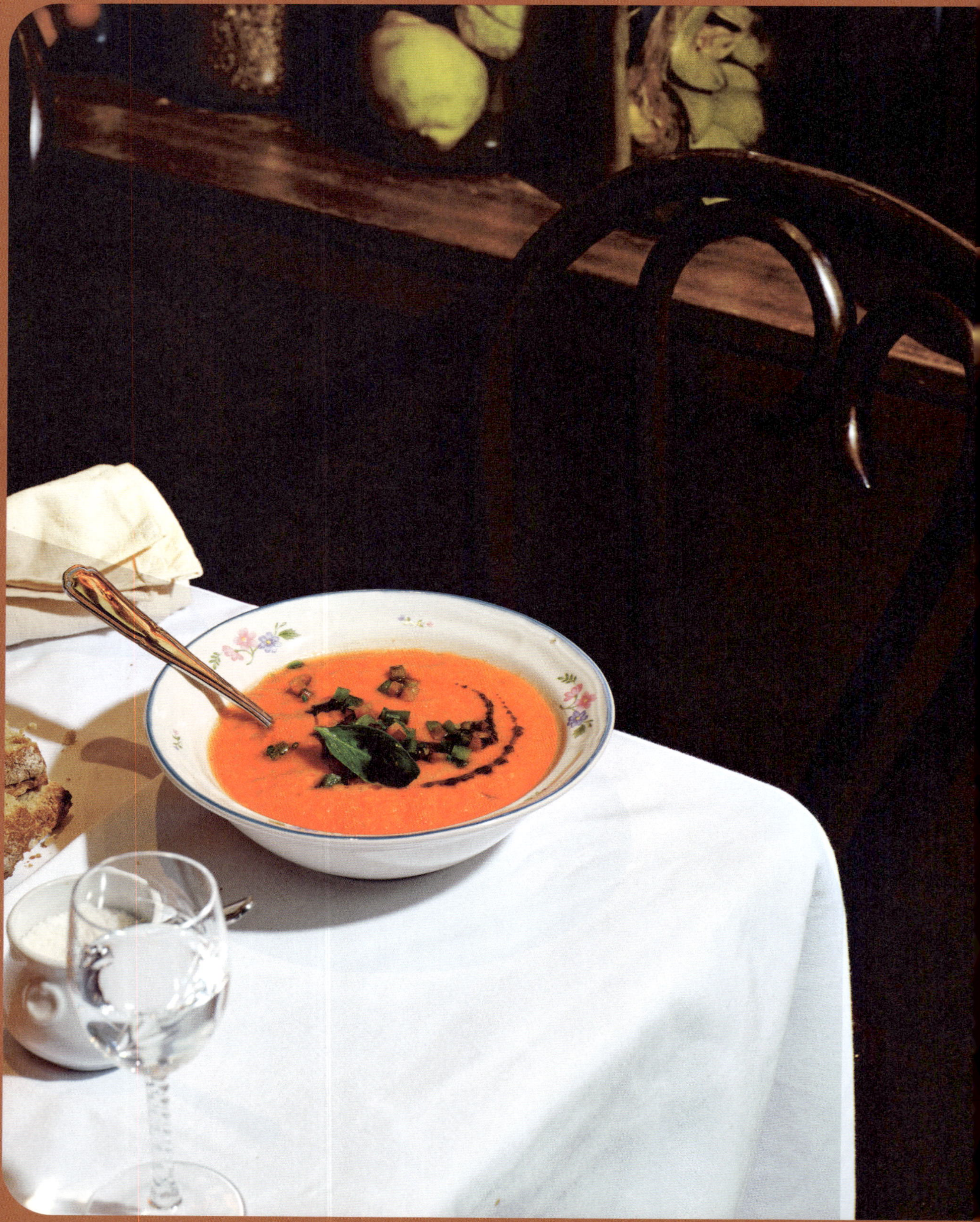

STARTERS

Chilled Tomato Soup

Soupe froide de tomates

PREP TIME
30 MINUTES

COOK TIME
1 HOUR
15 MINUTES

REST TIME
2 HOURS

SERVES 6

For the soup 4 carrots · 2 onions · 2¼ pounds (1 kg) heirloom tomatoes olive oil · ¼ cup red wine vinegar · 1 unpeeled garlic clove · salt and pepper **For the sauce vierge** 1 red pepper · 1 green pepper · 3 tablespoons olive oil 1 tablespoon red wine vinegar **For the croutons** 2 slices bread · 1 tablespoon olive oil · 1 garlic clove **For plating** olive oil · Herbed Oil (page 210) several basil leaves

THE SOUP —— Peel and finely chop the carrots and onions. Cut the tomatoes into quarters and remove the seeds. Sweat the carrots and onions in a pan with olive oil until they soften. Deglaze the pan with the vinegar, add the garlic clove, then add the tomatoes. Cook over low heat for 1 hour. Strain the mixture and set the solids aside. Reduce the strained liquid by half. Return the strained tomatoes to the pan with the reduced liquid, adjust seasoning to taste, and refrigerate for at least 2 hours.

THE SAUCE VIERGE —— Dice the peppers. Mix with the olive oil and vinegar and adjust seasoning to taste.

THE CROUTONS —— Preheat the oven to 350°F (180°C). Brush each side of the bread with oil and toast in the oven. Rub the toasted bread with the cut side of a garlic clove. Wrap in parchment paper and gently break into bite-sized pieces.

TO PLATE —— Pour the chilled tomato soup into the bowls. Top with 2 tablespoons of sauce vierge and a handful of croutons. Finish with a dash of olive oil and herbed oil and a few basil leaves.

STARTERS

Haricots Verts with Gribiche

Salade de haricots verts sauce gribiche

PREP TIME 30 MINUTES

COOK TIME 4 HOURS 20 MINUTES

SERVES 4

1 fresh Crottin de Chèvre (about 2 ounces / 60 g)

14 ounces (400 g) haricots verts

For the gribiche sauce

4 eggs

2 teaspoons Dijon mustard

1 teaspoon red wine vinegar

1 ⅔ cups (400 ml) sunflower oil

12 cornichons

2 teaspoons capers

1 shallot

1 tablespoon each parsley, chervil, and tarragon

THE GOAT CHEESE —— Preheat the oven to 175°F (80°C). Bake the goat cheese for 2 hours 30 minutes to dehydrate, then refrigerate for at least 1 hour.

THE HARICOTS VERTS —— Trim the haricots verts. Add to a large pot of boiling water and cook until al dente, 2 to 3 minutes. Once cooked, transfer to an ice bath. Drain and set aside.

THE GRIBICHE SAUCE —— Cook the eggs in a pot of salted boiling water for 9 minutes 40 seconds, then transfer to an ice bath. Peel the eggs, then separate the yolks from the whites. Put the yolks in a bowl and mash with a fork, then add the mustard and vinegar. Whisk in a small drizzle of oil as you would to thicken a mayonnaise. Finely chop the cornichons, capers, shallot, and herbs, then stir into the yolk mixture. Roughly chop the egg whites and mix in last. Adjust seasoning to taste, pour into a gravy boat, and set aside.

TO PLATE —— Plate the haricots verts and crumble the goat cheese over them. Finish with the gribiche sauce.

Around THE TABLE

FREQUENTLY PAIRED WITH TÊTE DE VEAU (CALF'S HEAD), gribiche is a vinaigrette made from cooked egg yolks mixed with capers, cornichons, shallots, cooked and diced egg whites, and fresh herbs. It is the undisputed mascot of French sauces. A guild of master *sauciers* (sauce makers) is said to have existed in the 19th century. They were known as *compositeurs de sauce* (literally, "composers of sauce") and operated within France's guild of vinegar makers. When it comes down to it, we're inclined to agree with Balzac, who declared that "sauce is the mastery of flavor in cooking."

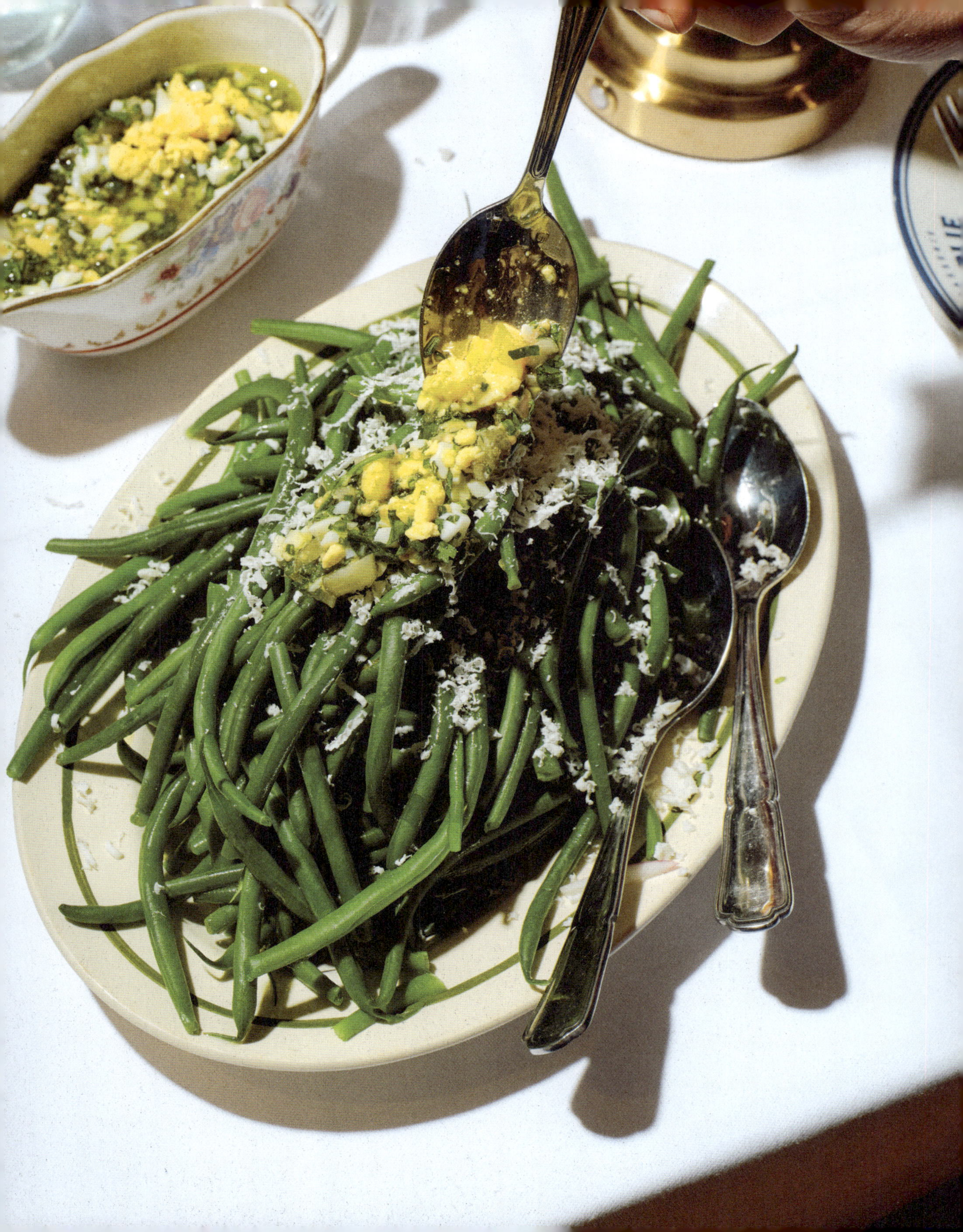

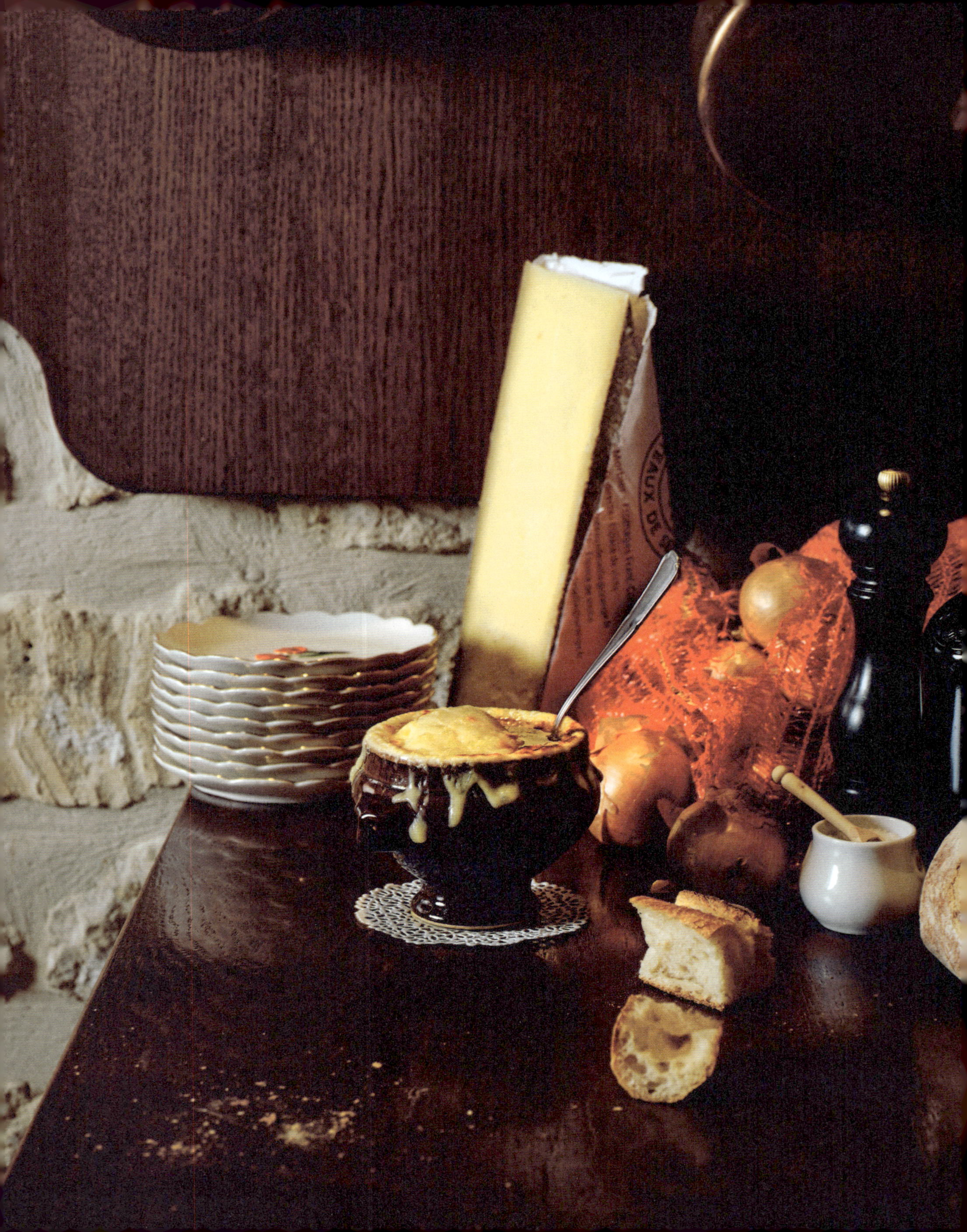

STARTERS

French Onion Soup

Soupe à l'oignon

> **PREP TIME**
> **30 MINUTES**

> **COOK TIME**
> **1 HOUR**

SERVES 4

For the soup

¾ pound (350 g) yellow onions

1 tablespoon (15 g) unsalted butter

1 pinch salt

1 pinch mignonette pepper

1 tablespoon (15 ml) red port

4¼ cups (1 L) veal stock

For the croutons

2 slices bread

2 tablespoons (30 g) butter

1 thyme sprig

1 garlic clove, crushed

For the assembly

7 ounces (200 g) grated Comté

THE SOUP —— Finely chop the onions. Sweat in a pot with butter until lightly caramelized. Season with salt and pepper. Add the port and reduce by half. Add the veal stock. Bring to a boil and simmer for 45 minutes. Adjust seasoning.

THE CROUTONS —— Cut the bread into 1-inch (2 to 3 cm) cubes. Melt the butter in a pan, then add the thyme and crushed garlic. Season with salt. Toast the croutons until golden brown. Remove from the pan and place on paper towels to drain. Lightly season the croutons with salt.

TO ASSEMBLE —— Fill 4 oven-proof bowls ¾ full of soup. Top each bowl with 3 or 4 croutons and ¼ of the Comté. Place under the broiler in a preheated oven until the cheese is melted and bubbly.

Around THE TABLE

This "poor person's soup" has been eaten since Roman times, particularly by peasants, because onions were easy to grow. It wasn't until the 19th century that onion soup became popular and earned the title "la gratinée des Halles." In fact, it is in Paris' Les Halles market where the brilliant idea to add grated cheese to the base recipe and then melt it in the oven first appeared. Onion soup has gained a reputation as a staple for workers ending a graveyard shift and as a hearty meal after a long night of partying.

STARTERS

Country Terrine

Terrine de campagne

(PREP TIME 30 MINUTES)   (COOK TIME 2 HOURS)   (REST TIME OVERNIGHT)

MAKES 1 TERRINE

For the white wine onions 1 large onion · 1 large pat butter · ½ cup (100 g) white wine · 1 pinch pepper **For the terrine** ⅓ pound (150 g) pork shoulder · 1¾ pounds (800 g) pork belly · 1 pound (500 g) pork liver · 3⅓ cups (800 ml) milk · ½ cup (130 g) heavy cream · 2 eggs · 3 parsley sprigs, finely chopped · leaves from 1 thyme sprig · 1 tablespoon (15 ml) cognac · 1 pinch nutmeg · 1 tablespoon (20 g) salt pepper · a few bay leaves

THE WHITE WINE ONIONS —— Finely chop the onion and sweat in a pan with butter. Add the white wine and pepper and bring to a boil, then reduce until the liquid has completely evaporated. Cool.

THE TERRINE —— Ask your butcher to chop the meat for you. Add all of the meat to a bowl and mix to combine. Mix in the rest of the ingredients, including the onions, except for the bay leaves. Season with pepper and mix well. You have what is called a *mêlée*. Fry a very small portion in a skillet as a test and adjust the seasoning. Transfer the mêlée to a terrine and round the top. Arrange a few bay leaves on top for presentation.

TO COOK —— Preheat the oven to 400°F (200°C). Bake the terrine for 10 minutes, then reduce the heat to 225°F (110°C) and continue baking for 1 hour 30 minutes. Once cooled to room temperature, cover with parchment paper, add weight on top (a carton of milk, for example), and refrigerate overnight. Note: the terrine will taste much better after a few days in the refrigerator.

TO PLATE —— Serve the terrine sliced, with a few pickled vegetables (page 210) and a dash of freshly ground pepper.

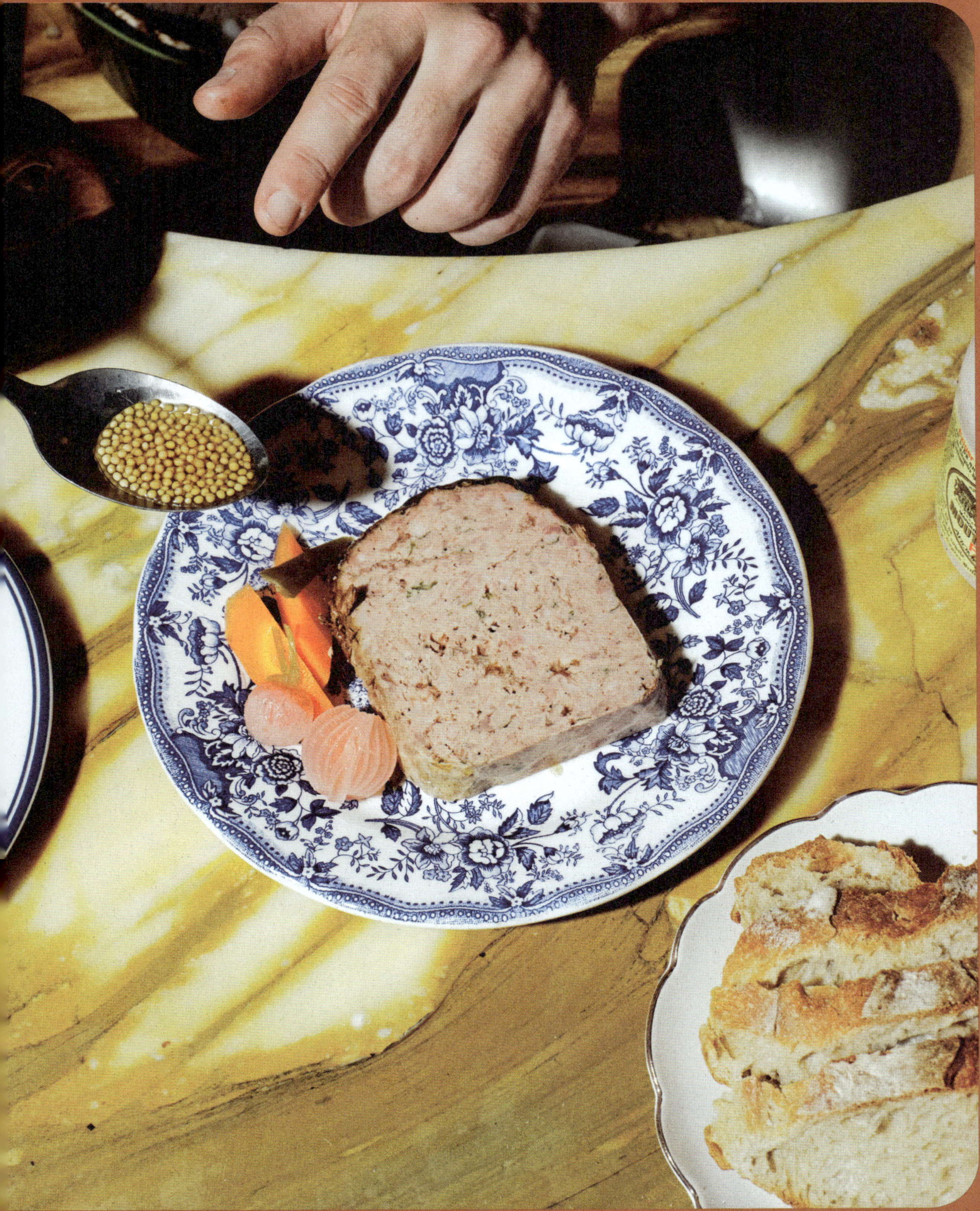

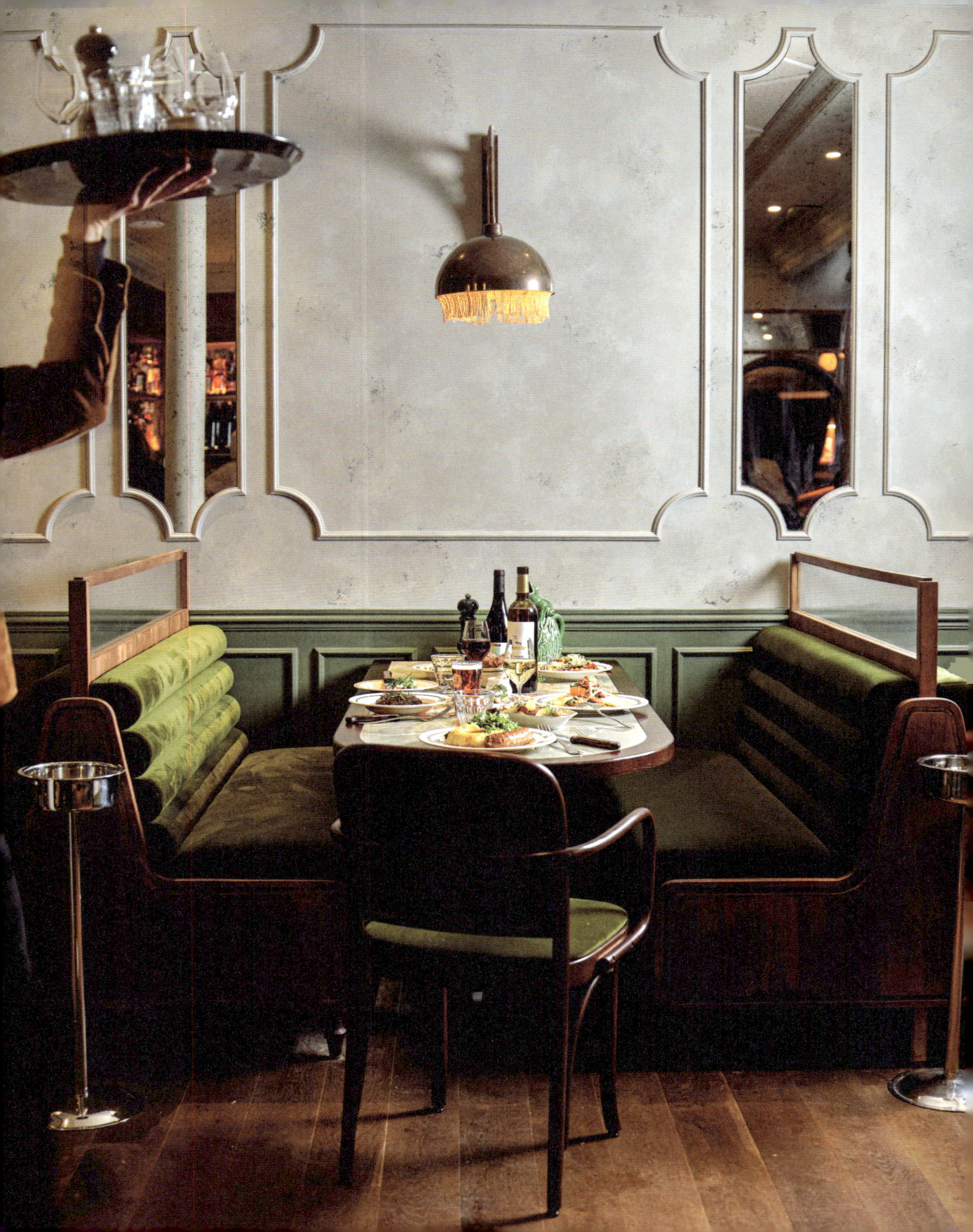

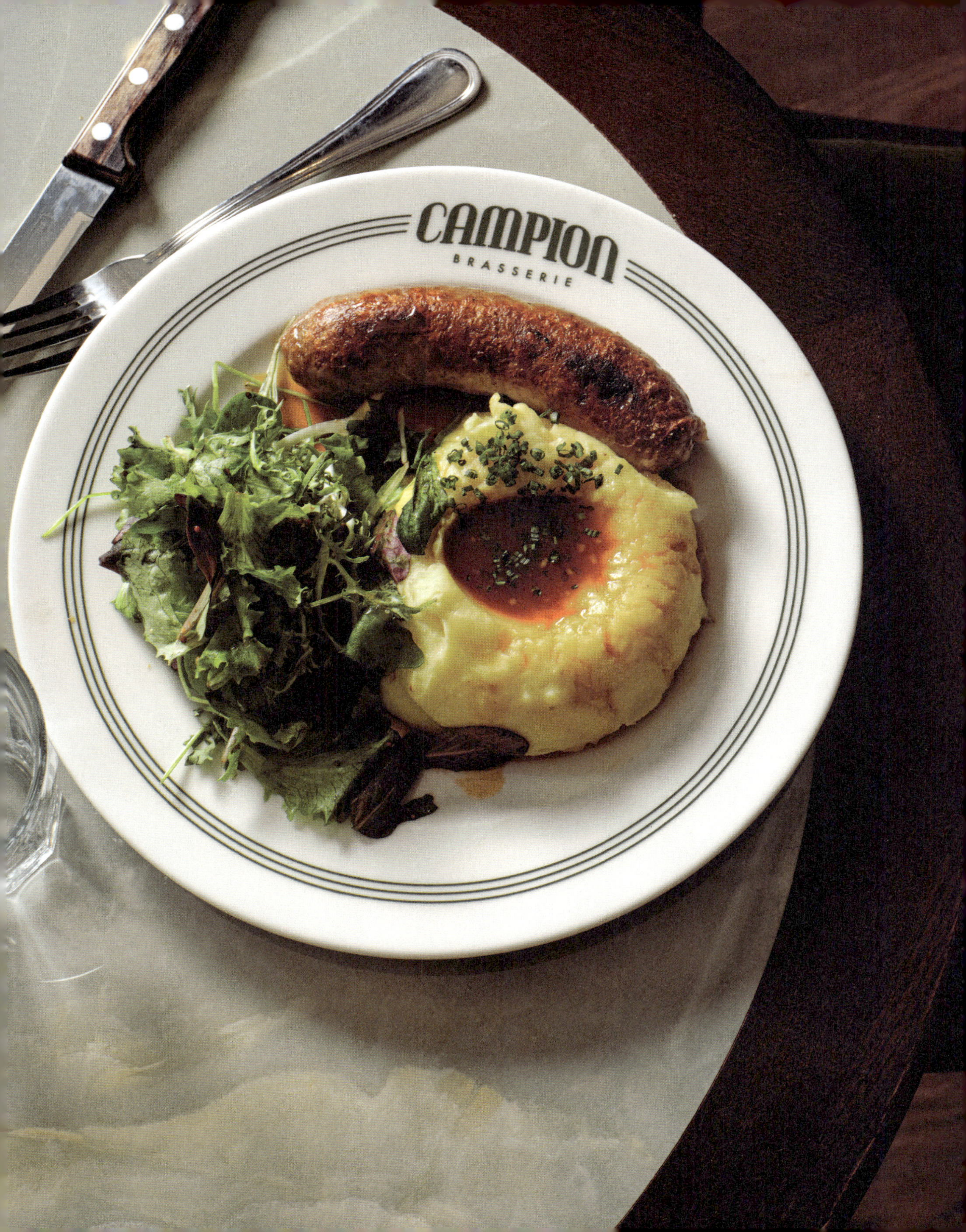
CAMPION
BRASSERIE

STARTERS

Frisée and Lardon Salad

Frisée aux lardons

PREP TIME
30 MINUTES

COOK TIME
10 MINUTES

SERVES 4 TO 6

For the dressing
About 11 ounces (300 g) bacon, cut into slices
1½ tablespoons (20 g) crème fraîche
2 tablespoons plus 2 teaspoons (40 ml) vinaigrette (page 209)

For the croutons
2 slices bread
2 tablespoons (30 g) butter
1 thyme sprig
1 garlic clove, crushed

For the salad
4 to 6 eggs (1 per person)
1 tablespoon vinegar
1 head frisée, leaves separated

THE DRESSING —— Cut the bacon into lardons. Add to a pan and cook until browned. Remove the lardons from the pan and transfer the fat to a bowl. Allow to cool, then mix the crème fraiche and vinaigrette into the fat.

THE CROUTONS —— Cut the bread into ⅓-inch (1 cm) cubes. Melt the butter in a pan, then add the thyme and crushed garlic. Season with salt. Add the bread to the pan and toast until golden brown. Remove from the pan and place on paper towels.

THE EGGS —— Fill a large pot with water and 1 tablespoon of vinegar and bring to a boil. Gently submerge the eggs in the boiling water. Cook for 6 minutes 30 seconds, then remove the eggs and place them in an ice bath. Carefully remove the shells.

TO PLATE —— In a salad bowl, toss the frisée with the dressing. Add the lardons and toss again to combine. To serve, top each bowl with one egg.

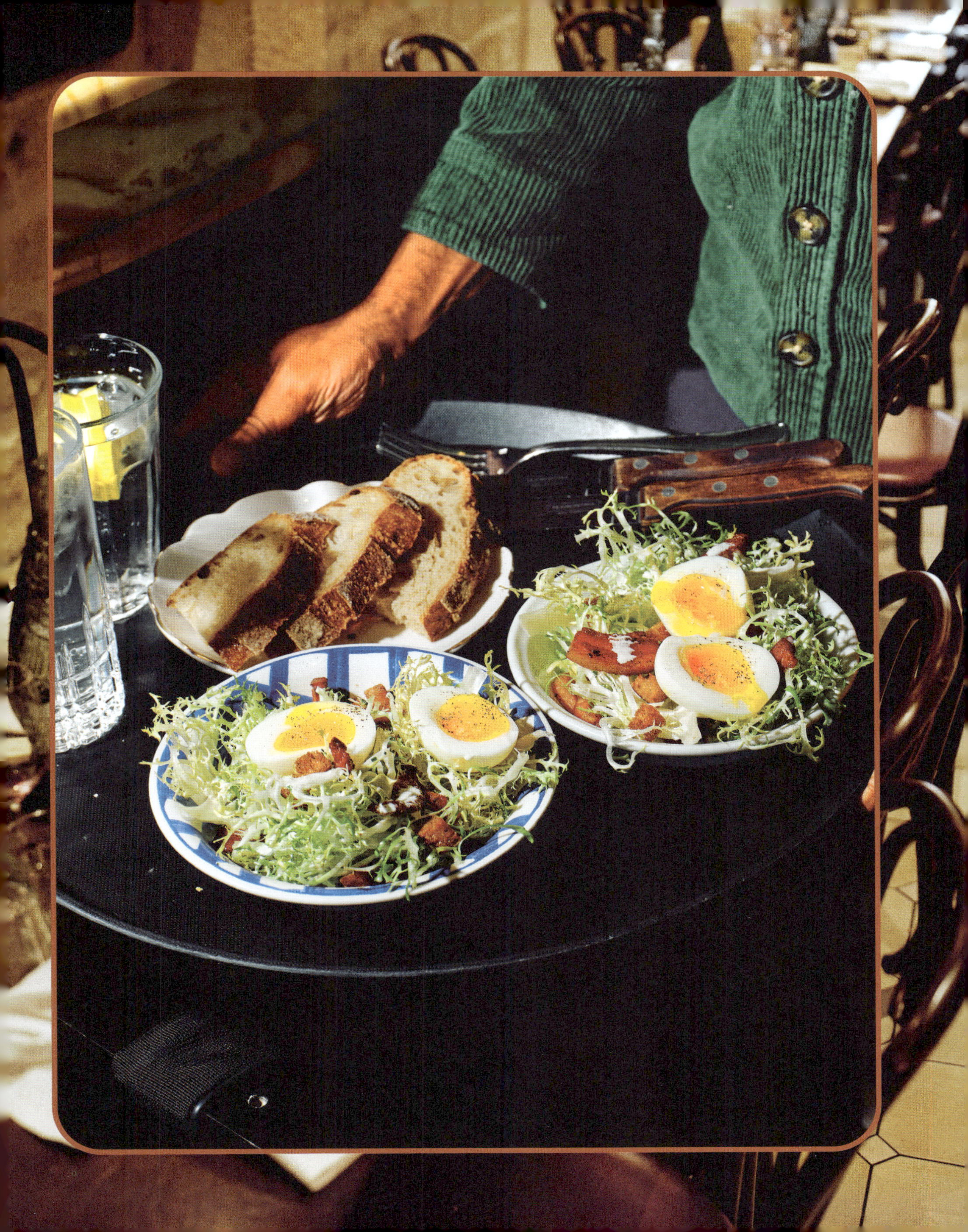

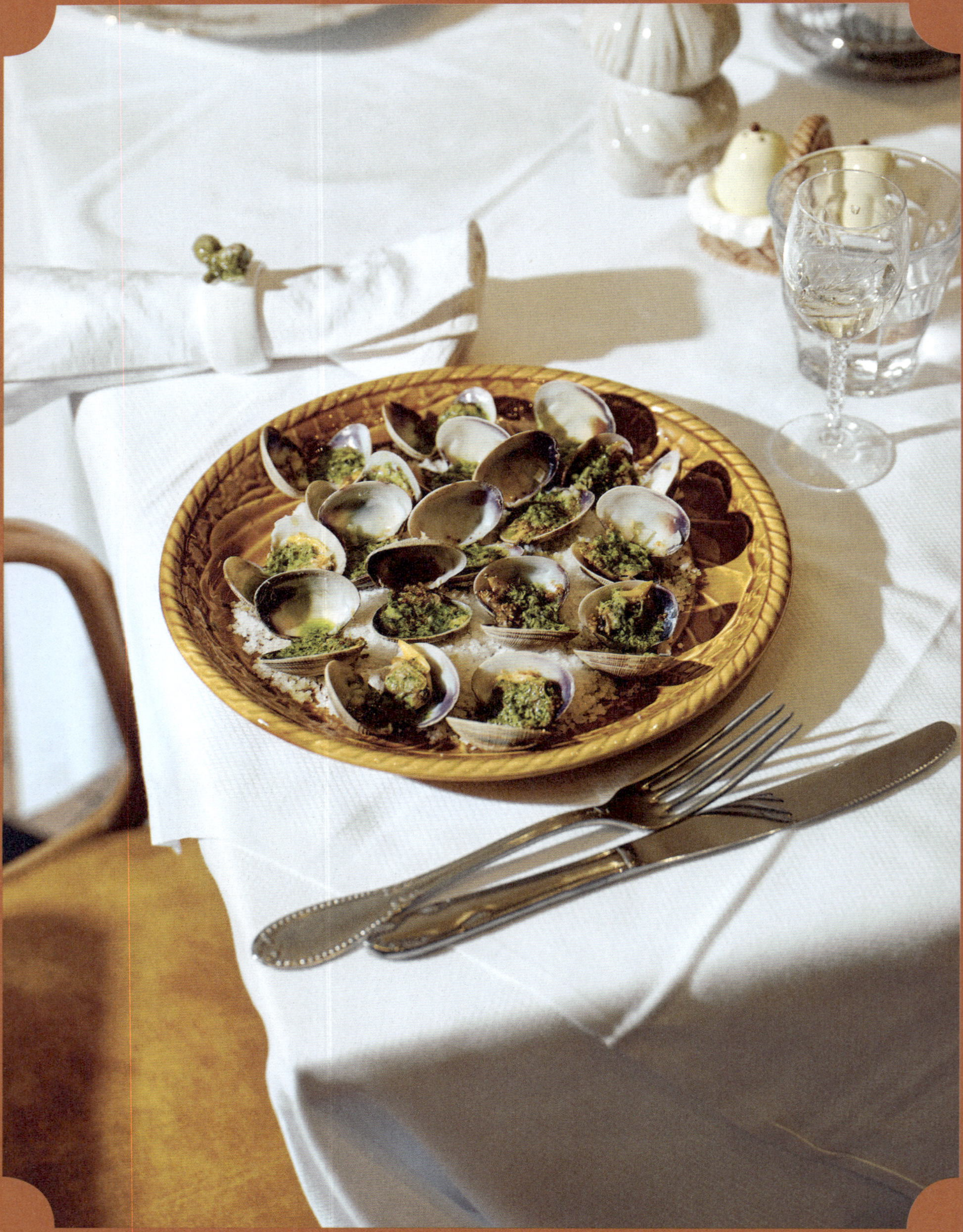

STARTERS

Stuffed Clams
Palourdes gratinées

PREP TIME
15 MINUTES
+2 HOURS TO PURGE THE CLAMS

COOK TIME
5 MINUTES

SERVES 2

For the herb butter
2¼ cups (500 g) unsalted butter
2 shallots, roughly chopped
2 garlic cloves, minced
2 bunches parsley, leaves only
Juice of 1 lemon
2½ teaspoons (15 g) salt
1 pinch mignonette pepper

For the clams
½ pound (200 g) clams
3 tablespoons plus 1 teaspoon (50 ml) olive oil
Coarse salt
¼ cup (30 g) breadcrumbs

THE HERB BUTTER —— Combine the softened butter, shallots, garlic, parsley leaves, lemon juice, salt, and pepper in a bowl. Adjust seasoning to taste.

THE CLAMS —— Begin by purging the clams: submerge them in a bowl of cold salted water (add 1 pinch of salt per quart/liter) and soak for 30 minutes, then repeat the operation three times for a total of 2 hours. Heat the oil in a pot over high heat. Once the pot is hot, add the clams and cover. With the pot still covered and still on the burner, shake lightly to stir the clams. They should open quickly. Stop cooking as soon as they open. Pick through the clams and dispose of any that remain closed.

TO PLATE —— Preheat the oven to 400°F (200°C). Pour coarse salt onto a rimmed baking sheet. Add 1 teaspoon of herb butter to each clam. If you have any butter left over after you've garnished your clams, roll it into a ball and refrigerate for later use. Sprinkle breadcrumbs on top, then place the baking sheet in the oven. Remove the clams from the oven once they are golden brown.

STARTERS

Celery Root Remoulade

CÉLERI RÉMOULADE

PREP TIME
15 MINUTES

COOK TIME
30 MINUTES

SERVES 5 TO 6

For the remoulade 18 ounces (500 g) celery root · ¼ cup plus 1 tablespoon (70 g) mayonnaise (page 209) · 3 tablespoons (45 ml) vinegar · 2 teaspoons (10 g) Dijon mustard · 1 teaspoon Worcestershire sauce **To serve** 1 smoked pork sausage, such as kielbasa · ½ cup (50 g) pickled mustard seeds (page 210) · horseradish

THE REMOULADE —— Peel and thinly julienne the celery root. In a salad bowl, mix the celery root with the mayonnaise, vinegar, mustard, and Worcestershire sauce. Add the sausage last and mix well.

TO SERVE —— Cook the sausage in a pot of boiling water for 30 minutes. Drain. Peel the casing from the sausage once it has cooled slightly. Dice the sausage and store in the refrigerator.

Place the celery root mixture on a serving platter. Top with pickled mustard seeds and a bit of horseradish, freshly grated if possible.

STARTERS

Poached Eggs in Red Wine

ŒUFS MEURETTE

PREP TIME 1 HOUR

COOK TIME 45 MINUTES

REST TIME 2½ HOURS

SERVES 2

For the brioche 1 teaspoon active dry or 10 g baker's yeast · 2 cups (250 g) flour + extra for kneading · 4 teaspoons (15 g) sugar · 4 eggs · 1 pinch salt 5 teaspoons (25 ml) milk · ⅔ cup (150 g) butter, melted + extra to toast the brioche before serving **For the meurette sauce** 1 onion · 3 tablespoons (40 g) butter, softened + extra for cooking the onion · 1 large garlic clove, minced · 1 bottle red wine (preferably a well-balanced wine like syrah) ⅓ cup (40 g) flour · salt and pepper **For the garnish** 20 button mushrooms butter · 2 slices smoked bacon **For the eggs** 4 very fresh eggs · vinegar

**THE BRIOCHE
(PREPARE 2 HOURS AHEAD)** — Add a bit of warm water to the yeast to activate. Mix together the flour, sugar, eggs, salt, milk, melted butter, and yeast. With floured hands, knead the dough until you have a stretchy, smooth, evenly textured ball. Cover the ball tightly in plastic wrap and let rest for 30 minutes at room temperature. Punch down the dough, then cover once more with plastic wrap. Refrigerate for at least 2 hours. Bake at 325°F (160°C) for 30 minutes in a generously buttered and floured rectangular loaf pan. Allow to cool for 5 minutes before removing from the pan.

THE MEURETTE SAUCE — Finely chop the onion and sauté quickly with a bit of butter. Add the garlic. Add the wine and reduce to a syrupy consistency. Strain the sauce through a sieve and set aside. Next, make a *beurre manié*: mix the flour and melted butter together. Heat the sauce over low and gradually add the beurre manié while whisking continuously, until the sauce coats the back of a spoon. Season with salt and pepper, then set aside.

THE GARNISH — Cut the mushrooms into quarters and sauté in a pan with a bit of butter over high heat until they are browned, then set aside. Dice the bacon to create lardons and sauté until crisp, then combine with the mushrooms.

THE EGGS — Poach the eggs one at a time. Fill a large pot with water, add a splash of vinegar, and bring to a boil. Crack the egg into a ramekin. Use a spatula to swirl the water in the pot until you create a vortex, then pour the egg into the center. Once the egg white is set, use a spoon to remove it from the water. Place on a paper towel to drain. Repeat the operation for each egg.

TO PLATE — Cut two nice slices of brioche. Toast in a pan with a little butter. Place two poached eggs on each slice of brioche. Cover with meurette sauce, then sprinkle the mushroom-lardon mixture on top.

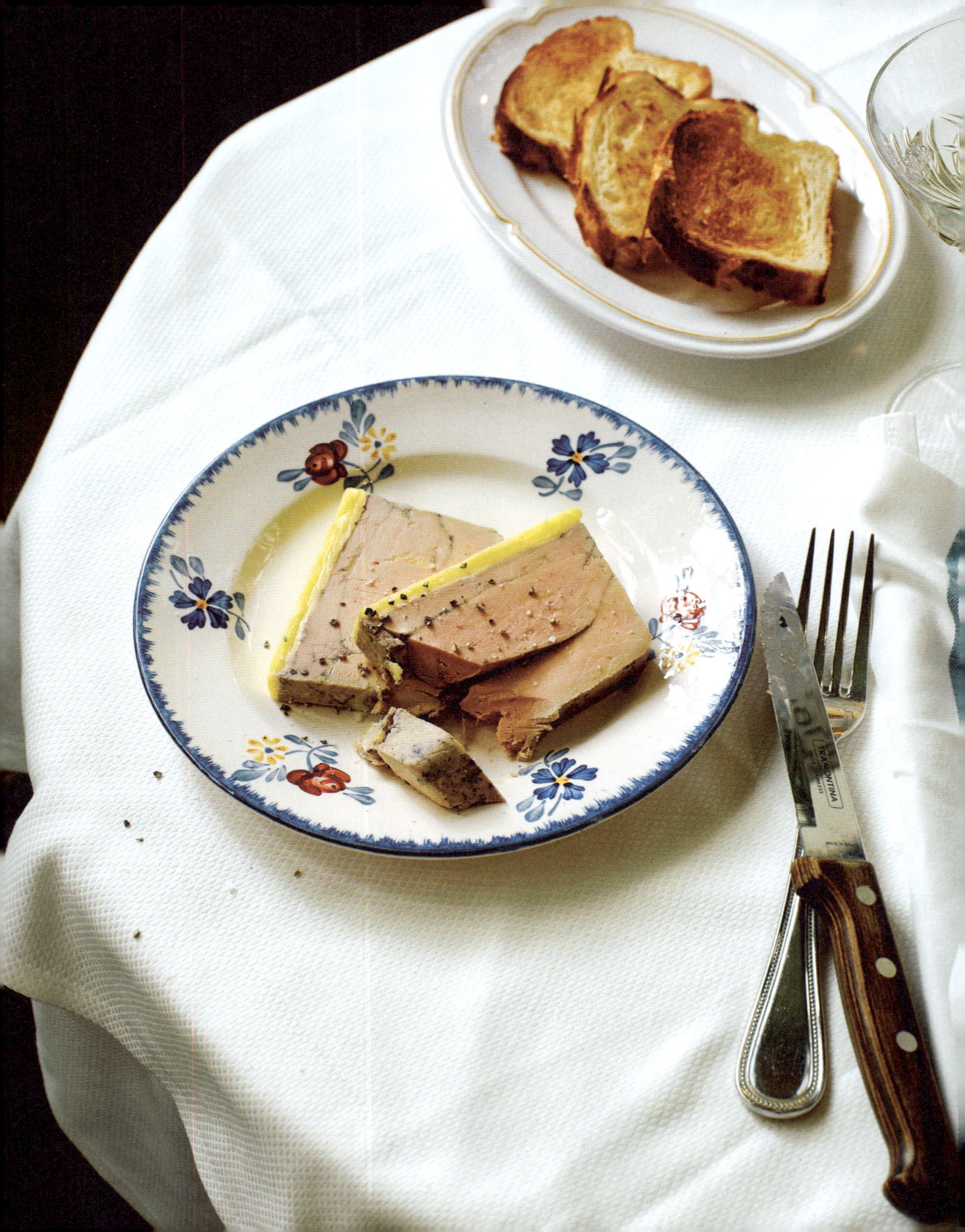

STARTERS

PREP TIME
10 MINUTES

COOK TIME
2 HOURS

REST TIME
2 HOURS
+ 1 NIGHT + 6 HOURS

Foie Gras

MAKES 1 TERRINE

2¼ pounds (1 kg) deveined foie gras
1 tablespoon salt
1 teaspoon pepper
1 teaspoon sugar
1 tablespoon cognac
1 tablespoon port

THE MARINADE —— Open the lobes of foie gras, dust with salt, pepper, and sugar, pour the cognac and port on top, and massage. Marinate in the refrigerator for at least 2 hours. Transfer the lobes to a terrine mold or a loaf pan and press firmly to pack down.

TO COOK —— Preheat the oven to 150°F (65°C). Bake the terrine for 2 hours.

TO TURN OUT —— Remove the terrine from the oven. Use a ladle to remove the accumulated fat from the top, transfer the fat to a bowl, and store in the refrigerator. Place a weight on top of the terrine and chill in the refrigerator overnight. The next day, reheat the fat in a pot, then pour on top of the chilled terrine. Return to the refrigerator for at least 6 hours. Serve sliced, with a dash of freshly ground pepper.

Around THE TABLE

WEB-FOOTED BIRDS HAVE BEEN RAISED DOMESTICALLY SINCE ANTIQUITY. Scenes depicting force-fed geese have even been found painted in Egyptian tombs. While observing wild geese, Egyptians noticed that they instinctively overate to endure winter migration—and that the plumpest birds happened to be the most delicious. The practice of fattening geese was passed on to the Romans and later to the Gauls. *L'Art culinaire* ("Culinary Art") is a collection of Roman recipes attributed to Apicius (though likely written later). The book makes reference to foie gras: *jecur ficatum*, or liver with figs, in particular. After all, figs are one of the main foods used to fatten up geese.

STARTERS

Mackerel Escabèche

Maquereaux à l'escabèche

(PREP TIME
30 MINUTES)   (COOK TIME
10 MINUTES)   (REST TIME
1 HOUR)

SERVES 4

2 carrots · 4 medium-sized Yukon Gold potatoes · ½ white onion · 1 celery rib · about 10 coriander seeds · about 10 fennel seeds · 2 star anise · 1 thyme sprig · 1 bay leaf · 1 garlic clove, crushed · ¾ cup plus 4 teaspoons (200 ml) white vinegar · 3 cups (700 ml) sauvignon blanc · 4 mackerel fillets, 7 to 10 ounces (200 to 300 g) each · ½ red onion, sliced thinly

THE MARINADE —— Peel the carrots and cut into thin slices. Peel the potatoes and cut into ¼-inch (5 mm) rounds. Place in a bowl of cold water and set aside. Peel and thinly slice the white onion. Cut the celery into thin slices. Place a pot over low heat and add the carrots, white onion, celery, potatoes, coriander and fennel seeds, star anise, thyme, bay leaf, and crushed garlic. Pour in the vinegar and wine and simmer about 10 minutes. Pierce the potatoes with a knife to ensure they are cooked, then remove from the marinade with a slotted spoon and allow to cool.

TO MARINATE —— Debone the mackerel fillets. Arrange on a baking dish. Season with salt, then cover with the hot marinade. Let cool for a few minutes, then refrigerate for 1 hour.

TO PLATE —— Remove the mackerel from the marinade and cut into 2 or 3 pieces, depending on the size of the fillets. Place the potatoes on a deep plate and top with the mackerel pieces, then add the carrots and celery from the marinade. Pour the marinade onto the mackerel and top with the sliced red onion to finish.

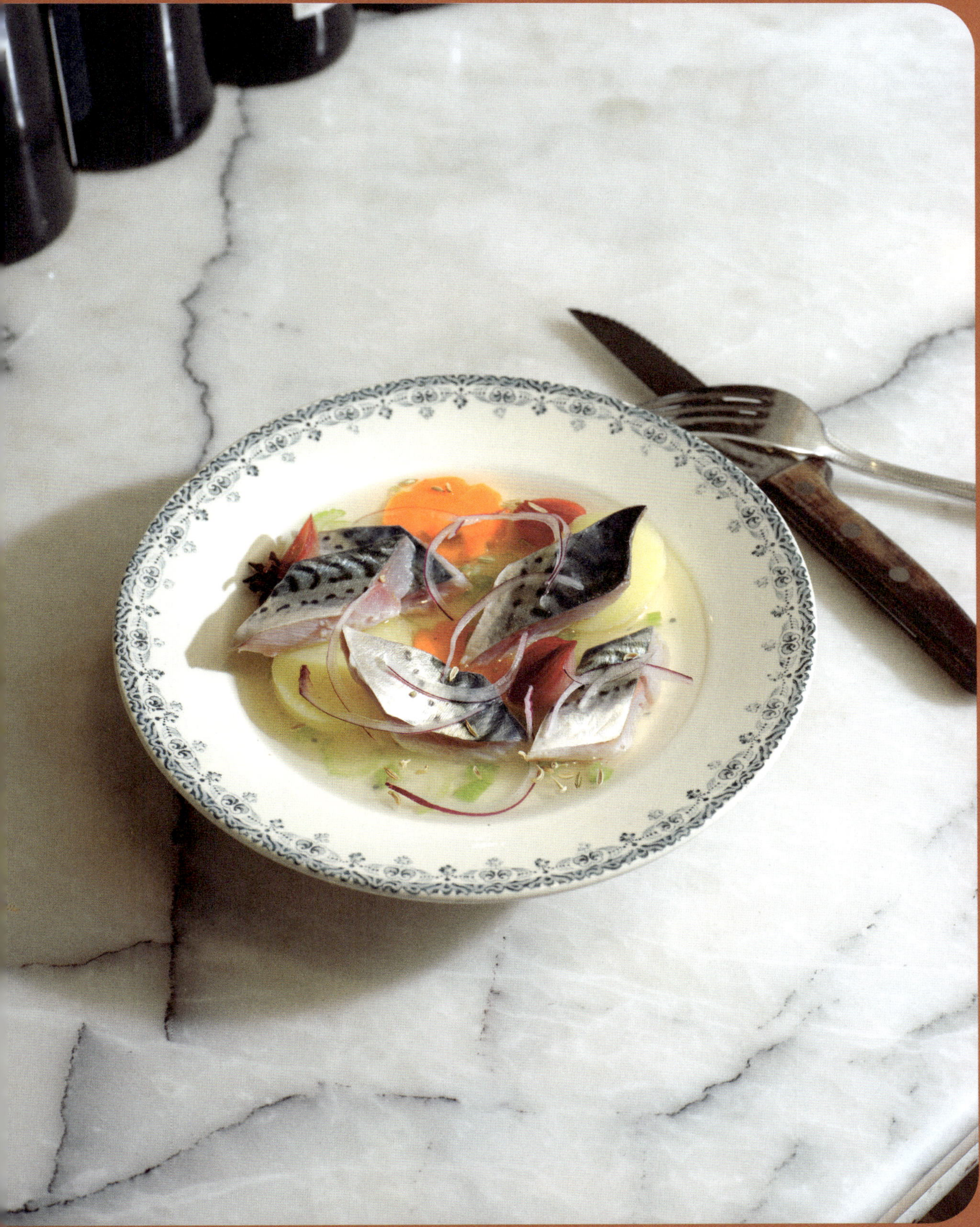

Around THE TABLE

① TERRINE
— *recipe page 36*

At the most basic level, a *terrine* refers to a preparation cooked in an earthenware vessel of the same name. Pâtés and terrines became popular with the development of the canning industry in the 18th century. At the time, Napoleon Bonaparte's troops were being decimated more by hunger and scurvy than by combat, so he offered a prize to anyone who could invent a method of preserving food. Confectioner Nicolas Appert took the prize with the invention of appertisation, the process of using heat to preserve food in sealed jars. He also wrote a book called *The Art of Preserving Animal and Vegetable Substances for Many Years*, which was published in Paris and sold 6,000 copies.

② POACHED EGGS IN RED WINE
— *recipe page 46*

The name "meurette" comes from the Latin *muria*, meaning "brine" or "salted water" and has "gastropolitical" origins. In the 17th century, salt was the only ingredient for preserving food. In France, the Ancient Regime imposed *la gabelle*, or a salt tax, making salt unaffordable for most. In its place, leftover sauces from previously salted dishes (such as beef bourguignon) were used to season foods, leading to the development of this legendary dish.

③ MACKEREL ESCABÈCHE
— *recipe page 50*

The French *escabèche* comes from the Provençal *escabassa*, meaning "to decapitate." This Mediterranean technique for preserving fish involves removing the head, organs, and bones, then marinating what remained in vinegar and herbs. It was a brilliant discovery in the 13th century that not only keeps fish fresh longer, but also adds flavor.

④ LEEKS WITH VINAIGRETTE
— *recipe page 56*

This classic dish is a pillar of French cuisine and can be found on nearly every menu—certainly thanks to the irresistible vinaigrette. As early as the 14th century, it was described in *The Good Wife's Guide* (*Le Ménagier de Paris*) as "a sauce made of oil, vinegar and various condiments." Its real rise to fame, however, is owed to the chevalier d'Albignac. While exiled in London during the French Revolution, he was entrusted with preparing a vinaigrette at a high-society dinner—à la Française, of course. His recipe was a hit. The savvy businessman began offering his services to restaurants and wealthy English families and was often referred to as "the fashionable salad maker."

⑥ TOMATO AND OCTOPUS PIE (TIELLE SÉTOISE)
— *recipe page 67*

In the late 19th century, Italian fishermen from the small coastal town of Gaeta settled in Sète. Arriving empty-handed was not an option, so they packed this famous recipe for octopus pie into their suitcases. The name "tielle Sétoise" comes from the terracotta dish, or *teglia*, and city (Sète) in which it was baked. Adrienne Virduci was the first Sétoise to commercialize the dish in the 1930s, cementing its status as a beloved local specialty in the Sétois region.

⑤ STUFFED MUSHROOMS
— *recipe page 62*

It was Jean-Baptiste de La Quintinie, the legendary gardener of King Louis XIV and mastermind of the famous Versailles kitchen garden, who was the first to experiment with the cultivation of button mushrooms in the royal gardens. His efforts paid off, yielding results spectacular enough to earn a place on the Sun King's table. Under the reign of Napoleon Bonaparte, mushrooms were grown in former quarries in the Parisian suburbs as well as in the heart of the city itself, notably in the catacombs beneath the Place d'Italie. However, with the arrival of the metro in the early 1900s, mushroom production gradually shifted from these urban tunnels and suburban caves to the open fields of the Pays de la Loire region. Today, only a small number of mycologists, or mushroom farmers, are still active in the Île-de-France region.

STARTERS

Asparagus with Mousseline Sauce

PREP TIME 30 MINUTES

COOK TIME 10 TO 15 MINUTES

Asperges sauce mousseline

SERVES 4

About 12 green or white asparagus spears

For the mousseline sauce

⅓ cup plus 4 teaspoons (100 ml) heavy cream
2 egg yolks
⅔ cup (150 g) butter
Juice of 1 lemon

THE ASPARAGUS —— For green asparagus: trim away the woody bottoms. For white asparagus: peel from top to bottom using a vegetable peeler, then trim away the tough ends.

THE MOUSSELINE SAUCE —— Whisk the cream in a chilled bowl until it reaches soft peaks. Prepare a sabayon with the egg yolks and butter (page 208) and mix in the lemon juice. To finish, gently fold the whipped cream into the sabayon. Transfer to a gravy boat and set aside.

TO COOK —— Bring a pot of salted water to a boil. Add the asparagus and cook for 10 to 15 minutes, depending on the thickness of the asparagus spears. Drain and transfer to an ice bath. Once cool, dry with a clean towel.

TO PLATE —— Arrange the asparagus side by side on a serving platter and top with the desired amount of mousseline sauce.

Around THE TABLE

THE COLOR OF ASPARAGUS—white, green, or purple—is determined by its growing conditions. White asparagus grows entirely underground, sheltered from the sun. Purple asparagus begins the same way but gains its distinctive hue as its tips break through the soil and are exposed to the sun. Green asparagus, on the other hand, basks in the blazing sun and develops its color through photosynthesis. The Greeks were so convinced of asparagus's aphrodisiac powers that they dedicated the vegetable to Aphrodite, the goddess of love.

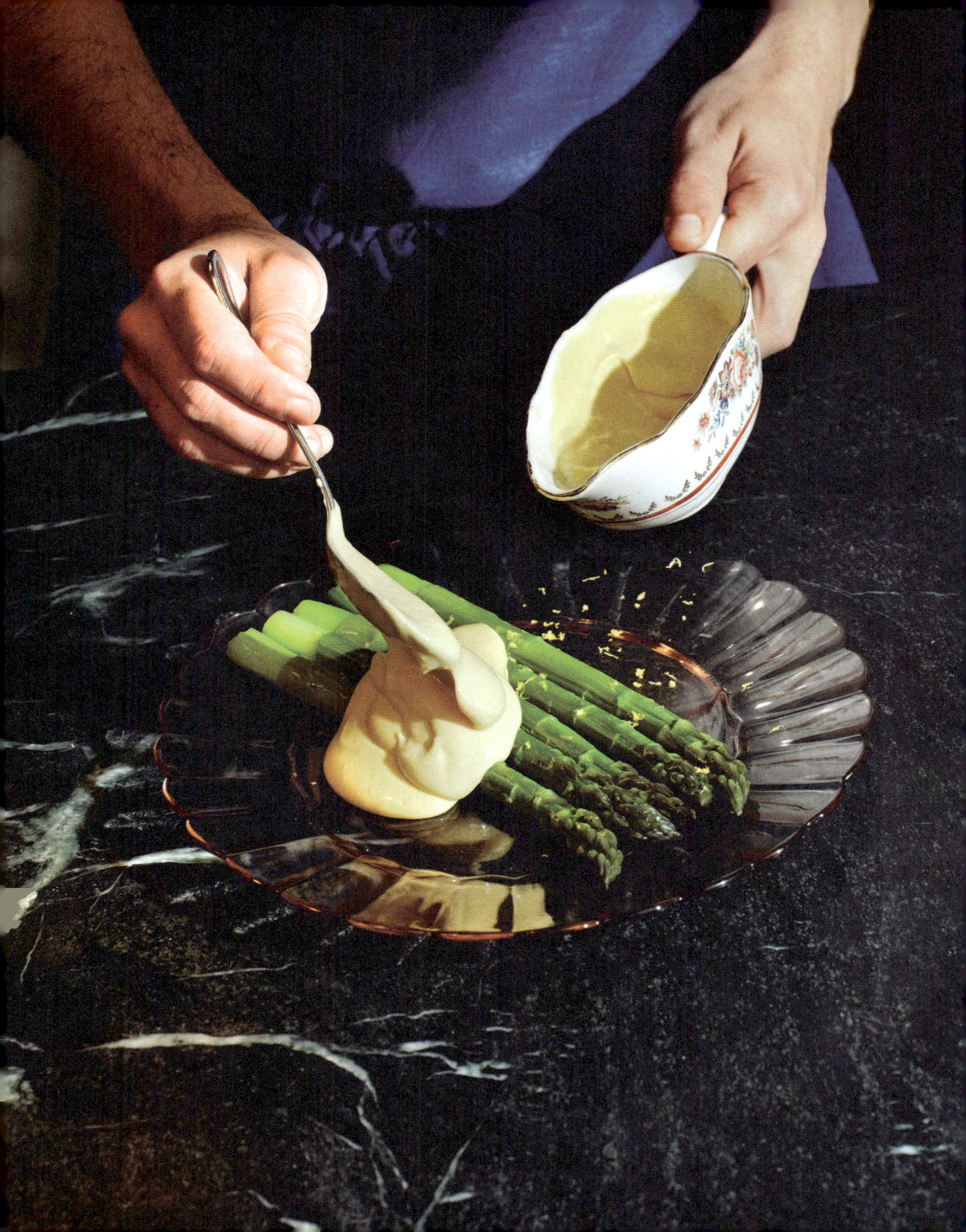

STARTERS

Leeks in Vinaigrette

POIREAUX VINAIGRETTE

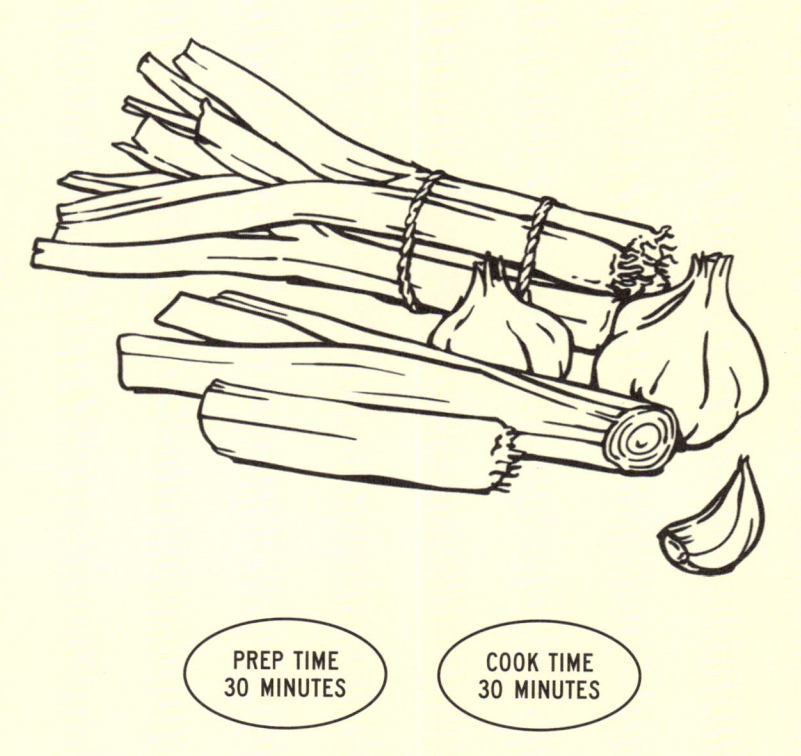

PREP TIME
30 MINUTES

COOK TIME
30 MINUTES

SERVES 4

For the leeks 4 leeks · neutral oil **For the croutons** 1 slice bread · 1 tablespoon (15 g) butter · 1 thyme sprig · 1 garlic clove, crushed · salt **For the topping** 3 tablespoons (20 g) hazelnuts · ½ bunch chervil · ½ bunch parsley 3 tarragon sprigs **To serve** 2 cups plus 4 teaspoons (500 ml) vinaigrette (page 209)

THE LEEKS — Fill a large pot with salted water and bring to a boil. In the meantime, trim the greens from the leeks (save to use in a vegetable broth, page 207). Cut the white part of the leeks lengthwise into quarters, then rinse thoroughly under running water to remove any dirt. Add to the boiling water and cook about 15 minutes. Pierce the leeks to test for doneness: they should be very soft. Once cooked, strain through a colander and place on a dry towel to drain. Once dry, brown the leeks on each side in a pan with a little oil.

THE CROUTONS — Cut the bread into ⅓-inch (1 cm) cubes. Melt the butter in a skillet, then add the thyme, crushed garlic clove, and salt. Toast the croutons until golden brown, then transfer to a paper towel to drain.

THE TOPPING — Preheat the oven to 350°F (180°C). Place the hazelnuts on a baking sheet and roast in the oven for about 15 minutes, until they are browned. Chop the herbs, then transfer to a bowl and mix with the hazelnuts.

TO SERVE — Arrange the leeks on a serving platter. Pour the vinaigrette generously over the leeks, then spread the herb-hazelnut mixture evenly on top. Add the croutons and serve.

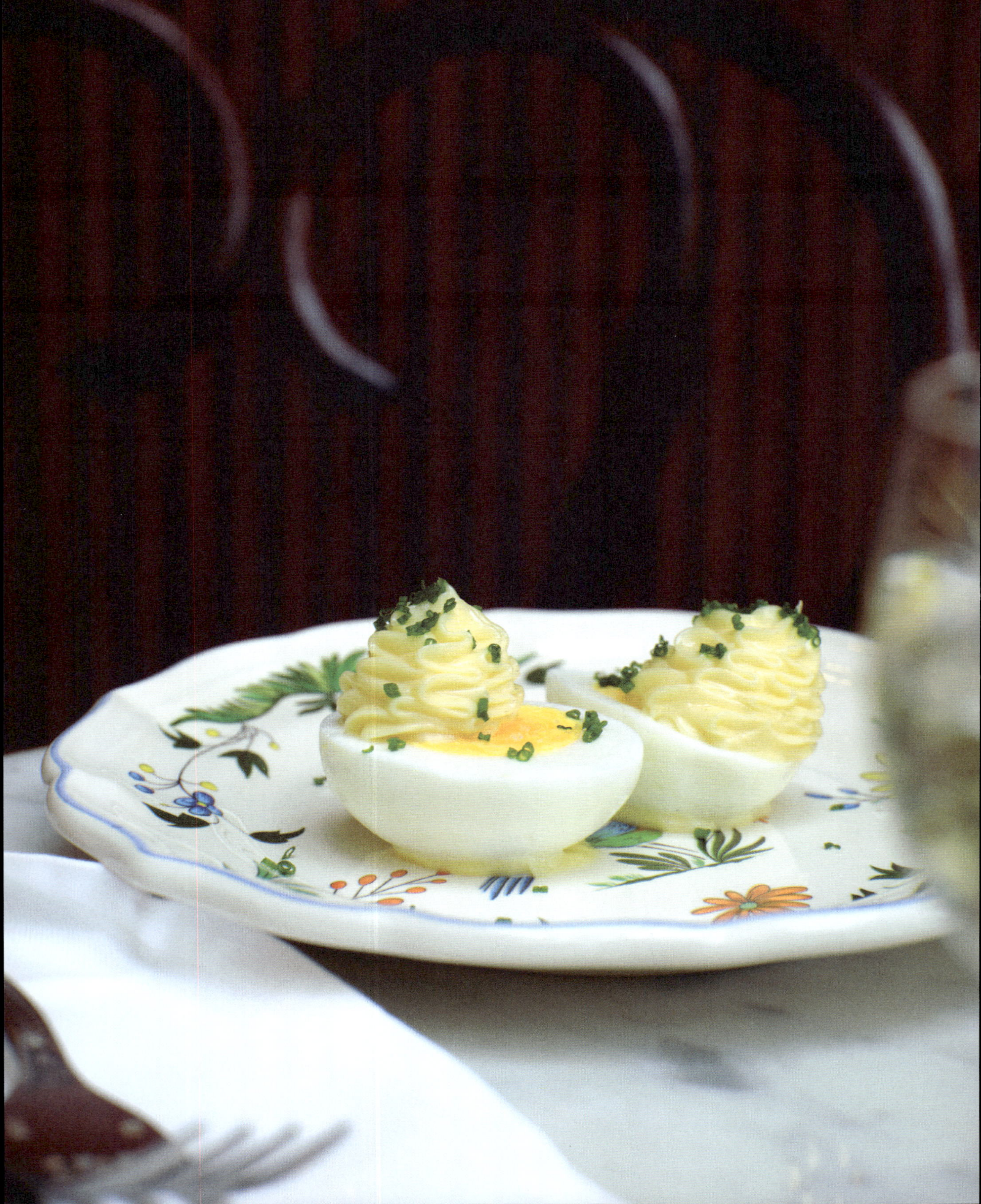

STARTERS

Eggs with Mayo

Œuf mayo

**PREP TIME
30 MINUTES**

**COOK TIME
9 MINUTES
40 SECONDS**

SERVES 4

Vinegar
4 eggs
1 bunch chives
Mayonnaise (page 209)
Sea salt

THE EGGS —— Fill a large pot with water and 1 tablespoon of vinegar and bring to a boil. Carefully place the eggs in the boiling water and cook for 9 minutes 40 seconds. Once the time is up, transfer the eggs to an ice bath. Crack each egg and soak in water for a few minutes before peeling to remove the shell more easily.

THE CIBOULETTE —— Wash the chives and arrange the sprigs on a cutting board. With a sharp knife, finely chop a small handful at a time.

TO PLATE —— Cut the eggs in half. Place one drop of mayonnaise on the plate for each egg and arrange the halves on top so they stay in place. Sprinkle a pinch of sea salt on each yolk, then pipe or place a dollop of mayonnaise on each half. Garnish with a pinch of chives.

Around THE TABLE

NOT TO WHISK UP CONTROVERSY, but the history of mayonnaise, crowned the "mother sauce" by Escoffier, is hazy. Its origins have long been the subject of debate. In Antonin Carême's 1833 work *The Art of French Cooking in the 19th Century* (*L'Art de la cuisine française au XIXe siècle*), the chef of kings and king of chefs called it "magnonaise" in reference to its preparation, since it must be *manié* ("handled" or "mixed") carefully. Grimod de La Reynière, considered to be one of France's first great gastronomic critics, maintains in his 1808 book that it's "bayonnaise," because Bayonne makes really good stuff. A less tangy and slightly more militaristic theory traces "mahonnaise" to 1756, when the Duke of Richelieu invaded Mahon, the capital of the island of Minorca, during the Seven Years' War. To celebrate his victory, his cook whipped up this new sauce using the ingredients he had on hand. Last but not least, pharmacists may have also had something to do with it: some suggest the name comes from the Old French *moyeu*, meaning "egg yolk." As far back as the Middle Ages, pharmacists began using cold egg yolk emulsions, and in the 18th century, they discovered the concept of creating an emulsion by gradually adding oil . . . a scientific breakthrough that inspired chefs everywhere.

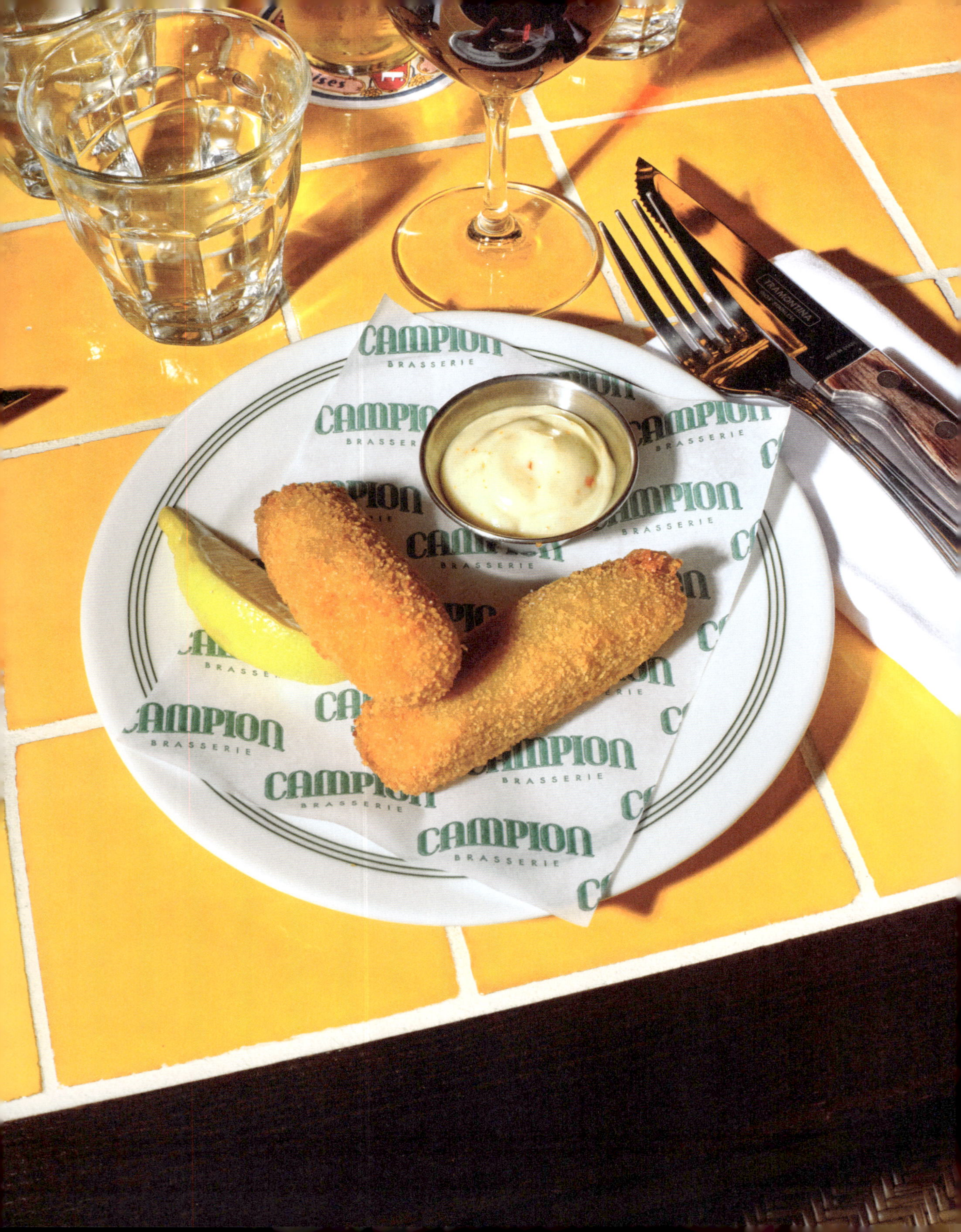
CAMPION
BRASSERIE

STARTERS

Shrimp Croquettes
Croquettes de crevettes

PREP TIME
30 MINUTES

COOK TIME
1 HOUR
15 MINUTES
REST TIME: OVERNIGHT

SERVES 6

1 recipe fish fumet (page 207)

Oil for frying

Spicy mayonnaise for serving (page 209)

For the shrimp croquettes

¾ cup plus 2 tablespoons (200 g) butter

1½ cups plus 3 tablespoons (200 g) flour

Pepper

1 pinch nutmeg

9 ounces (250 g) brined bay shrimp

5 teaspoons (25 g) heavy cream

1 egg yolk

½ cup (50 g) Comté cheese

For the breading

¼ cup (30 g) flour

¾ cup (100 g) breadcrumbs

2 eggs

THE FUMET —— Reduce the fish fumet by half. You should have about 2 cups (500 ml).

THE CROQUETTES —— Start by making a roux. Melt the butter in a pot, then add the flour all at once and stir for several minutes. Gradually mix in the fish fumet, then season with pepper and nutmeg. Roughly chop the shrimp and add it to the mixture. Remove the pot from the heat and whisk in the cream and egg yolk, then finally the grated Comté. Chill in the refrigerator overnight.

TO ASSEMBLE —— Roll the shrimp mixture into 2-ounce (50 g) croquettes. Pour the flour for the breading into one bowl. Pour the breadcrumbs into a second bowl. Crack the eggs into a third bowl and beat with a whisk or fork. Dredge each croquette in flour, then dip in the eggs and breadcrumbs. Repeat the operation until all croquettes have been coated.

TO COOK —— Heat the oil to 350°F (180°C) in a frying pan or pot. Add the croquettes and fry until golden brown. Remove from the oil and season with salt. Serve with spicy mayonnaise.

TIP —— Make a larger batch of shrimp croquettes and freeze for future use.

STARTERS

Stuffed Mushrooms

CHAMPIGNONS FARCIS

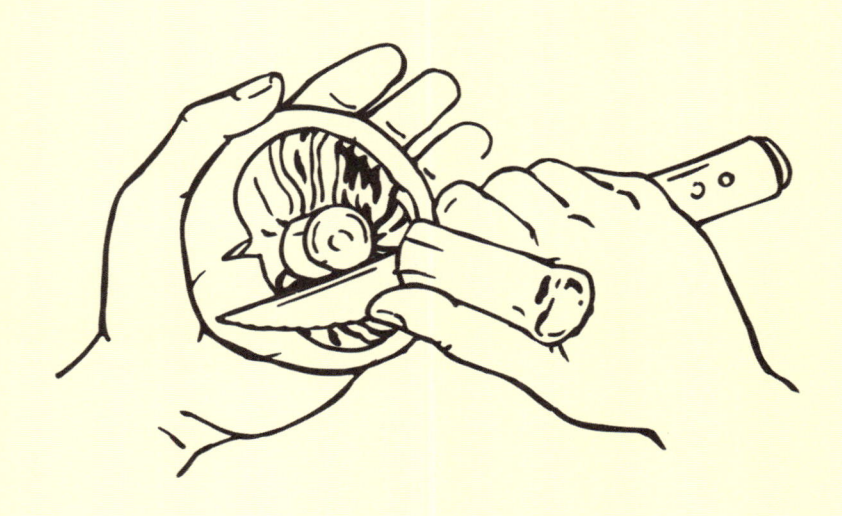

PREP TIME
30 MINUTES

COOK TIME
3 HOURS
30 MINUTES

SERVES 4

For the pigs' feet 2 pigs' feet · vegetable bouillon (page 207) · 2 shallots
2 garlic cloves · ½ bunch parsley · 2 teaspoons (10 g) butter **For the filling**
11 ounces (300 g) ground sausage · salt and pepper **For the mushroom cream**
8 brown button mushrooms (the biggest you can find) · 1 pat butter · ⅓ cup
(80 g) light cream **To assemble** 4 teaspoons (10 g) toasted breadcrumbs

THE PIGS' FEET —— Blanch the pigs' feet for 3 minutes, then rinse with cold water and add to the vegetable bouillon. Bring to a boil and then reduce the heat to low, cover, and cook for at least 3 hours. Remove the pigs' feet after cooking and reserve the stock for future use. Once cool, remove the cartilage from the pigs' feet and chop the meat. Finely chop the shallots and chop the garlic and parsley. Sweat in a skillet with the butter, then cool.

THE FILLING —— Mix the ground sausage with the pigs' feet mixture and season with salt and pepper.

THE MUSHROOM CREAM —— Separate the stems from the caps of the mushrooms. Set the caps aside for stuffing. Wash and dry the stems thoroughly, then chop them and sweat them in butter. Season with salt and pepper, add the cream, and reduce by half. Process everything in a blender and allow to cool.

TO ASSEMBLE —— Preheat the oven to 375°F (190°C). Fill each mushroom cap with the stuffing mixture. Sprinkle breadcrumbs on top and bake 10 to 15 minutes, depending on the size of the mushrooms. While the mushrooms are baking, add one dollop of mushroom cream on the plate for each mushroom. Once cooked, place one mushroom on top of each dollop of cream.

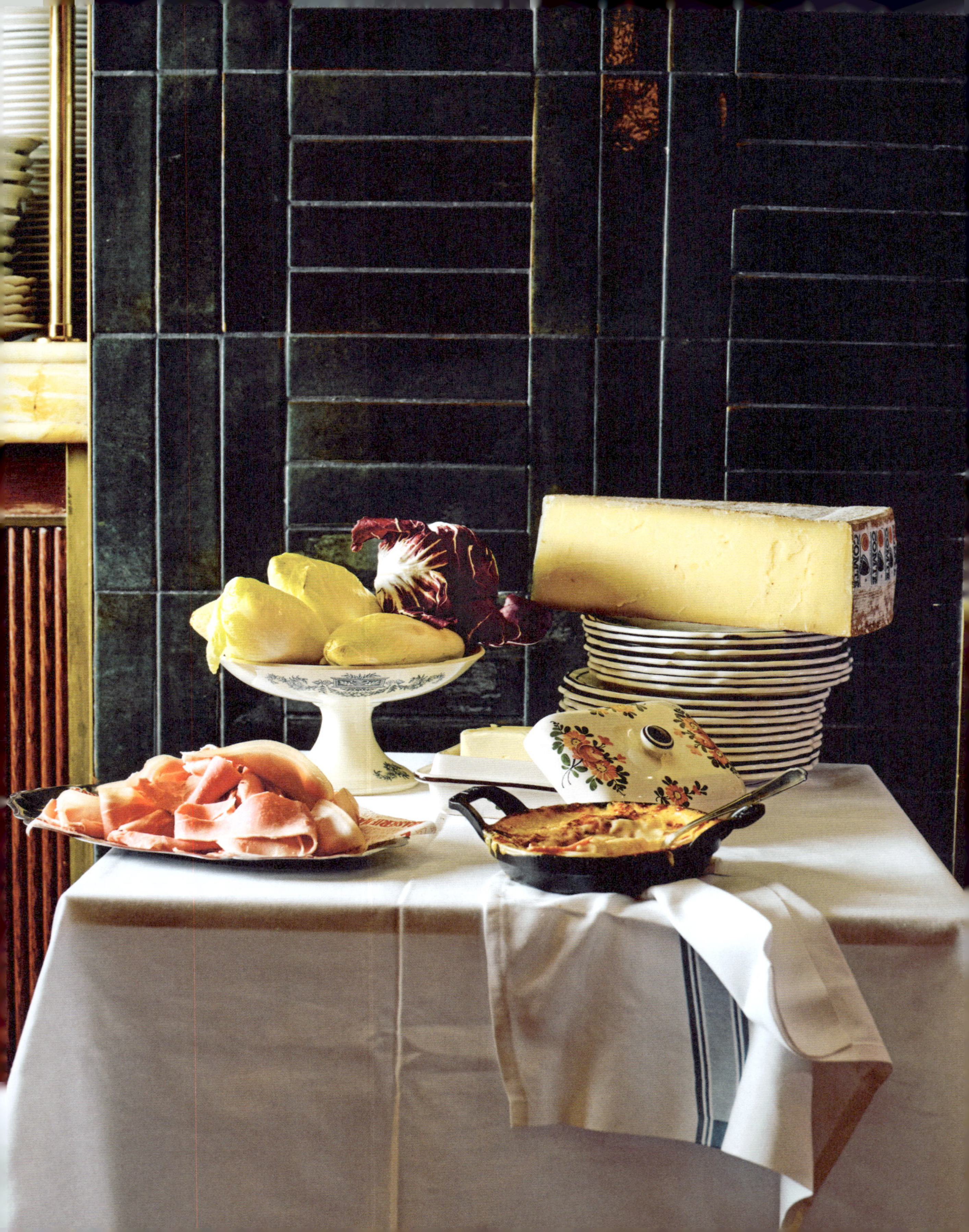

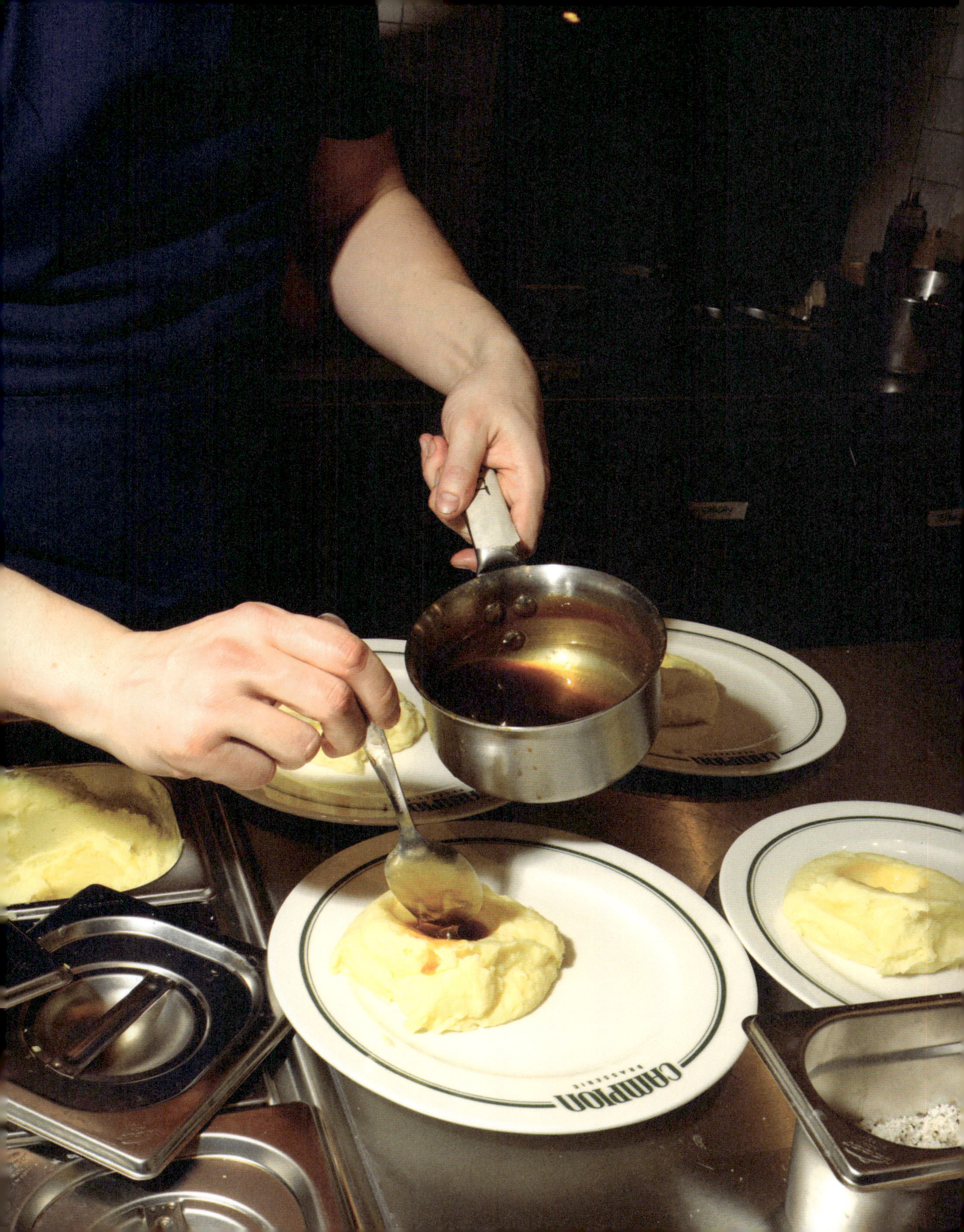
CAMPION

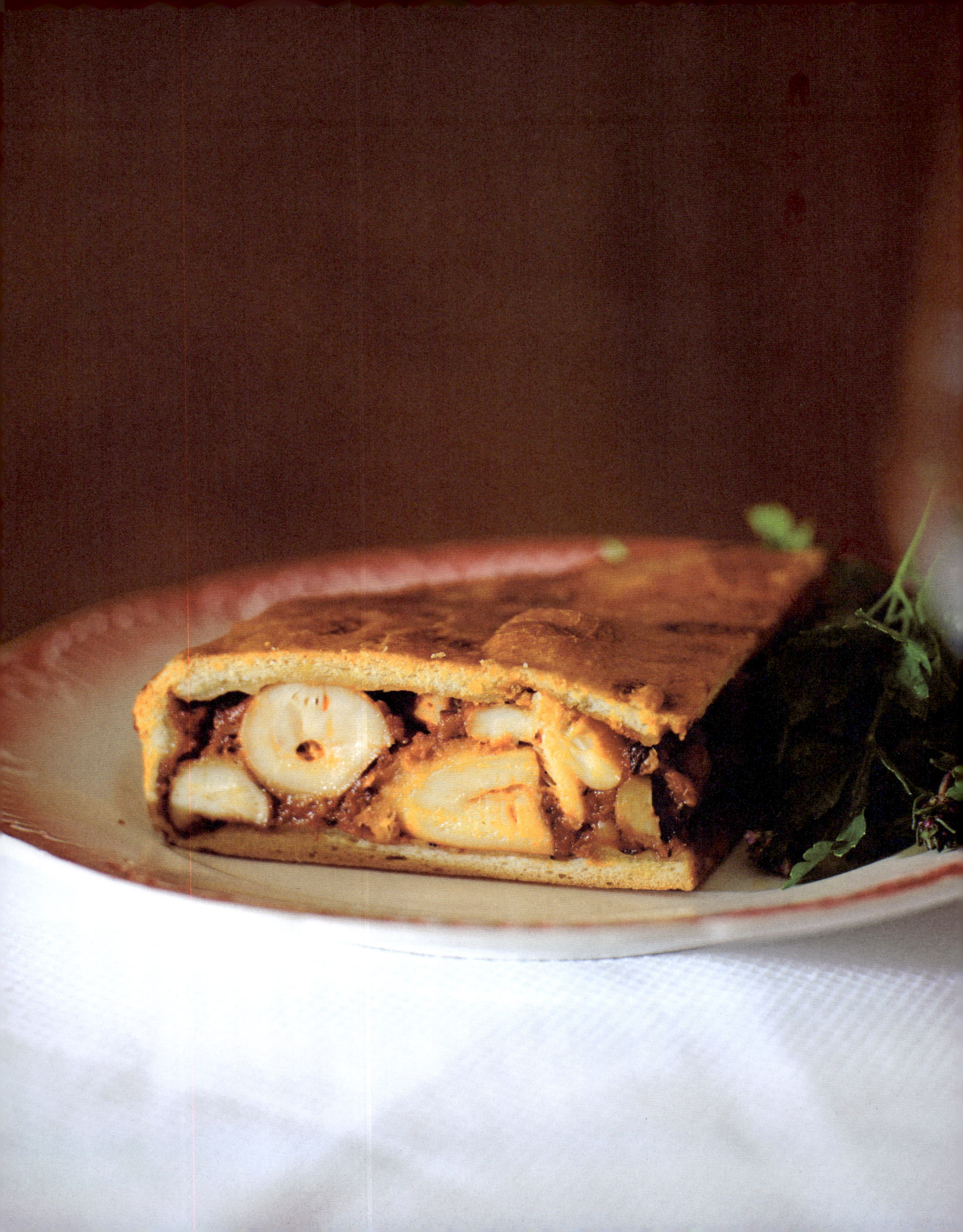

STARTERS

PREP TIME
40 MINUTES

COOK TIME
3 HOURS
25 MINUTES

REST TIME
1 HOUR

Octopus and Tomato Pie
Tielle sétoise

SERVES 8

For the dough

3 ⅓ cups (400 g) flour

½ cup (120 g) olive oil

1 tablespoon (10 g) fresh baker's yeast or 1 teaspoon active dry yeast

For the octopus ragout

1 recipe fish fumet (page 207)

1 medium-sized octopus

2 carrots

2 white onions

1 celery rib

½ cup plus 2 tablespoons (150 ml) olive oil

1 cup white wine

1 tablespoon tomato paste

1 can peeled tomatoes

1 garlic clove, unpeeled

1 thyme sprig

1 bay leaf

1 teaspoon Espelette pepper

Salt and pepper

THE BREAD —— Mix ¼ cup (50 g) lukewarm water with ½ cup (50 g) flour to make the starter. Let stand at room temperature for 1 hour. Pour the remaining flour into a mixing bowl and form a well. Pour the olive oil and yeast into the well. Mix together, add the starter, and then knead the dough. If it sticks to your fingers, add a small amount of flour; if it is too dry, add a small amount of olive oil. Form it into a ball and transfer it to a bowl. Cover the bowl with a kitchen towel and let it rest until it doubles in size.

THE OCTOPUS —— Make a fish fumet. Pour the fumet into a pot and bring to a boil. Clean the octopus and add it to the pot. Simmer on a low boil for about 2 hours. Pierce the tentacles: they will be tender when the octopus is cooked. Drain and allow to cool. Cut into pieces.

THE OCTOPUS RAGOUT —— Finely chop the carrots, onions, and celery. Sweat in olive oil until soft. Add the wine and reduce until the pot is almost completely dry. Add the tomato paste and heat for 1 to 2 minutes. Add the peeled tomatoes, unpeeled garlic, thyme, bay leaf, Espelette pepper, and octopus and stir. Simmer at a low boil for about 45 minutes. Remove from the heat and allow to cool.

TO ASSEMBLE —— Divide the dough in half. Roll out one half and line a pie pan, leaving ⅓-inch (1 cm) of overhang. Pierce the dough with a fork. Spread the octopus ragout onto the dough, then place the other half of rolled-out dough on top. Pinch and roll the dough around the outer edge to seal. Pierce the top of the dough to allow steam to escape.

TO BAKE —— Bake at 350°F (180°C) for 40 minutes. Serve hot or cold, depending on your preference.

BRASSERIE
Dubillot

222 rue Saint-Denis - Paris 02
CUISINE AU CHARBON DE BOIS

TEAM

MEAT

Steak with Peppercorn Sauce

PREP TIME 20 MINUTES

COOK TIME 10 TO 20 MINUTES

Fillet de bœuf sauce au poivre

SERVES 2

For the meat

2 steaks, about 7 ounces (200 g) each

1 teaspoon salt

2 tablespoons (20 g) mignonette pepper

Sunflower oil

3 tablespoons (40 g) butter

1 garlic clove, crushed

1 thyme sprig

For the peppercorn sauce

½ finely chopped shallot

1 tablespoon (10 g) whole mignonette peppercorns

½ cup cognac

½ cup plus 2 tablespoons (150 g) heavy cream

Salt and pepper

THE MEAT —— Salt the steaks generously on each side. Pour the pepper onto a plate and roll the steaks in the pepper to coat the sides. Heat a pan over high and sear the steaks in oil. Reduce the heat to medium and add the butter. Once the butter is melted, add the garlic and thyme, then baste the meat with the butter for a few minutes. For steaks cooked to medium, finish in the oven for a few minutes at 350°F (180°C). Cover with foil and set aside to rest.

THE PEPPERCORN SAUCE —— Sweat the shallot and roast the peppercorns in the same skillet. Add the cognac, then flambé. Cook until the liquid has nearly evaporated. Add the cream and reduce once more, until the consistency has thickened. Adjust seasoning to taste and transfer to a gravy boat.

Around THE TABLE

CHRISTENED THE "KING OF SPICES" BY ROMAN GOURMET APICIUS, pepper was a symbol of wealth in the Middle Ages. A fortune could therefore be measured in terms of gold . . . or pepper. Beginning in the 7th century, Arabs commercialized pepper and even used it as a currency, which is where the French expression *payer en espèces* ("to pay in cash") is derived: *espèces* and *épices* ("spices") share the same etymology. Many ransom payments were settled in pepper throughout history, and legend has it that the Crusaders who captured the Palestinian city of Caesarea were rewarded with 1 kilo of this prized spice.

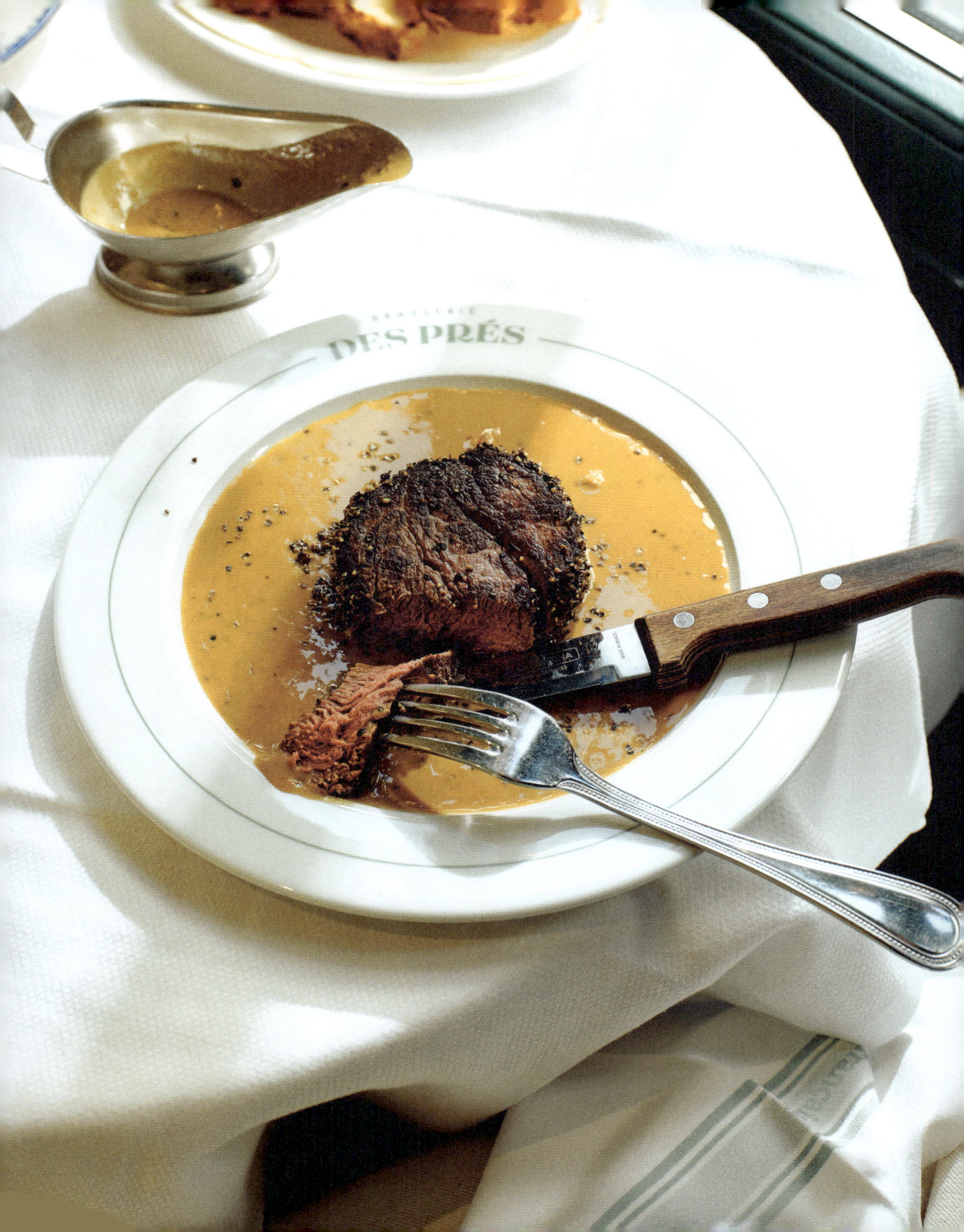
BRASSERIE
DES PRÉS

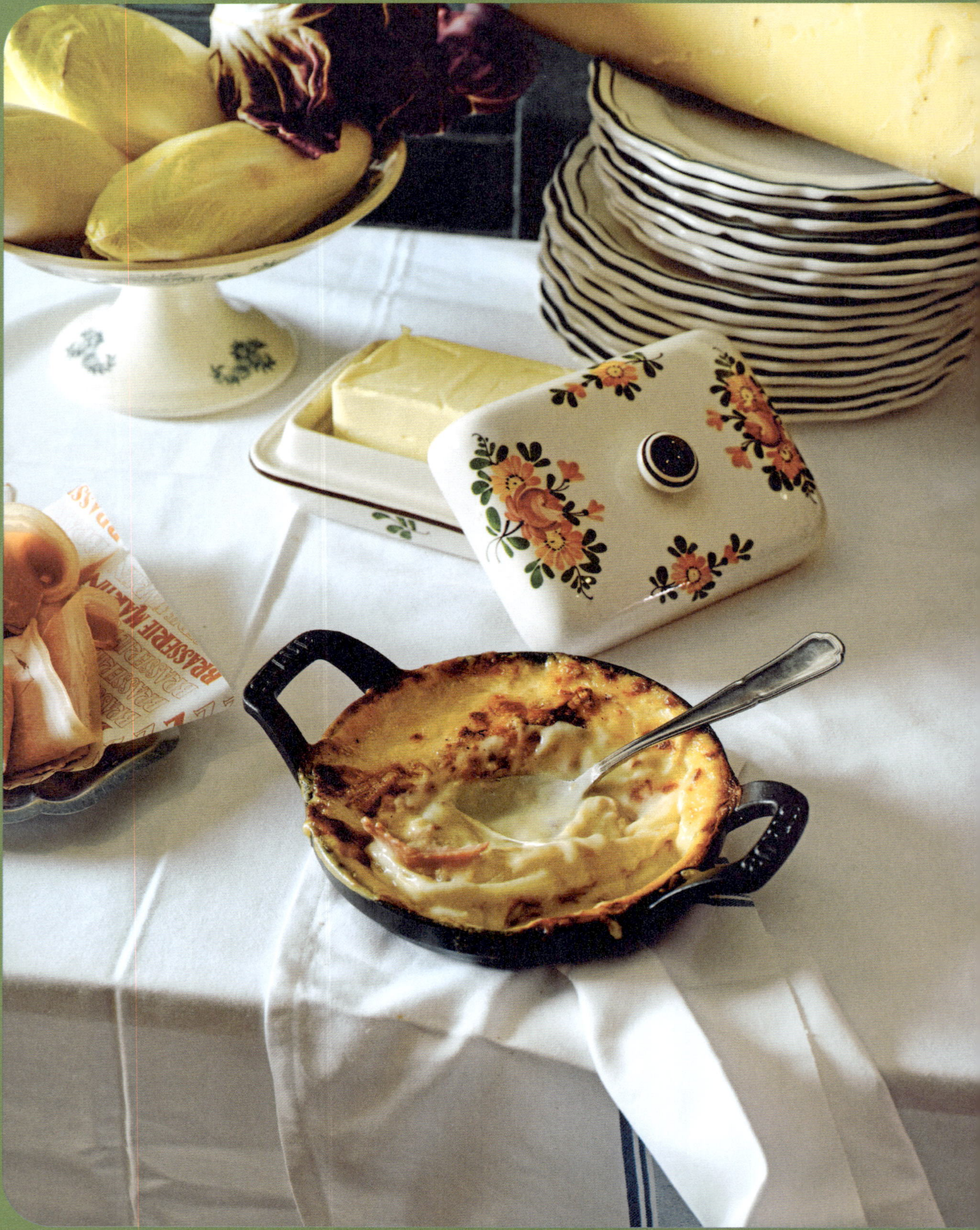
BRASSERIE

MEAT

Endive and Ham Gratin

Endives au jambon

(PREP TIME 20 MINUTES)   SERVES 4   (COOK TIME 40 MINUTES)

For the béchamel sauce 3 tablespoons (40 g) butter · ⅓ cup (40 g) flour · ¾ cup plus 4 teaspoons (200 ml) milk · 2 pinches mignonette pepper · salt · nutmeg **For the endives** 4 large endives · butter · 8 slices cured or smoked ham · ¼ cup (30 g) grated Comté

THE BÉCHAMEL SAUCE —— To prepare the béchamel, first make a roux. Melt the butter in a saucepan, then add the flour all at once and whisk until combined. Pour the milk in gradually while whisking continuously. Season with pepper, salt, and nutmeg. Set aside.

THE ENDIVES —— Preheat the oven to 350°F (180°C). Remove and discard the outer leaves from the endives, slice the endives in half lengthwise, then wash and dry well. Melt a little butter in a pan and brown the endives on the cut side. Roll a slice of ham around each endive half, then arrange in a gratin dish with the seam on the bottom to seal it. Cover with béchamel sauce and sprinkle Comté on top.

TO BAKE —— Bake for 30 minutes. Serve hot, with a mesclun salad.

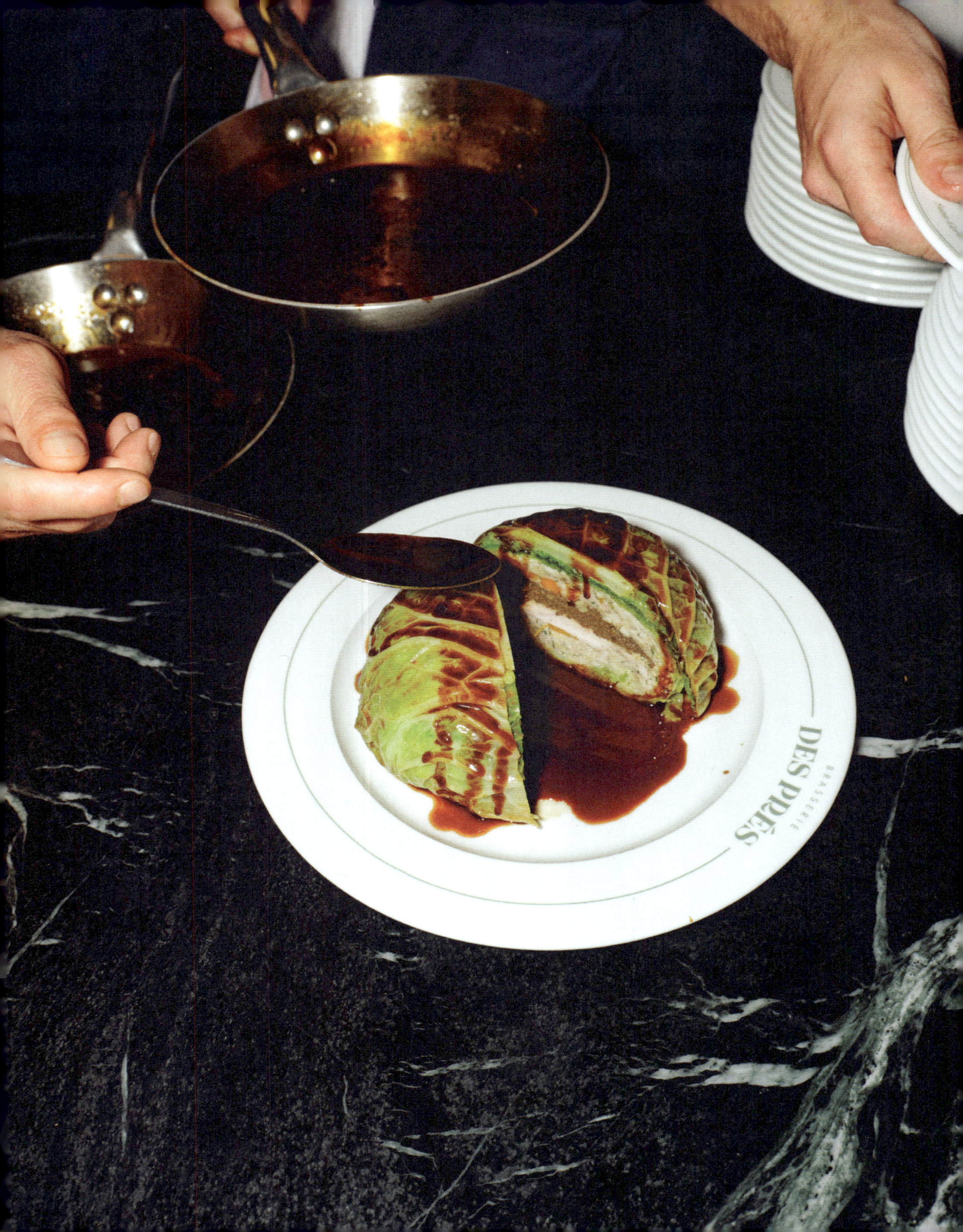
BRASSERIE
DES PRÉS

MEAT

Stuffed Cabbage
Chou farci

PREP TIME
1 HOUR

COOK TIME
1 HOUR
20 MINUTES

SERVES 2
1 head green cabbage
Vegetable bouillon (page 207)

For the mushroom duxelles
1 shallot
18 ounces (500 g) mushrooms
1 garlic clove
2 parsley sprigs
7 ounces (200 g) prosciutto
Salt

For the filling
1 slice smoked bacon
1 carrot
½ onion
1 celery rib
⅓ cup plus 4 teaspoons (100 ml) milk
3 slices (100 g) day-old bread
1 egg
11 ounces (300 g) ground sausage
2 parsley sprigs, chopped
Salt and pepper

THE CABBAGE —— Remove the leaves from the cabbage, then blanch them with the heart in boiling water for 4 minutes. Transfer to an ice bath, then arrange on a clean kitchen towel to dry.

THE MUSHROOM DUXELLES —— Finely chop the shallot. Thinly slice the mushrooms. Mince the garlic and parsley and finely dice the prosciutto. Sweat the shallot in a pan, then add the mushrooms. Season with salt. Continue to cook until the all the liquid has cooked off the mushrooms. To make the *duxelles*, a very dry mushroom paste, process the shallot and mushrooms in a blender or food processor. Transfer to a bowl and mix in the garlic, parsley, and prosciutto.

THE FILLING —— Slice the bacon into matchsticks. Dice the carrot, onion, and celery. Finely chop the cabbage heart. Sweat this mixture in a pan. Purée the milk, bread, and egg in a blender or food processor. Transfer to a bowl and add the ground sausage, chopped parsley, salt, and pepper. Mix by hand. Season to taste.

TO ASSEMBLE —— Preheat the oven to 400°F (200°C). Line the inside of a bowl with the cabbage leaves. To assemble the dish, spread alternating layers of filling and duxelles on top of the cabbage leaves. Press the mixture to pack it down, then cover and seal with the remaining cabbage leaves.

TO COOK —— Place the stuffed cabbage in a gratin dish and pour in enough vegetable bouillon to cover the bottom of the dish. Bake for 15 minutes at 400°F (200°C), then finish at 175°F (80°C) for 30 minutes.

MEAT

Beef Stew

POT-AU-FEU

PREP TIME
30 MINUTES

COOK TIME
3 ½ TO 4 ½ HOURS

REST TIME
OVERNIGHT / 1 NIGHT

SERVES 4

For the marrow bones 4 marrow bones · vinegar **For the meat** about 2 ½ pounds (1.2 kg) stew meat (chuck, shank, short ribs, etc.) **For the aromatic garnish** 3 carrots · 1 leek · 3 onions · 1 celery rib · 4 whole cloves 2 garlic cloves · **For the vegetables** 1 bunch young turnips · 1 bunch carrots with their stems · ¼ head green cabbage · 4 yellow potatoes · brown stock or vegetable stock (pages 206–207) · 1 bouquet garni

THE MARROW BONES — Place the marrow bones in an ice bath with a bit of vinegar and store in the refrigerator overnight to release the blood and other impurities.

THE MEAT — Trim the meat. Cut into ½-inch (1.5 cm) cubes.

THE AROMATIC GARNISH — Cut the carrots and leek into large pieces (page 57), then finely chop 1 onion and the celery. Peel another onion and stud it with cloves. Cut the last onion in half widthwise and sear the cut sides on a hot, dry pan. Crush the garlic cloves.

THE VEGETABLES — Wash the turnips and carrots. Cut the turnips in half and the carrots in thirds at an angle. Chop the cabbage into 2-inch (5 cm) pieces. Peel the potatoes and cut in half widthwise.

TO COOK — Brown the meat in a large pot or dutch oven, then remove from the pot and set aside. In the same pot, sauté the aromatic garnish for a few minutes without letting it brown. Return the meat to the pot and cover with brown stock, vegetable bouillon, or water. Add the bouquet garni and bring to a boil. Cover and cook at a low boil for 3½ to 4½ hours, until the meat is fork-tender. Try to skim the fat from the top occasionally during cooking. With 30 minutes left on the timer, add the marrow bones to the pot, followed by the rest of the vegetables in the order of required cooking time: potatoes, carrots with their stems, turnips, cabbage.

TO PLATE — Fill a soup tureen with broth. Slice the pieces of meat and arrange them on a plate with the vegetables and marrow bones. Serve with cornichons, mustard, and horseradish if you have it. FYI: it's even better reheated the next day.

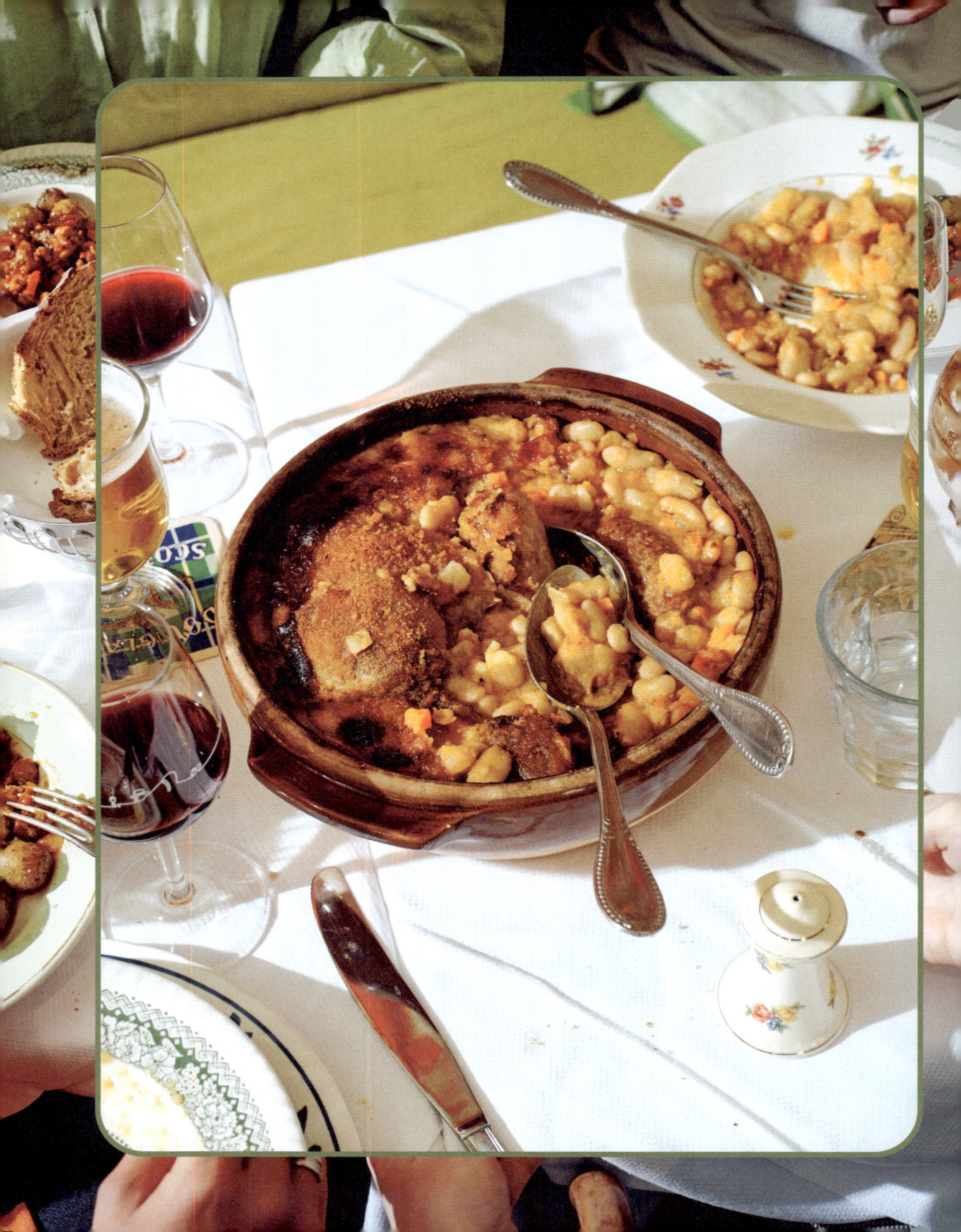

MEAT

Cassoulet

**PREP TIME
1 HOUR**

**COOK TIME
3 HOURS**
REST TIME: OVERNIGHT

SERVES 6

For the base

18 ounces (500 g) Tarbais (cassoulet) beans

3 white onions, divided

4 whole cloves

½ head of garlic

4 carrots

7 ounces (200 g) fresh pork belly

¼ cup (70 g) tomato paste

½ bunch thyme

1 celery rib

For the meat

3 Toulouse sausages

6 large slices garlic sausage

3 confit duck legs

2 garlic cloves

Salt and pepper

1 ¼ cups (160 g) breadcrumbs

THE BASE —— Soak the beans in water overnight. The next day, cut an onion in half and stud it with cloves. Crush the half head of garlic, peel the carrots, and slice the pork belly. Add the beans and studded onion to a pot and cover with water. Add the tomato paste, thyme, crushed garlic, celery, carrots, and pork belly. Cook over low heat for 2 hours, then remove the carrots and celery. Dice the carrots and celery once they are cool enough to handle.

THE MEAT —— While the beans and vegetables cook, sear the sausages in a pan with the fat from the duck confit, then set aside. Finely chop the remaining two onions and set those aside as well. Add the onions to the pan with the sausages and cook just until softened. Add the minced garlic and cooked carrots and celery. Pour the mixture into the pot on top of the beans and stir to combine. Season with salt and pepper.

TO ASSEMBLE —— Chop the Toulouse sausage into large pieces. Spread a layer of beans into the bottom of a ceramic casserole dish, then layer the pork belly and garlic sausage on top. Add another layer of beans, then the Toulouse sausage. Add a final layer of beans, place the duck thighs on top, and cover with a light layer of breadcrumbs. Rest for 1 hour.

TO BAKE —— Bake at 350°F (180°C) for about 1 hour, until the crust is golden brown. Remove from the oven and let rest for a few minutes before serving.

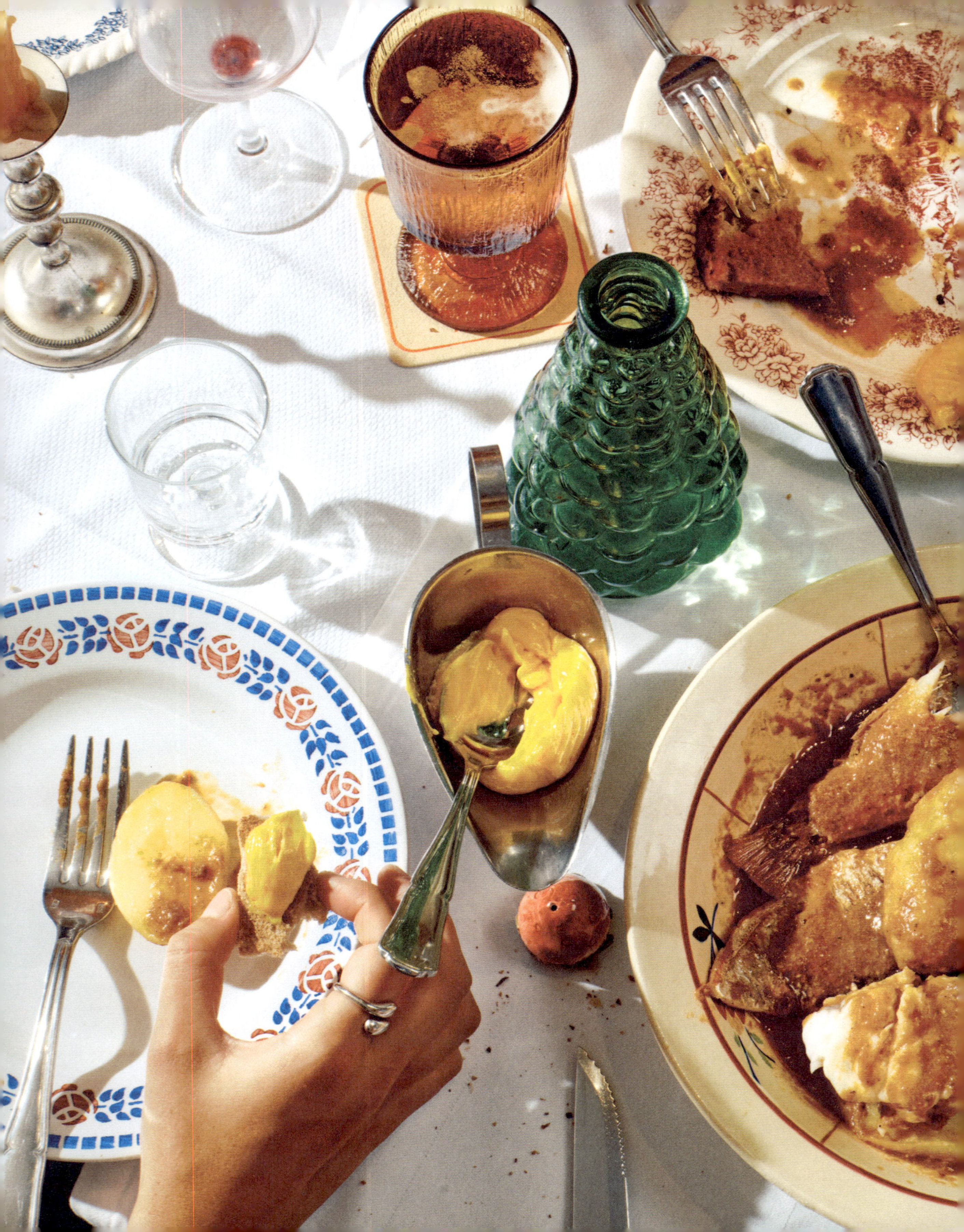

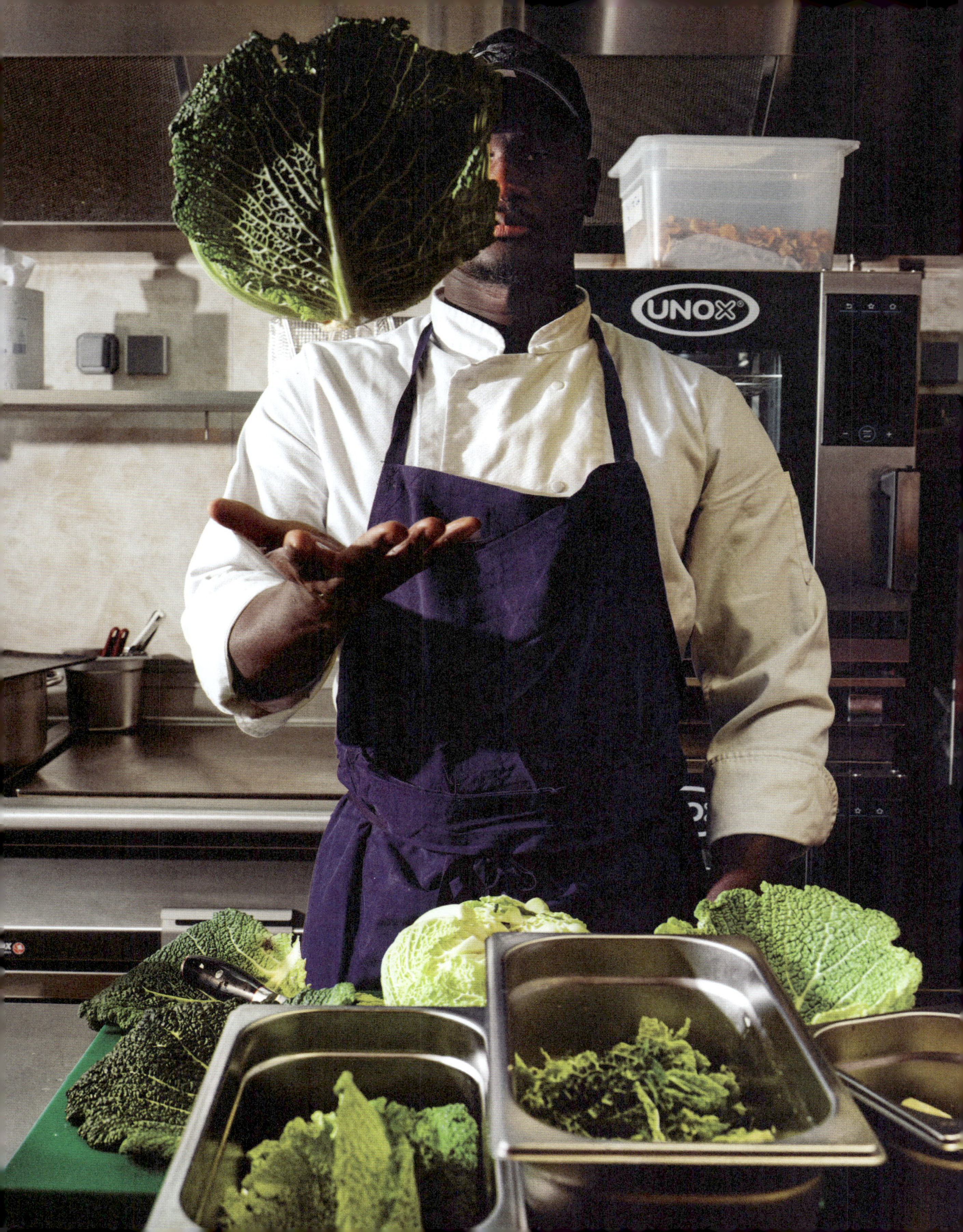
UNOX

MEAT

Roast Chicken with Lemon Confit

POULET RÔTI CONTISÉ CITRON CONFIT

PREP TIME 1 HOUR

COOK TIME 3 HOURS

SERVES 4

For the lemon confit 8 to 10 lemons · 4¼ cups (1 L) olive oil · 1 garlic clove 1 thyme sprig **For the herbed butter** 1 cup plus 2 tablespoons (250 g) unsalted butter, softened · 1 shallot, finely chopped · ½ garlic clove, minced · ¼ bunch parsley · ¼ bunch chervil · juice and zest of 1 lemon 1 teaspoon (7 g) salt · ½ pinch mignonette pepper **For the chicken** 1 free-range chicken · 2 garlic cloves, unpeeled · 3 thyme sprigs · 2 slices day-old bread · sunflower oil · salt **For the sauce** 1 large handful green olives 4 cups chicken stock (page 206) · 2 slices day-old bread torn into pieces

THE LEMON CONFIT —— Add all the ingredients to a pot and bring to a boil. Reduce the heat and let the lemons cook for at least 2 hours. Transfer to an airtight container once cooled. Preserved lemons will keep for several weeks.

THE HERBED BUTTER —— Combine the softened butter, finely chopped shallot, minced garlic, parsley and chervil leaves, and lemon zest and juice in a bowl. Season with salt and pepper and adjust seasoning to taste.

THE CHICKEN —— Preheat the oven to 375°F (190°C). Lay the bird flat, skin side up. Beginning at the neck, use your fingers to separate the skin from the meat. Gently insert the butter under the skin, then press firmly to seal. Cut 2 preserved lemons into quarters. Flip the chicken over and insert the garlic, thyme, lemon quarters, and bread into the cavity. Cover the entire chicken with oil and season generously with salt.

TO COOK —— Bake for 50 minutes to 1 hour, until the chicken is golden brown. Once cooked, remove the chicken from the dish, strain the liquid, and set aside.

THE SAUCE —— Finely dice the remaining preserved lemons and finely chop the green olives. Combine the lemons, olives, chicken stock, bread, and chicken roasting juices in a pot. Stir over low heat, then transfer to a gravy boat.

MEAT

Croque-monsieur

PREP TIME 30 MINUTES

COOK TIME 15 MINUTES

SERVES 4

For the Mornay

4 teaspoons (20 g) butter

2 tablespoons plus 2 teaspoons (20 g) flour

⅓ cup plus 4 teaspoons (100 ml) milk

Salt

1 pinch mignonette pepper

Nutmeg

1 ¾ ounces (50 g) young Comté, grated

To assemble

4 teaspoons (20 g) butter

8 thick slices white sandwich bread

1 teaspoon Dijon mustard

8 slices (200 g) young Comté

4 thick ham slices

THE MORNAY —— Make a roux: first melt the butter in a pot, then add the flour all at once and stir for several minutes. Gradually incorporate the milk, whisking constantly. Season with salt, pepper, and nutmeg. Remove from the heat and mix in the grated cheese, then store in the refrigerator.

TO ASSEMBLE —— Melt the butter. Use a pastry brush to generously butter one side of each slice of bread. Working with one slice at a time, top the other side of 4 slices of bread with Dijon and a slice of Comté, then spread with 2 heaping spoons of Mornay sauce, one slice of Comté, and one slice of ham. Be sure to reserve some sauce for serving. Top each sandwich with the remaining slices of bread, butter-side up.

TO COOK —— Preheat the oven to 400°F (200°C). Melt a little butter in a pan and toast the sandwiches on each side.

TO PLATE —— Remove the pan from the heat and spread 1 tablespoon of Mornay sauce onto each sandwich, then bake in the oven for 4 to 6 minutes. Serve with a fresh salad or portion of fries.

Around THE TABLE

A BRASSERIE CLASSIC, the name "croque-monsieur" speaks for itself. The French *croquer* means "to munch" and a *monsieur* is, well . . . a man. Legend has it that in the 1910s on Paris' Boulevard des Capucines, the owner of the Bel Âge brasserie made bread that was as good as his gossip. One evening, when he ran out of baguettes, he improvised these smashing sandwiches on sliced white bread. When asked what was inside, he replied with a smirk: "Man meat."

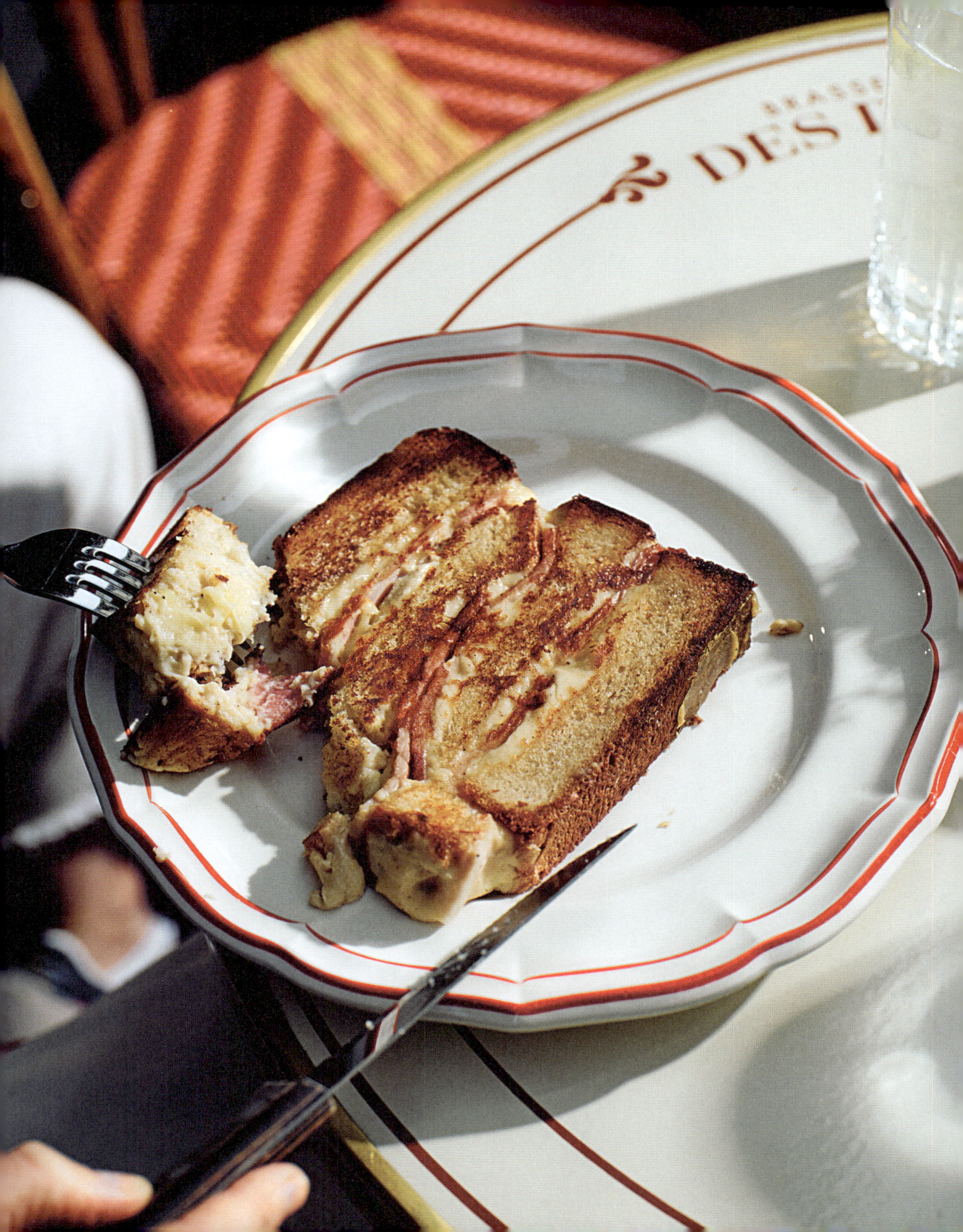
DES

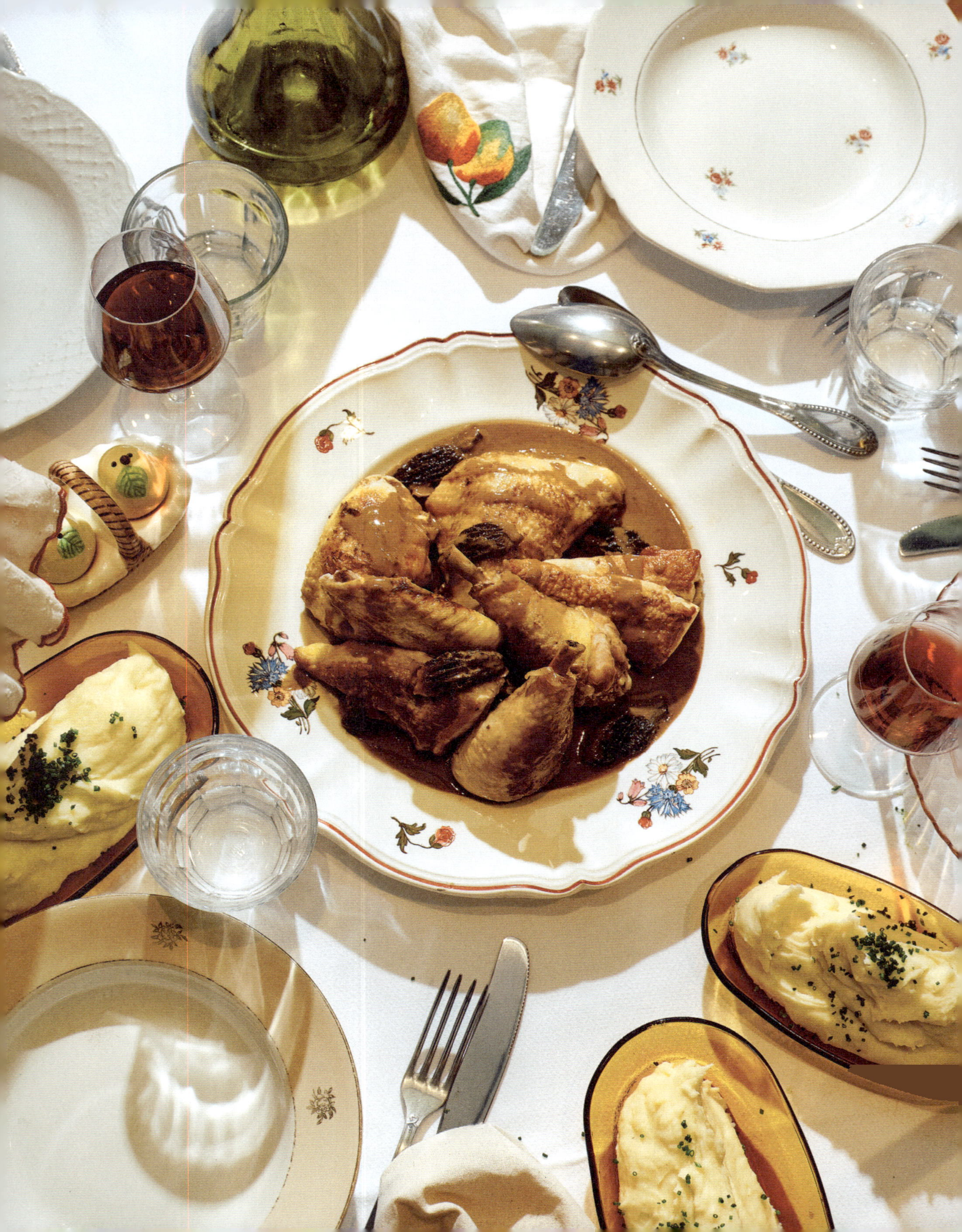

MEAT

Braised Chicken
with Morels and Vin Jaune

Volaille au vin jaune et aux morilles

PREP TIME 10 MINUTES

COOK TIME 45 MINUTES

SERVES 4

For the chicken

1 free-range chicken, about 4 pounds (1.8 kg)
2 teaspoons (10 g) butter
1 cup (240 ml) vin jaune
1 ¼ cups (300 ml) white stock
1 ⅔ cups (400 ml) heavy cream
Salt and pepper

For the morels

About 30 fresh morel mushrooms
1 shallot
2 teaspoons (10 g) butter
½ cup (120 ml) vin jaune

THE CHICKEN —— Ask your butcher to cut your chicken into 8 portions. Preheat the oven to 350°F (180°C). Season the skin side of the chicken with salt. Melt the butter in a dutch oven over medium heat and brown the chicken pieces on each side. Pour in the wine and the white stock. Bake about 15 minutes. Remove the chicken and set aside. Pour the cream into the pot and reduce over low heat until the consistency is thick enough to coat the back of a spoon. Season with salt and pepper.

THE MORELS —— Wash the morels thoroughly in a bowl of vinegar water, then dry with a clean towel. Finely chop the shallot. Sauté the mushrooms in a pan with butter over high heat until nearly all the liquid has evaporated. Add the shallots and sauté quickly. Add the wine and reduce until nearly all the liquid has evaporated.

TO PLATE —— Plate the morels and chicken, then drizzle with the sauce and serve.

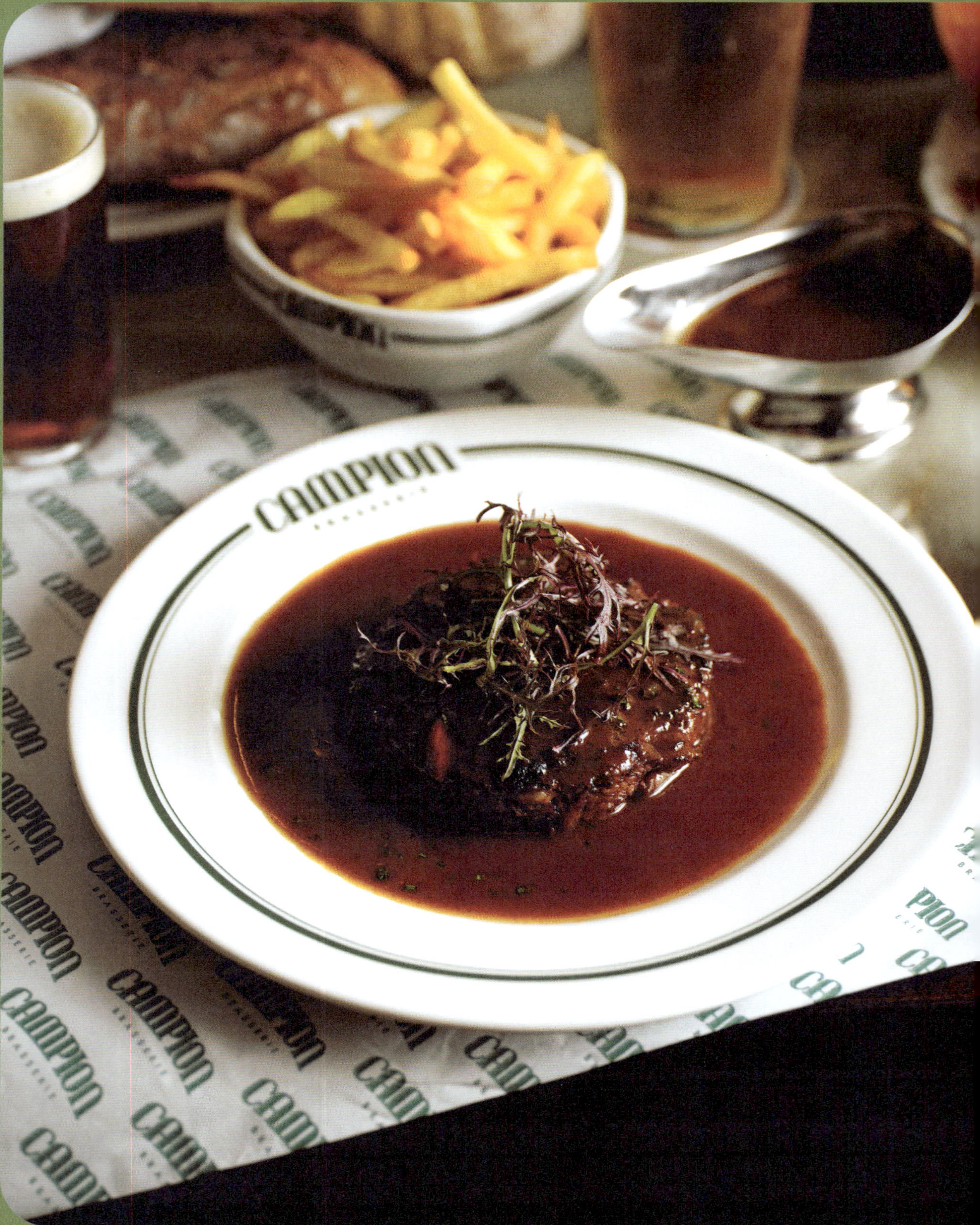
CAMPION

MEAT - EAT HEARTY BEFORE THE PARTY

Beef and Beer Stew

Carbonade

PREP TIME 20 MINUTES — **SERVES 6** — **COOK TIME 3 HOURS**

For the meat 4½ pounds (2 kg) flat iron steak · 1¾ pounds (800 g) beef cheeks · oil **For the sauce** 3 onions · 2 garlic cloves · 3 tablespoons plus 1 teaspoon (50 ml) red wine vinegar · ½ cup (100 g) brown sugar · ¼ cup plus 3 tablespoons (100 g) whole-grain mustard · 4¼ cups (1 L) dark beer · 4¼ cups (1 L) brown stock (page 206) or water

THE MEAT —— Trim the fat and nerves from the meat (your butcher can do this for you) and cut into large 2-inch (5 cm) cubes. Brown the meat in a pan with oil, then transfer to a large pot.

THE SAUCE —— Slice the onions thinly and chop the garlic. Sweat the onions and garlic in the same pan you used to brown the meat, then add to the pot with the browned meat. Add the vinegar to the pan to deglaze, then pour the liquid into the pot and add the brown sugar, mustard, beer, and stock. Bring to a boil, cover, and cook at a low boil for at least 3 hours, until the meat is tender. Strain the sauce, then reduce to your desired consistency.

TO PLATE —— You can shred the meat or leave it in chunks. Either way, reheat the meat in the reduced sauce before serving.

Around THE TABLE

THIS BEEF AND BEER STEW IS A TRADITIONAL FLEMISH DISH. It is considered the beef bourguignon of the north, except it's made with beer... and only beer. From the Latin *carbo* meaning "coal," the dish got its name from the miners who cooked leftover meat over coal embers.

MEAT

Braised Rabbit in Mustard Sauce

Lapin à la moutarde

PREP TIME
15 MINUTES

COOK TIME
1 HOUR
15 MINUTES

SERVES 4

For the rabbit
1 rabbit
1 tablespoon neutral oil
4 teaspoons (20 g) butter
3 shallots

For the sauce
1 tablespoon red wine vinegar
½ bottle white wine
2 garlic cloves, crushed
2 thyme sprigs
1 ¼ cups (300 g) heavy cream
½ cup (125 g) Dijon mustard
Salt and pepper

THE RABBIT —— Ask your butcher to carefully separate each part of the rabbit: the thighs, saddle, and legs. Add the oil and butter to a frying pan. Over high heat, sear the salted rabbit cuts on each side. While the rabbit cooks, peel and finely chop the shallots.

THE SAUCE —— Once the rabbit is golden brown, transfer it to a platter. Add the shallots to the same pan and cook until translucent. Add a splash of vinegar. Add the wine, crushed garlic, and thyme and season with pepper. Reduce until ¼ of the liquid remains.

TO FINISH —— Once the liquid has reduced, return the rabbit to the pan. Add the cream and mustard. Cover and cook over low heat for about 1 hour. Season with salt and pepper and add more mustard to taste.

Around THE TABLE

THE CITY OF DIJON: THE UNDISPUTED KINGDOM OF MUSTARD? Dijon's connection to mustard dates to Philippe Le Hardi, Duke of Burgundy. As the story goes, in gratitude for the city's support during the Flemish war of 1392, he bestowed up on it his motto: *Moult me tarde* or *Y me tarde*, depending on the account. Mustard was also apparently a guilty pleasure of Louis XI, known as "Louis the Prudent," who allegedly never left home without it.

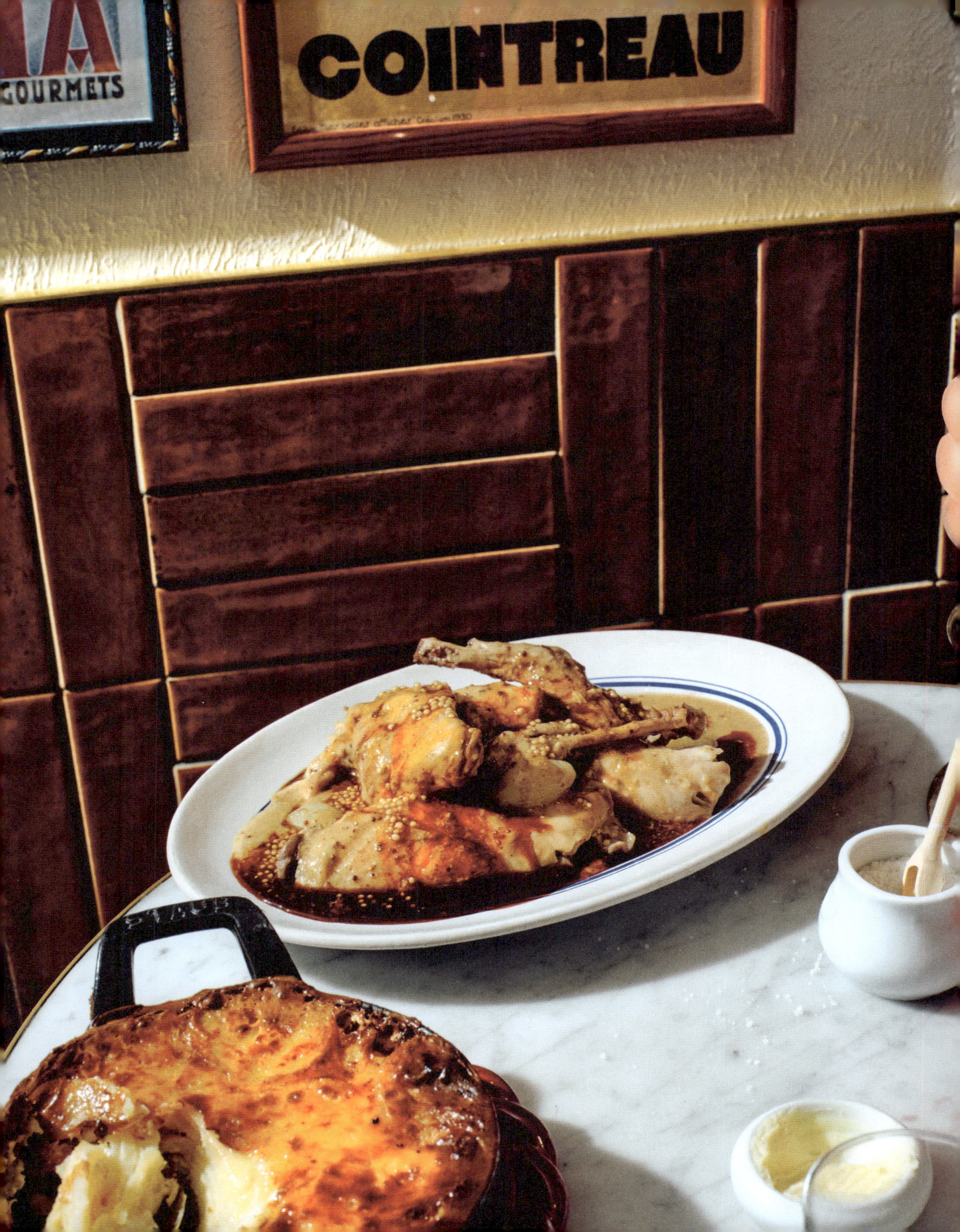
GOURMETS
COINTREAU

Around THE TABLE

① STUFFED CABBAGE (CHOU FARCI)
— *recipe page 73*

There are certain dishes where what you see is what you get, but like a cereal box surprise for grown-ups, stuffed cabbage can be filled with an endless variety of ingredients. These ingredients were once a reflection of social class. Jean Gabin himself savored the dish in *La Tatoué* (1968), though not before ensuring it was served "at room temperature." Originally a humble peasant dish, stuffed cabbage has since spread throughout many regions of Eastern and Central Europe.

② BEEF STEW (POT-AU-FEU)
— *recipe page 76*

Few dishes evoke a sense of nostalgia quite like a Sunday beef stew. In the late 18th century, Michel Honoré Bounieu captured its essence in a still life titled "Preparations for a Stew" (*Les Apprêts du pot-au feu*) that's displayed at the Louvre—which goes to show the number of times he enjoyed the dish. Alexandre Dumas called it "the cornerstone of [our] gastronomy." Marcel Rouff's 1942 novel *The Passionate Epicure* (*La Vie et la Passion de Dodin-Bouffant, gourmet*) immortalized the dish through its fictional gouramand, Dodin-Bouffant, who prepared a "magnificently complicated" four-course version. Throughout the years, many great chefs like Guy Savoy, Jean-François Piège, Yannick Alléno, and Pierre Gagnaire have each put their own spin on this classic French dish.

③ CASSOULET
— *recipe page 79*

Declared the "king of Occitan cuisine" by Prosper Montagné, author of the first *Larousse gastronomique*, cassoulet is steeped in legend. Gourmands claim that it was first created during the Hundred Years' War, when Castelnaudary was besieged by the English. The residents refused to surrender. They threw all the food they had left into a pot and simmered it overnight to nourish their troops... and cassoulet was born. Traditionally, those without home ovens would bring their cassoulet to their local baker to be cooked. Cassoulet rose to Hollywood star status on the evening of the 2009 United States presidential election thanks to pranksters from French newspaper *Le Petit Journal*. Hidden among the crowd, the journalists raised a massive sign that read "CASSOULET" in capital letters.

④ VEAL STEW (BLANQUETTE DE VEAU)
— *recipe page 96*

It's tough to separate fact from fiction when it comes to the origins of blanquette when several regions in France claim it as their own. What is certain, however, is that the name of the dish comes from its signature white (*blanc*) sauce. Blanquette becomes spy jargon in French film *OSS 117: Cairo, Nest of Spies* when used as a code word between Hubert Bonisseur de la Bath and the barman at the watering hole OSS 117 visits upon arriving in Cairo.

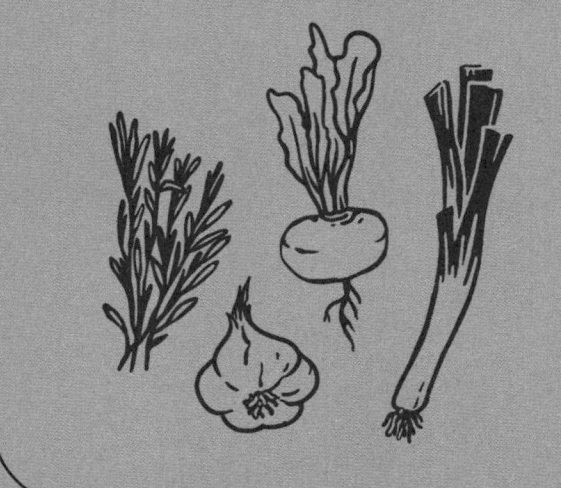

⑤ FAIRE CHABROT ("TO ADD RED WINE")
— *general*

Faire chabrot, faire godaille, boire à chabrot... there are so many expressions for adding a little wine to your leftover soup, then drinking it straight from the bowl. In this delicious tradition from the south of France, it is customary for the wine to be precisely measured: the spoon must be completely covered when resting in the bowl. "Chabrot" is said to come from the Latin *capreolus*, because the act is reminiscent of the way a goat drinks water.

DUCRETET
THOMSON
BEC-KINA
APERITIF DES SPORTIFS
Boire et manger à la française

MEAT

Braised Lamb Shoulder
with White Bean Ragout

Épaule d'agneau de 7 heures et ragout de cocos de paimpol

PREP TIME 30 MINUTES

COOK TIME 8 HOURS

SERVES 5 TO 6

For the lamb

1 lamb shoulder
Oil
1 onion
3 carrots
1 celery rib
1 shallot
1 head of garlic
1 cup white wine
1 tablespoon tomato paste
1 cup brown stock or vegetable bouillon (pages 206–207)
2 thyme sprigs
1 bay leaf branch
Espelette pepper
Mignonette pepper
Salt

For the white bean ragout

3 carrots
2 onions
1 celery rib
1 tablespoon tomato paste
2¼ pounds (1 kg) shelled Coco de Paimpol beans or Haricot Tarbais (cassoulet)
2 cups (500 g) brown stock or vegetable bouillon
7 tablespoons (100 g) butter, cubed
1 pinch mignonette pepper
Chicken stock (optional)

THE LAMB —— Preheat the oven to 250°F (120°C). Heat a pot over high and sear the lamb shoulder in oil on two sides, then remove and set aside. Cut the onion, carrots, celery, and shallot into thick slices. Cut the head of garlic in half. Add these aromatics to the pot and sweat until soft, then add the white wine. Cook until nearly all the liquid is reduced. Add the tomato paste and cook for 1 minute. Return the lamb shoulder to the pot and fill halfway with stock or bouillon. Add the herbs, the Espelette pepper, and the mignonette pepper. Season with salt. Cover and bake in the oven for 7 hours.

THE WHITE BEAN RAGOUT —— Dice the carrots, onions, and celery. Sweat the vegetables in a pan heated over low, then add the tomato paste and cook for 1 minute. Add the beans, cover with brown stock or vegetable bouillon, and bring to a boil. Simmer until the beans are tender, about 40 minutes. Transfer the mixture to a platter. Mix in the cubed butter and allow it to melt. Season with pepper.

THE SAUCE —— Remove the lamb from the oven and strain the cooking juices. Place the lamb on a baking sheet and broil in the oven until golden brown. In the meantime, reduce the cooking juices in a saucepan until the liquid is thick enough to coat the back of a spoon.

TO PLATE —— Transfer the beans to a serving platter and place the lamb in the center. Top with a drizzle of the reduced cooking juices and chicken stock, if desired.

MEAT

Veal Stew

BLANQUETTE DE VEAU

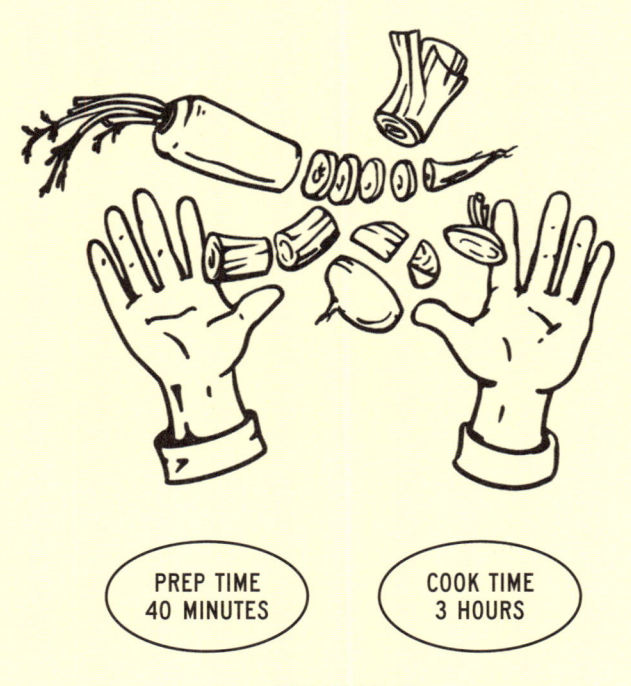

PREP TIME
40 MINUTES

COOK TIME
3 HOURS

SERVES 6

For the meat About 4½ pounds (2 kg) veal stew meat · **For the vegetables** 3 carrots · 3 onions · 4 whole cloves · 1 leek · 1 celery rib · 1 garlic clove 4 teaspoons (20 g) butter · 8½ cups (2 L) white stock · 1 bouquet garni **For the roux and sauce** 3 tablespoons (40 g) butter · ⅓ cup (40 g) flour 1¼ cups (300 g) heavy cream · 1 egg yolk · juice of ½ a lemon · salt and mignonette pepper **For the sides** 1 bunch carrots with greens · about 10 ounces (300 g) pearl onions · about 14 ounces (400 g) button mushrooms vegetable bouillon (or water) · 2 tablespoons (30 g) butter · 1 pinch salt 1 pinch sugar · olive oil

THE MEAT —— Cut the meat into large pieces. Place in a pot and cover with cold water. Bring to a boil and skim away the fat as it accumulates. Remove the meat from the pot and rinse with cool water. Discard the cooking liquid.

THE VEGETABLES —— Peel and cut the carrots into large pieces. Thinly slice 2 onions and stud the third with the cloves. Cut the leek and celery into large pieces. Peel and chop the garlic. Add the vegetables to the pot used to prepare the meat and sweat with butter. Add the meat to the pot and cover with white stock. Add the bouquet garni and bring to a boil. Cook at a low boil for 2 hours 30 minutes, skimming frequently.

THE ROUX —— Melt the butter in a large pot. Add the flour and stir for a few minutes. Let cool.

THE SIDES —— Wash the carrots and slice them diagonally. Peel the onions. Wash the mushrooms, remove the stems, then cut the caps into quarters. Add the mushroom stems to the pot with the rest of the vegetables. Cook the carrots and onions in a separate pot filled halfway with bouillon or water. Add the cubed butter, salt, and sugar. Bring to a boil and pierce the vegetables frequently to test for doneness. The vegetables are ready when they're soft and nearly all the liquid has evaporated—at this point, the vegetables will be glazed. Sauté the mushroom caps in a pan with a dash of oil until they are dry and browned.

THE BLANQUETTE SAUCE —— Retrieve the cooked meat and set aside. Strain the cooking broth from the meat and reduce until about 4¼ cups (1 L) of liquid remain. Pour the hot broth into the pot with the roux and whisk over high heat until smooth; the sauce will thicken. Cook at a low boil for 5 minutes. Remove the pot from the heat and whisk in the cream and egg yolk. Mix in the meat and aromatics, then add the lemon juice and reheat gently. Adjust seasoning to taste. Transfer the blanquette to a pretty soup tureen to serve.

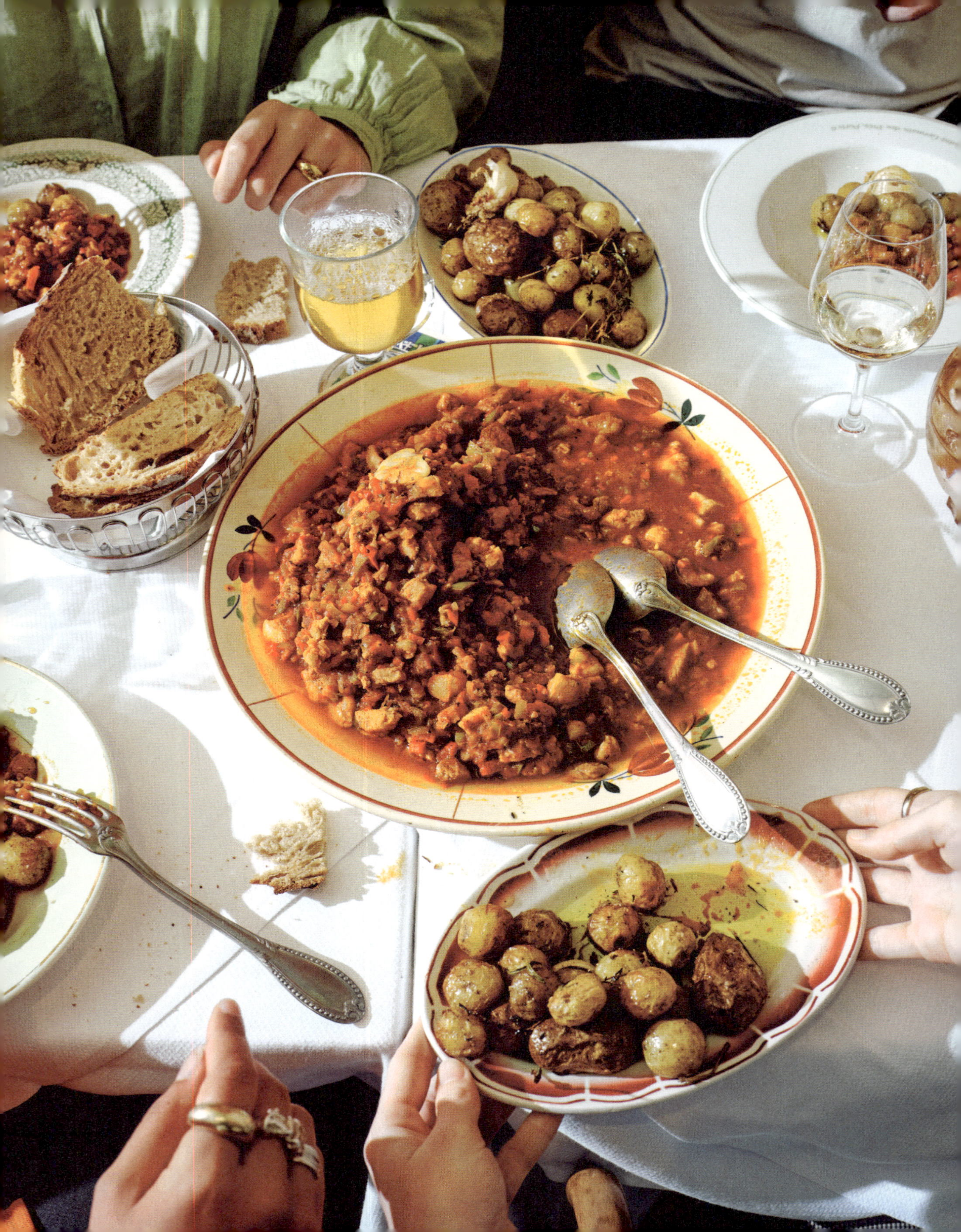

MEAT

Veal Axoa
Axoa de veau

PREP TIME 30 MINUTES — **SERVES 6** — **COOK TIME 1 HOUR 15 MINUTES**

- 4½ pounds (2 g) veal shoulder
- 5 yellow onions
- 11 ounces (300 g) green peppers
- 5½ pounds (2.5 kg) heirloom tomatoes
- 3 tablespoons olive oil
- 3 tablespoons red wine vinegar
- 8½ cups (2 L) veal stock
- 3 thyme sprigs
- Salt and pepper
- Espelette pepper

TO PREP —— Cut the veal shoulder into small cubes and then refrigerate. Peel and finely chop the onions. Deseed and finely chop the green peppers. Use a knife to slice an X into the end of each tomato. Submerge the tomatoes in boiling water for 30 seconds, then remove and transfer to an ice bath. Peel the tomatoes and chop them into large pieces.

TO COOK —— Pour the olive oil into a frying pan heated over high. Add the veal and cook until browned. Add the vinegar, then add the peppers and onions and cook until soft. Add the tomatoes and thyme, cover with veal stock, and cook over low heat for 1 hour. Season with salt and pepper, add the Espelette pepper, then transfer to a serving platter.

Around THE TABLE

PRONOUNCED "ACHOA," *axoa* is the Basque word for "chopped." This traditional dish from the Labourd province was originally made with beef, but restaurateur Mayi Darraïdou created a veal version in Espelette. Today, The Brotherhood of Pepper and Veal Axoa of Espelette swarms the streets every year in celebration of this beloved dish.

MEAT

Stuffed Veal

PAUPIETTES DE VEAU

PREP TIME
45 MINUTES

COOK TIME
1 HOUR
15 MINUTES

REST TIME
1 HOUR

SERVES 2

For the mousseline 1 shallot · ½ bunch parsley · 3 sage leaves · 18 ounces (500 g) button mushrooms · 14 ounces (400 g) breast of veal (ask your butcher to chop) · ⅔ cup plus 2 teaspoons (170 g) heavy cream · 1 egg white salt and pepper **For the paupiettes** 1 ⅓ pounds (600 g) veal escalope · about 2 ounces (50 g) caul fat · vegetable bouillon or brown stock (pages 206–207) 1 garlic clove, crushed · 1 thyme sprig · oil **For the mushrooms** vinegar 18 ounces (500 g) shiitake mushrooms · 18 ounces (500 g) button mushrooms **For serving** Potato Purée (page 151) or peas

THE MOUSSELINE — Finely chop the shallot and chop the herbs. Dice the mushrooms, add to a pan, and sauté until they release all their moisture. Mix half of the breast of veal with the cream and egg white. Transfer the mixture to a bowl and use your hands to incorporate the rest of the veal, the shallot, mushrooms, and herbs. Season with salt and pepper. To test the seasoning, cook a small portion of the mixture in a pan and sample it.

THE PAUPIETTES — Trim the veal escalope, if necessary, then cut into 8 thin slices. Place the slices in between two pieces of parchment paper and pound lightly with the base of a pot. Spread the caul fat onto your work surface. Place 4 veal slices on the fat, evenly spaced. Divide the mousseline into 4 portions and place 1 portion on each veal slice, then cover the mousseline with another slice of veal. Cut the caul fat so that you can wrap it around each paupiette, then roll each paupiette between your hands to form a ball. Refrigerate them for at least 1 hour.

THE SAUTÉED MUSHROOMS — Add a splash of vinegar to a bowl of cold water and use it to rinse the mushrooms. Add the mushrooms to a pan over high heat and cook until they have released all their moisture and the liquid has evaporated. Set aside.

TO COOK — Preheat the oven to 350°F (180°C). Brown the paupiettes in a pan with oil, then transfer to a baking dish and cover halfway with boiling vegetable bouillon. Add the crushed garlic clove and the thyme. Bake about 40 minutes. About 5 minutes before the cooking is finished, brown the mushrooms over high heat until they turn golden brown. Serve the paupiettes with Potato Purée or peas and top with the reduced braising liquid and mushrooms.

MEAT

Cordon Bleu

**PREP TIME
45 MINUTES**

**COOK TIME
15 MINUTES**

REST TIME: 2 HOURS – OVERNIGHT

SERVES 4

For the cordon bleu

2 veal escalopes, about 11 ounces (300 g)

7 ounces (200 g) Comté, sliced

3 ½ ounces (100 g) prosciutto

For the breading

⅓ cup plus 4 teaspoons (50 g) flour

2 eggs, lightly beaten with a fork

¾ cup (100 g) breadcrumbs

Frying oil

THE CORDON BLEU —— Slice each veal escalope halfway through the middle to butterfly it. Place each escalope between two pieces of parchment paper and tap with the bottom of a pan to flatten. Transfer the escalopes to a piece of plastic wrap and cover each with 3 ½ ounces (100 g) of Comté and 1 ¾ ounces (50 g) of prosciutto. Roll each escalope into a log and seal it carefully. Freeze it for 2 hours or refrigerate it overnight.

Preheat the oven to 250°F (120°C).

THE BREADING —— To bread the escalopes, first dredge each one in flour and shake off the excess, then dip in the beaten eggs and finally in the breadcrumbs. Repeat these steps one time.

TO COOK —— Heat a pot of oil to 350°F (180°C) and fry the escalopes for a few minutes. Transfer to the oven and bake for 10 minutes to finish.

Around THE TABLE

"CORDON BLEU" WAS ORIGINALLY THE NICKNAME FOR MEMBERS OF THE ORDER OF SAINT-ESPRIT, the most prestigious distinction of the French monarchy under the Ancient Regime. A predecessor to the Legion of Honor, the order took its name from the Maltese cross they carried, which hung from a blue ribbon. It was quite a time to be a noble, considering the lavish banquets they enjoyed. Today, the term "cordon bleu" remains synonymous with culinary excellence and refined gastronomy.

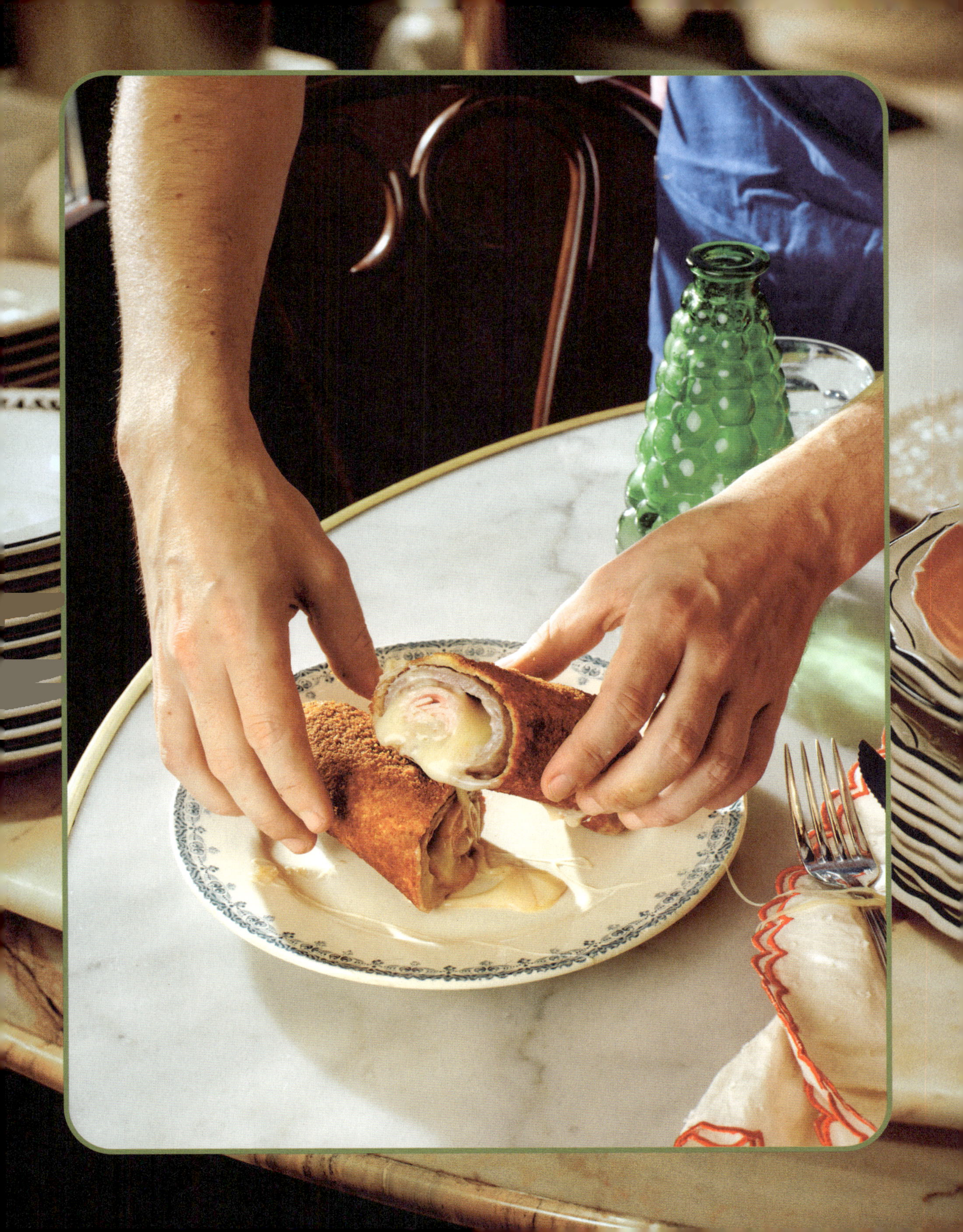

BRASSERIE MARTIN

24 rue Saint-Ambroise - Paris 11
CUISSON À LA BROCHE

1984

FISH

Monkfish Stew

LOTTE À L'AMÉRICAINE

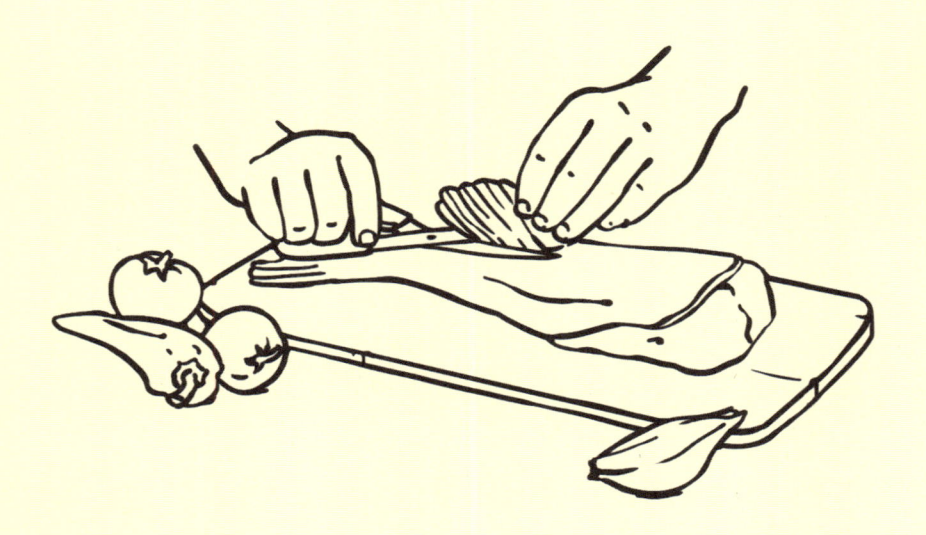

PREP TIME
15 MINUTES

COOK TIME
45 MINUTES

SERVES 4 TO 6

For the sauce 1 onion · 2 shallots · 4 large tomatoes on the vine **For the fish** 2¼ pounds monkfish · 4 teaspoons (20 g) butter · 2 tablespoons neutral oil 2 tablespoons (30 g) tomato paste · 3 tablespoons plus 1 teaspoon (50 ml) cognac · 2 garlic cloves, crushed · 3 thyme sprigs · 1¼ cups (300 ml) white wine · Espelette pepper · salt and pepper

THE SAUCE —— Peel and finely chop the onion and shallots. Use a knife to slice an X into the bottom of each tomato. Submerge the tomatoes in boiling water for 30 seconds, then transfer to an ice bath. Drain, then peel and roughly chop the tomatoes.

THE FISH —— Ask your fishmonger for one or two large monkfish fillets. Cut the fillets into large pieces and season with salt. Place a frying pan over high heat and add the butter and oil. Add the fish to the pan and brown evenly on each side. Remove from the pan and transfer to the refrigerator to stop cooking.

In the same pan, sweat the shallots and onions until translucent. Add the tomato paste. Add the cognac and flambé.

Stir in the tomatoes, crushed garlic cloves, thyme sprigs, and wine. Cook for about 10 minutes.

Arrange the fish in the pan with the tomatoes and continue cooking for about 30 minutes. Add the Espelette pepper and season with salt and pepper. Transfer to a platter to serve.

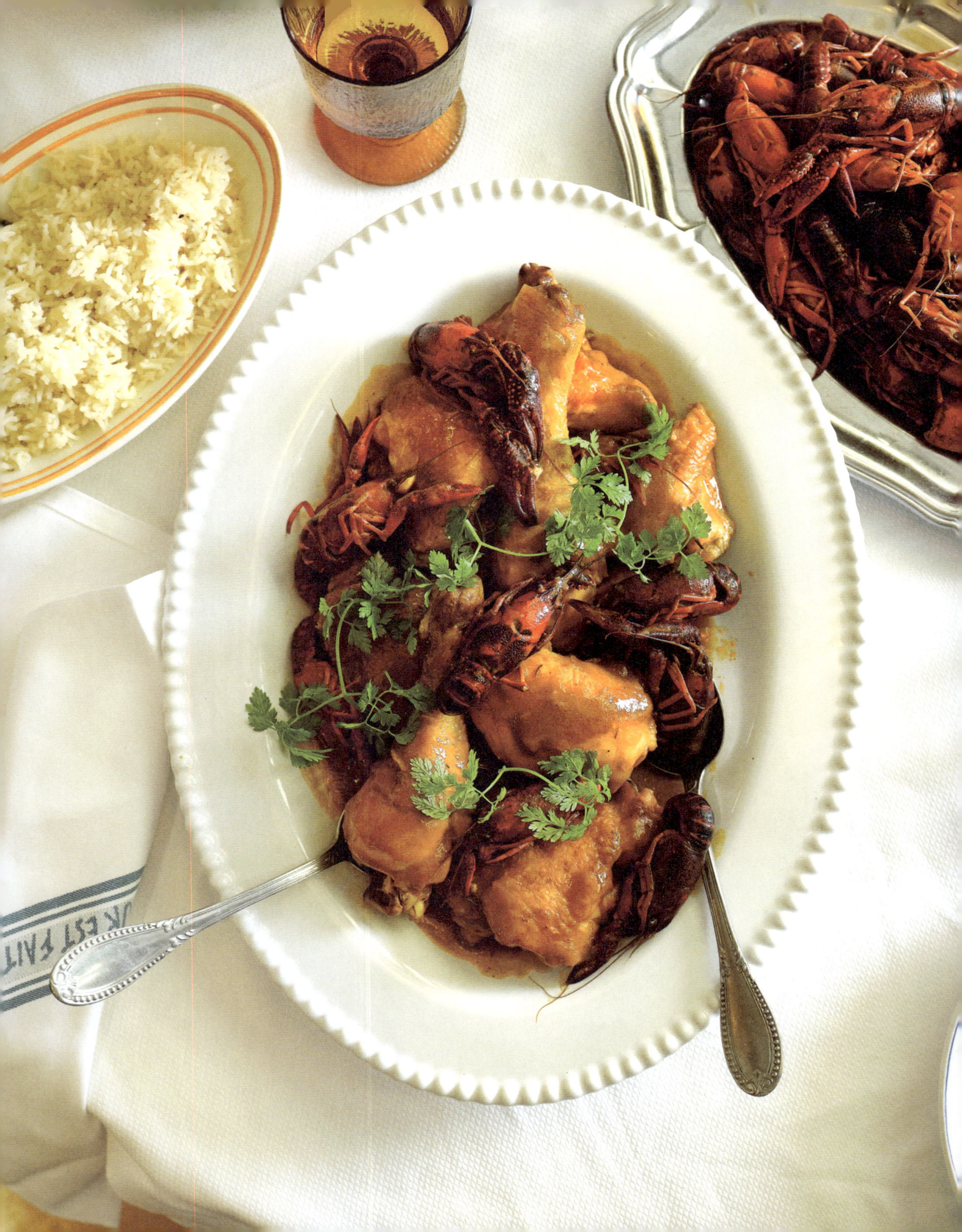

FISH

Braised Chicken with Crawfish

Volaille aux écrevisses

PREP TIME 30 MINUTES **SERVES 4** **COOK TIME 2 HOURS**

For the bisque

2¼ pounds (1 kg) crawfish
2 shallots
2 carrots
1 celery rib
½ fennel bulb
1 leek
2 garlic cloves
½ cup white wine
½ cup cognac
1 tablespoon tomato paste
1 bouquet garni

For the chicken

1 free-range chicken, about 4 pounds (1.8 kg)
1 shallot, minced
1 cup white wine

THE BISQUE —— Rinse the crawfish several times with cool water, then set aside one handful. Cut the shallots, carrots, celery, fennel, and leek into large pieces and crush the garlic cloves. Sweat these aromatics in a pan over low heat. Add the wine and reduce until the pan is dry. Add the crawfish (minus the handful set aside for later) and cook until they turn bright red. Add the cognac and flambé. Reduce until the liquid has evaporated. Add the tomato paste and continue cooking for 1 minute. Pour in enough water to fill the pot halfway, then add the bouquet garni. Bring to a boil, then cook at a low boil for at least 1½ hours. (In the meantime, prepare the chicken.) Once cooked, strain the bisque, then reduce the strained liquid until it is thick enough to coat the back of a spoon.

THE CHICKEN —— Ask your butcher to divide the bird into 8 pieces. Preheat the oven to 350°F (180°C). Salt the skin side of the chicken generously. Heat an oven-safe pan over high and brown the skin side of the chicken. Remove the chicken from the pan, add the shallot, and sweat it in the cooking juices. Add the white wine. Return the chicken to the pan with the skin side up and cover it halfway with the bisque. Bake for 20 minutes. While the chicken is cooking, fill a pot with salted water and bring to a boil. Add the reserved handful of crawfish and cook for about 1 minute.

TO PLATE —— Arrange the chicken and crawfish on a serving platter and cover with bisque. Pour the remaining bisque into a gravy boat and serve on the side.

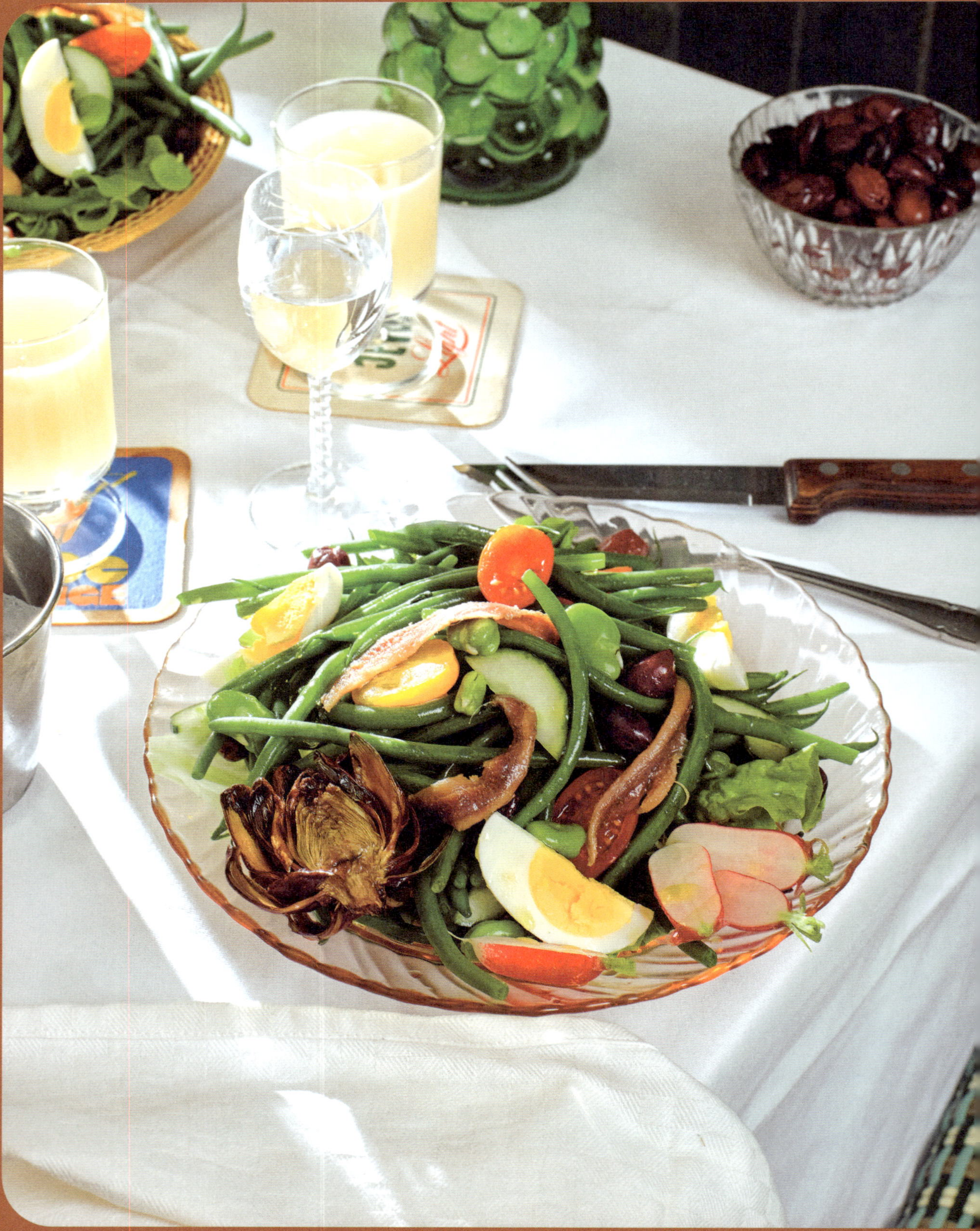

FISH

Salade Niçoise

PREP TIME 45 MINUTES **SERVES 2** **COOK TIME 20 MINUTES**

For the anchoïade (makes about 1 cup / 300 g) 1 garlic clove · 1 tin anchovies packed in oil · ¾ cup plus 2 tablespoons (200 g) olive oil · 1 tablespoon lemon juice · vinaigrette (page 209) **For the niçoise** 2 eggs · oil · 2 baby artichokes · salt · 3½ ounces (100 g) fresh haricots verts · 1 handful fava beans · 1 handful cherry or plum tomatoes · ¼ cucumber · 4 small radishes · 1 lemon · 1 small head lettuce · 4 anchovy fillets · 6 kalamata olives

THE ANCHOÏADE —— Fill a saucepan with cold water and add the garlic clove. Bring to a boil, then refresh with more cold water. Repeat this operation 2 times. Pour the entire tin of anchovies into a blender, including the oil. Add the garlic clove. Drizzle olive oil into the mixture while blending, until the consistency is similar to that of a vinaigrette. Add the lemon juice and blend. Transfer to an airtight container. To make the niçoise vinaigrette, combine 2 parts vinaigrette (page 209) with 1 part anchoïade.

THE NIÇOISE —— Cook the eggs in boiling water for 9 minutes 40 seconds, cool in an ice bath, then cut into quarters. Trim the stems from the artichokes, leaving ¾ inch (2 cm) at the base, and then cut them in half. Heat a pot of oil to 350°F (180°C) and fry the artichokes until the hearts are tender and the leaves are crispy. Transfer to a paper towel-lined plate and season with salt. Trim the haricots verts, then cook in a pot of salted boiling water until al dente. Remove from the pot and transfer to an ice bath, then drain and set aside. Shell the fava beans and add to the boiling water for a few minutes. Open one to test for doneness. Once cooked, transfer to an ice bath, drain, and remove the skin from the beans. Discard the skin and set the beans aside. Cut the tomatoes in half. Peel and deseed the cucumber. Sprinkle the cucumber with salt to draw out its water. Set aside for 10 minutes, then rinse. Cut the radishes into thin slices and store in iced lemon water so they stay fresh. Divide the lettuce leaves between two salad bowls and place the rest of the vegetables on top. Add the egg, anchovy fillets, and olives last, then drizzle with the anchoïade vinaigrette to finish.

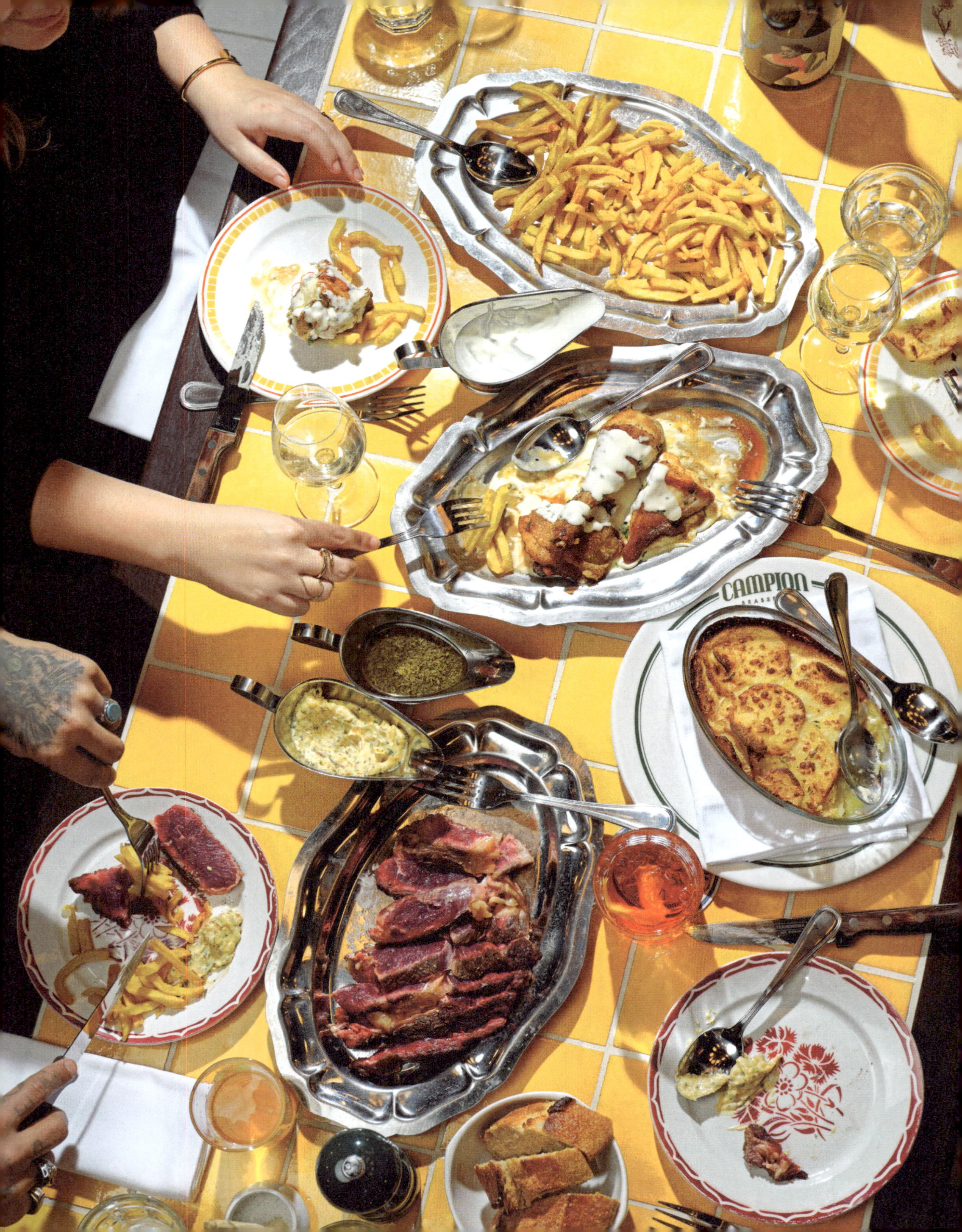
CAMPION

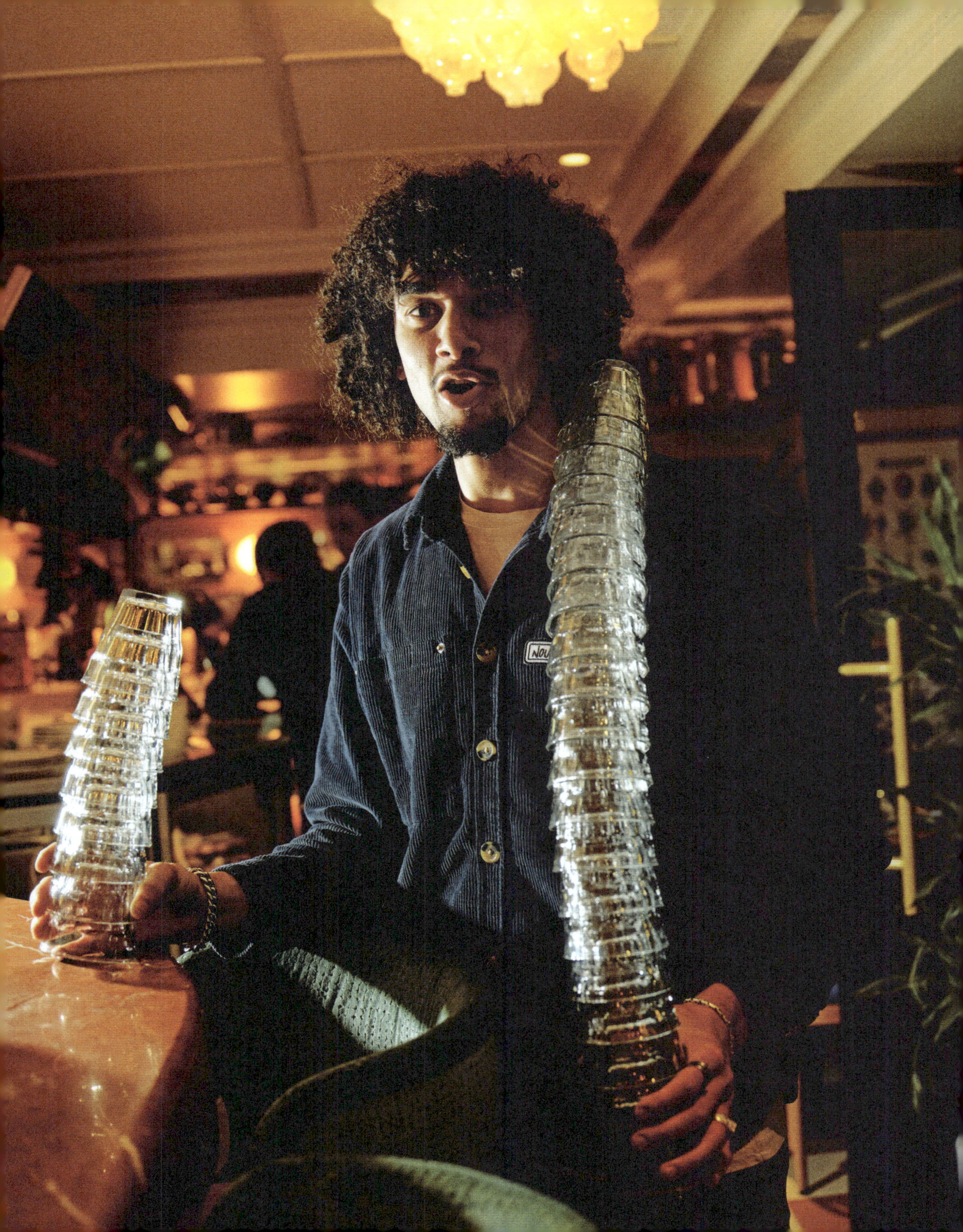

FISH

Salt-Baked Sea Bass

Bar en croute de sel

PREP TIME 10 MINUTES

COOK TIME 20 MINUTES

SERVES 4

1 sea bass, about 2¼ pounds (1 kg)
2 thyme sprigs
2 lemon slices
1 egg white
6½ pounds (3 kg) coarse salt

THE SEA BASS —— Ask your fishmonger to gut, scale, and trim the sea bass. Stuff the belly with the thyme and lemon.

TO COOK —— Preheat the oven to 350°F (180°C). In a bowl, mix the egg white and salt together with a splash of water. Pour half of the salt mixture into an oven-safe baking dish and place the fish on top. Cover the fish with the rest of the salt. Bake for 20 minutes. If the fish weighs more than 2¼ pounds (1 kg), increase the cooking time by 1 minute for each 3½ ounces (100 g)—and vice versa if the fish weighs less.

TO SERVE —— Let the fish rest for the same amount of time it cooked, about 20 minutes. Crack open the salt crust and serve.

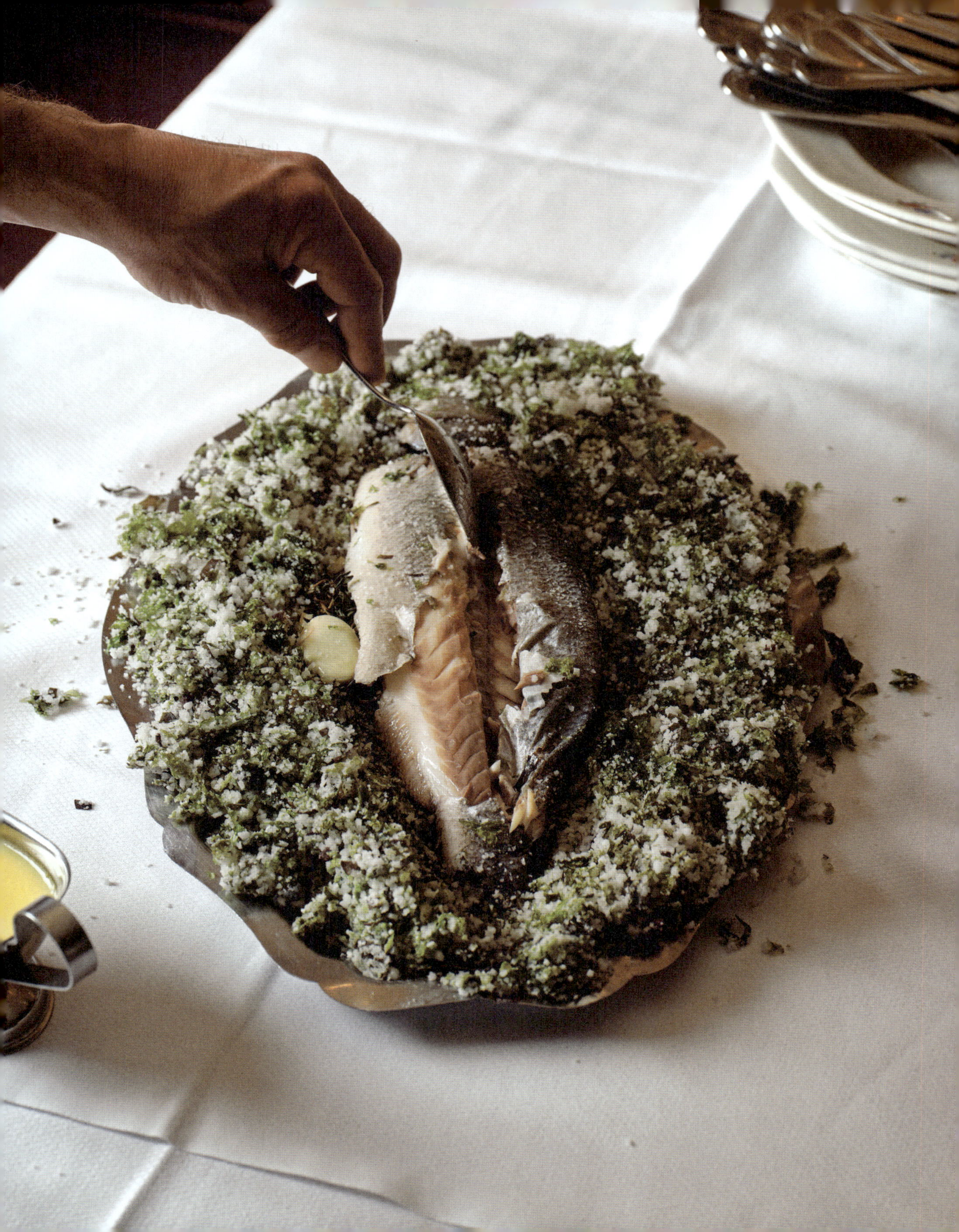

FISH

Bouilla-baisse

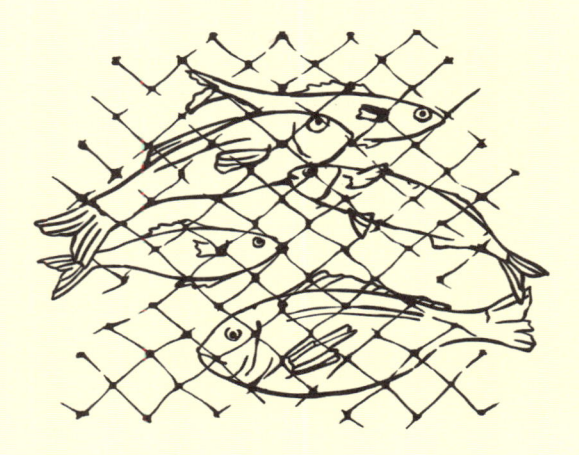

**PREP TIME
40 MINUTES**

**COOK TIME
2 HOURS
15 MINUTES**

SERVES 6

For the soup 6½ pounds (3 kg) small rockfish · 2 carrots · 1 leek · 2 shallots · 4 ripe tomatoes · olive oil · 2 garlic cloves, crushed · 1 bouquet garni
1 shot (1½ ounces) pastis · 1 tablespoon tomato paste · 1 recipe fish fumet (page 207) or water · mignonette pepper · 1 pinch coriander seeds · 1 pinch fennel seeds · 1 pinch saffron · a dozen thick-skinned potatoes · 2 red snapper fillets · 2 red mullet fillets · 6 monkfish pieces **For the rouille** 1 large potato
2 garlic cloves · ½ tin cod liver (optional) · ⅓ cup plus 4 teaspoons (100 ml) olive oil · 1 pinch saffron · 1 pinch salt · pepper · toasted bread, for serving

THE SOUP — Gut the rockfish, remove the gills, and rinse under running water. Cut each fish into 3 pieces.

Peel and chop the carrots. Clean and chop the leek and shallots. Deseed the tomatoes and cut into quarters. Sweat the aromatics with olive oil in a pot. Add the rockfish and cook for 2 to 3 minutes, then add the crushed garlic cloves and the bouquet garni. Add the pastis to flambé and add the tomato paste. Cook for 1 minute, then cover with fish fumet or water. Add the pepper, coriander and fennel seeds, and saffron. Bring to a boil, then reduce the heat and cook at a low boil for 1 hour 30 minutes.

Once cooked, pass the mixture through a food mill. Return the soup to the pot and bring to a boil. Peel and halve the potatoes, then add to the pot. Cook the potatoes until tender, about 30 to 40 minutes. Before the potatoes are finished, add the fish to the soup to cook: about 1 minute 30 seconds for the red snapper and red mullet and 2 minutes 30 seconds for the monkfish.

THE ROUILLE — Peel the potato. Cook in boiling water until very tender. Drain and cool.

Add the garlic cloves to a pot of cold water. Bring to a boil, then add cold water to cool it. Repeat this operation 2 times.

Mash the potato and garlic in a mortar until you have a smooth paste. Add the cod liver and mash again. Whisk a drizzle of olive oil into the mixture until the consistency is similar to that of mayonnaise. Mix in the saffron, salt, and pepper to finish. Serve with toasted slices of bread.

Around THE TABLE

① BRAISED CHICKEN WITH CRAWFISH
— *recipe page 109*

This Lyonnais dish exemplifies the sophistication of French gastronomy. As the story goes, Grimod de La Reynière, the father of gastronomic journalism, used to amuse his guests by painting live crawfish red and mixing them in with the ones that had been cooked. The tutorial can allegedly be found in one of the volumes of his *Almanach des gourmands*.

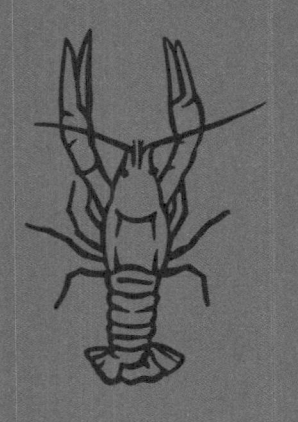

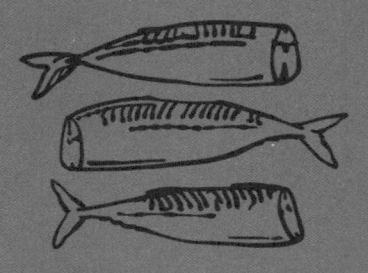

② BOUILLABAISSE
— *recipe page 106*

Legend has it that it was a bouillabaisse that the Roman goddess Venus gave to her husband, Vulcan, so that he would sleep while she seduced Mars. Bouillabaisse originated in Marseille, and here, the dish is sacred. It is so sacred that in 1980, the city's chefs and restaurateurs had the brilliant idea to draw up a "Bouillabaisse Charter" to maintain the integrity of the dish. The charter specifies the basic elements of the original recipe—for example, the species of fish required or rituals of service that must be performed.

③ SKATE WING WITH GRENOBLOISE SAUCE
— *recipe page 120*

This dish is a variation of a *meunière*, the name of which refers to the *meunier* ("miller") who processed the flour; this indicates cooking flour-coated fish in butter. This version includes capers, croutons, and diced lemon in the sauce. As the story goes, fish was once transported long distances before reaching the fishmonger's stalls in the mountains of Grenoble. It was not uncommon for the catch to arrive rotten during the warmer months, so it was cooked in this spicy, flavorful sauce to mask any unpleasant taste.

⑤ LA TABLE DE PRÊTS
— *general*

The king's meals were once attended by his "officers" (the "office" referred to the members of his court who were responsible for meal service) and held at what was known as the "*table des prêts*." This era was a time of revenge, and members of the French court could not take the risk of being poisoned. It was therefore customary for the king's servants to "*faire les prêts*" ("make the loans") in the presence of the king, using pieces of bread to test each dish he was about to eat.

④ THE CHEF'S TOQUE
— *general*

The high, pleated shape of a chef's hat is said to have been developed by Marie-Antoine Carême in the 1820s to combat the heat in the kitchen. However, it was not until Auguste Escoffier adopted the look that we would see the *toque* become a symbol of the kitchen. Escoffier rewrote all the rules and established a hierarchy within the profession, where each cook then had a very specific role. The kitchen brigade was born, and its uniform, inspired by those of Carême, became emblematic. The higher and more pleated the toque, the greater the chef's culinary knowledge and skills. It is even said that the number of pleats—100 at most—represents the number of ways a chef knows how to prepare an egg.

FISH

Skate Wing with Grenobloise Sauce

Aile de raie à la grenobloise

PREP TIME
20 MINUTES

COOK TIME
1 HOUR

SERVES 2

For the croutons
2 slices white bread
¼ cup (60 g) butter, divided
1 thyme sprig
1 garlic clove, crushed
Salt

For the potatoes
11 ounces (300 g) firm-skinned potatoes

For the skate
2 skate wing fillets, 11 ounces (300 g) each
1 lemon
2 parsley sprigs + extra to garnish
3 tablespoons capers
3 tablespoons (20 g) flour
Neutral oil

THE CROUTONS —— Cut the bread into ¼-inch (0.5 cm) cubes. Melt half of the butter in a pan, then add the thyme, crushed garlic clove, and salt. Add the croutons and toast until golden brown. Remove the from the pan and transfer to a paper towel-lined plate.

THE POTATOES —— Wash and peel the potatoes. Add the potatoes to a large pot of water and bring to a boil. Once cooked, drain and set aside.

THE SKATE —— Ask your fishmonger to prepare the fish for you. Juice one half of the lemon and peel and dice the other half. Finely chop the parsley and chop the capers. Dust each side of the fish with flour, then shake off the excess. Add a dash of oil to a hot pan and brown the fish on each side. Cut the remaining half of the butter into cubes, lower the heat to medium, and add the cubed butter to the pan. Once melted, baste each side of the fish for about 3 minutes. To check for doneness, try to lift the meat from the bone: if it separates easily, the fish is cooked. Remove the fish from the pan, turn off the heat, and prepare the Grenobloise sauce: stir the lemon juice, capers, parsley, and diced lemon into the melted butter.

TO PLATE —— Place the fish fillets in the center of a serving platter and arrange the potatoes around the fish. Top with a generous pour of Grenobloise sauce and finish with the croutons and a pinch of chopped parsley.

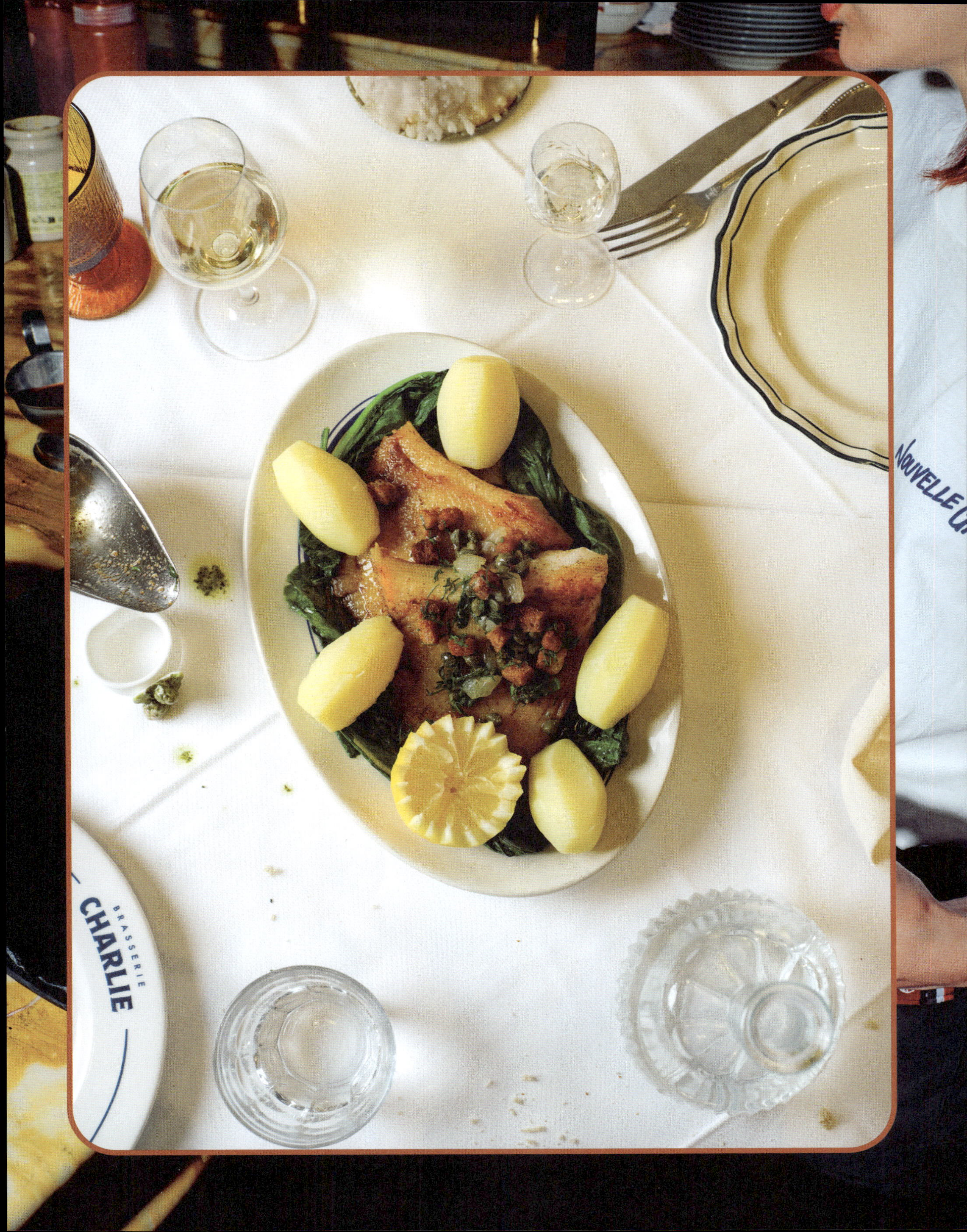
BRASSERIE
CHARLIE
NOUVELLE

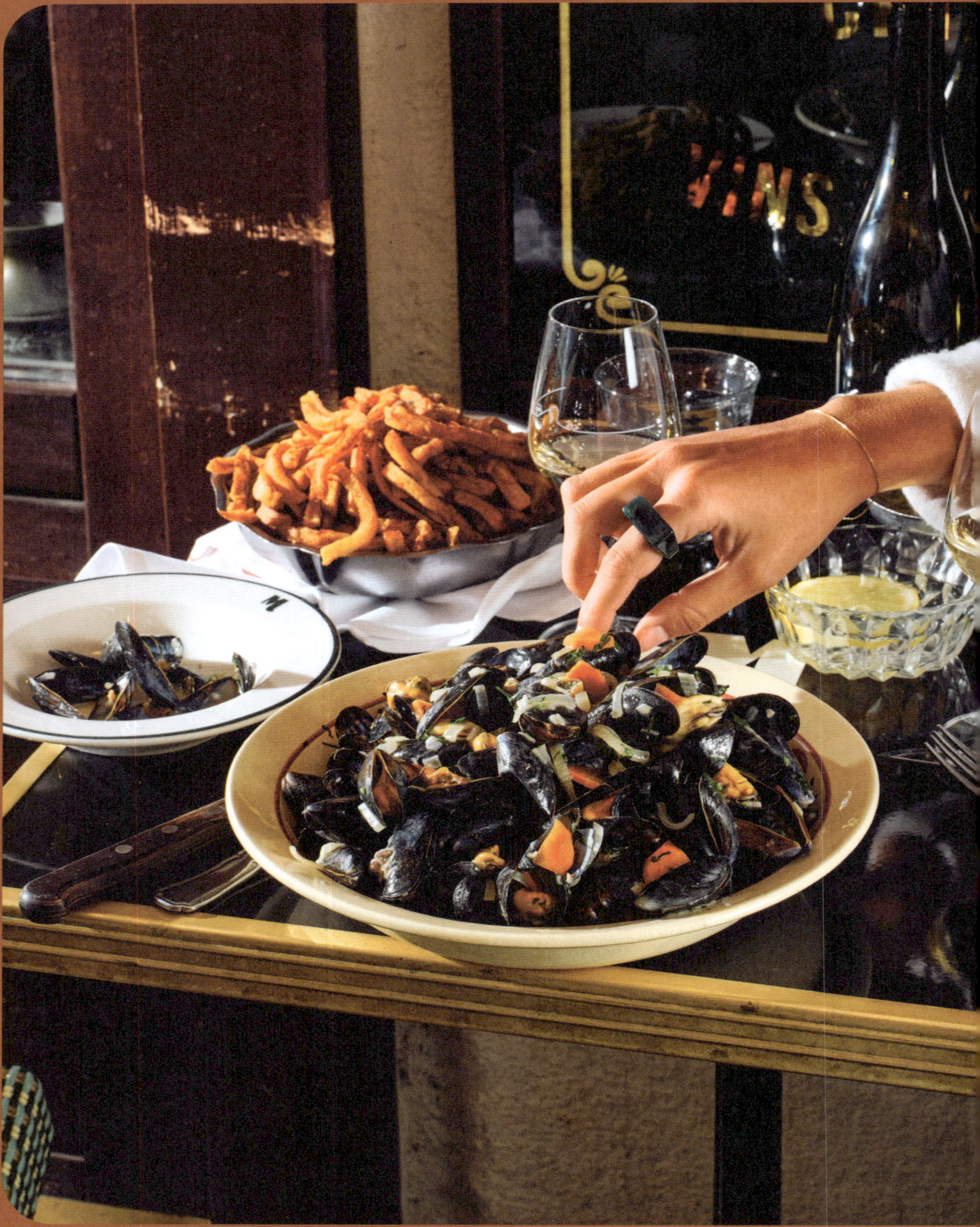

FISH - FINGER FOODS

Mussels with Poulette sauce

Moules façon poulette

PREP TME 15 MINUTES **SERVES 4** **COOK TIME 15 MINUTES**

For the mussels 4 ½ pounds (2 kg) Bouchot mussels · 2 shallots · 1 carrot 1 celery rib · 1 garlic clove · 1 pat butter · ½ cup dry white wine · 1 thyme sprig · 1 pinch mignonette pepper · 1 small bunch parsley, chopped **For the sauce** 1 ¼ cups (300 ml) chicken stock (page 206) · 2 tablespoons heavy cream · 1 egg yolk · salt

THE MUSSELS —— Rinse the mussels several times until the water runs clear. Finely dice the shallots and carrot. Chop the celery into small pieces. Crush the garlic clove. Add everything to a pot and sweat with a pat of butter. Add the wine, thyme, and pepper to the pot and bring to a boil. Add the mussels, then cover the pot. Once the mussels open (after about 1 minute of cooking), quickly mix in two-thirds of the chopped parsley. Use a slotted spoon to remove the mussels from the pot and transfer to a bowl. Cover and set aside.

THE SAUCE —— Pour the chicken stock into the pot, bring to a boil, and reduce by one-third. Remove the pot from the heat and strain the sauce. Away from the heat, return the sauce to the pan and whisk in the cream and egg yolk. Adjust seasoning to taste. Return the mussels to the pot to reheat and coat in sauce. Sprinkle the remaining parsley on top and serve.

Around THE TABLE

THE WORD "BUCHOT" refers to the traditional method of farming mussels using V-shaped wooden pilings planted in the sea. The technique has been credited to an Irish sailor who, upon finding himself shipwrecked in 1235 in the Bay of Aiguillon in Charentes-Maritimes, attempted to make a living by trapping seabirds using nets strung between partially submerged wooden beams. Little did he know, his wooden beams were worth their weight in gold once covered in mussels.

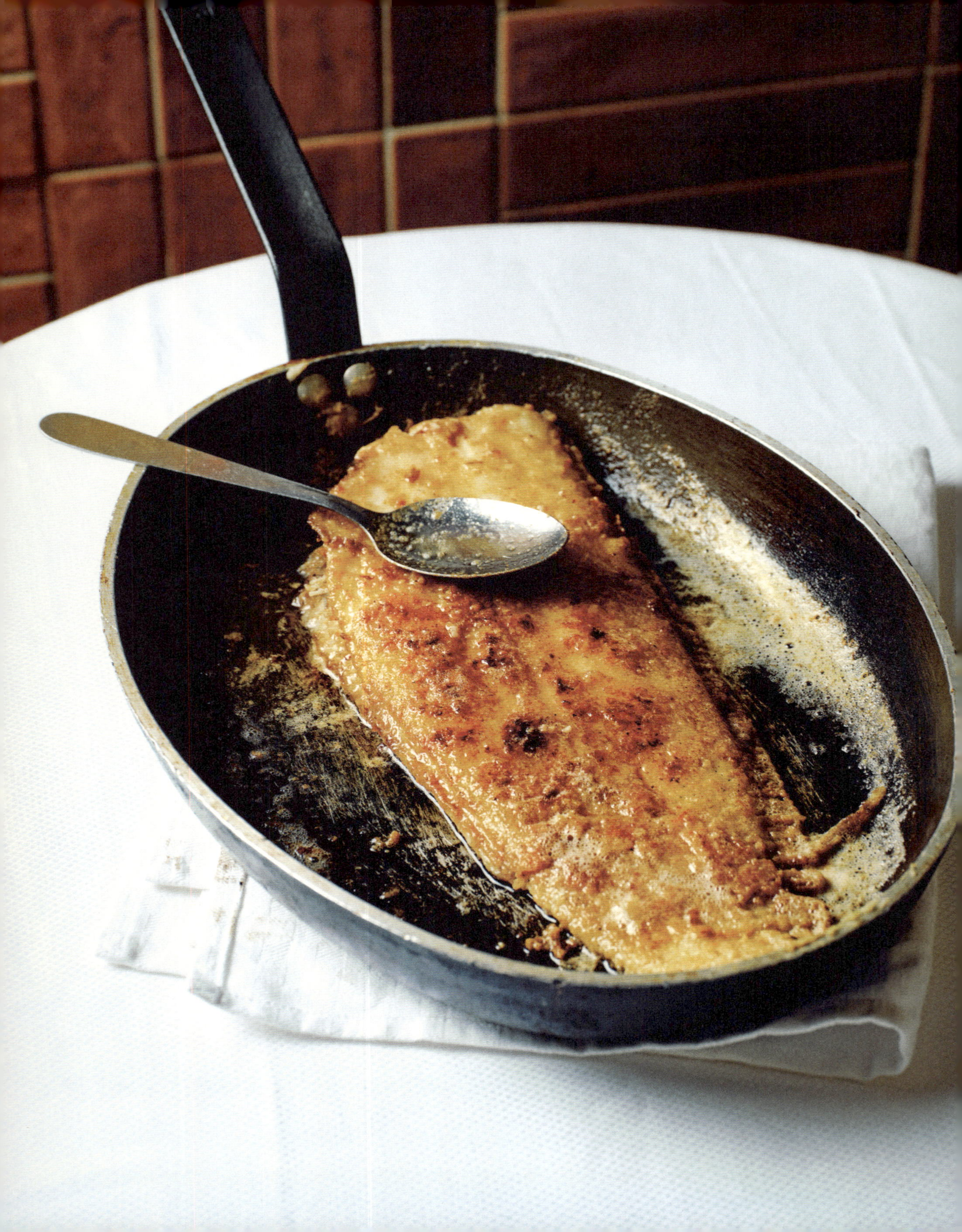

FISH

Sole Meunière

PREP TIME 5 MINUTES

COOK TIME 10 MINUTES

SERVES 2

1 sole, 1½ pounds (700 g)

¼ cup (50 g) flour

A little sunflower oil

7 tablespoons (100 g) butter, chilled

2 parsley sprigs

1 lemon

THE SOLE —— Ask your fishmonger to gut, trim, and skin the sole for you. Pour the flour onto a plate and dredge the fish in the flour to lightly coat each side. Shake off the excess.

TO COOK —— Pour a little sunflower oil into a very hot pan. Brown the sole for about 3 minutes on each side. Lower the heat to medium, then cut the butter into cubes and add it to the pan. Once the butter is melted, baste the fish with the butter for about 3 minutes on each side. To test for doneness, use a spoon to lift the meat from the spine: if it separates easily, the fish is cooked.

TO PLATE —— Transfer the sole to a serving platter to rest. Remove the pan from the heat and finely chop the parsley. To finish the meunière sauce, add 2 tablespoons of lemon juice and the parsley to the cooking butter. Pour the sauce on top of the sole and serve.

FISH

Scallops with Celery Root Purée

SAINT-JACQUES FAÇON DUBILLOT

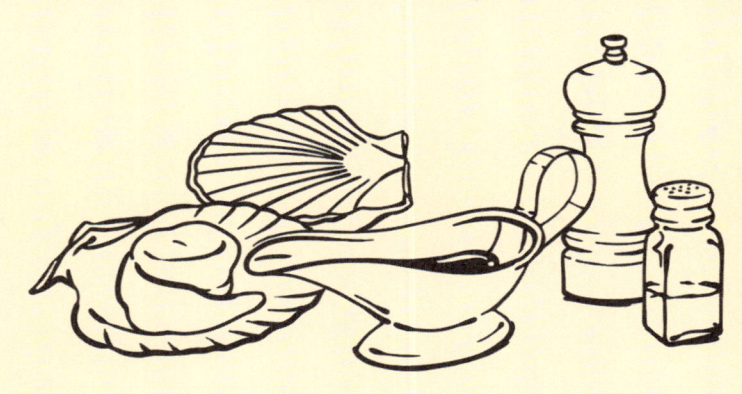

PREP TIME
30 MINUTES

COOK TIME
30 MINUTES

SERVES 2

For the celery root purée ¼ celery root (18 ounces / 500 g) · ⅓ cup plus 4 teaspoons (100 ml) milk · ⅓ cup plus 4 teaspoons (100 ml) water · 1 pinch salt · 1 pinch mignonette pepper · 1 bouquet garni **For the celery tartare** 2 ounces (60 g) celery root · 1 ounce (30 g) celery · 2 Saint-Jacques scallops 1 drizzle neutral oil · 1 teaspoon chicken stock · 1 teaspoon olive oil · 1 pinch salt · 1 twist freshly ground pepper **For the scallops** 2 Saint-Jacques scallops (save the shells for plating) · 1 drizzle olive oil · 2 tablespoons (30 g) butter, chilled **To plate** 2 thin slices lardons · 2 teaspoons chicken stock (page 206)

THE CELERY ROOT PURÉE — Roughly chop the celery root and add to a pot with the milk and water. Add the salt, pepper, and bouquet garni and bring to a boil. Cook until the celery root is very soft. Strain through a colander and set the cooking liquid aside. Blend the cooked celery root with a bit of the cooking liquid at medium speed, adding more if necessary, until the purée is smooth and evenly textured. Season with salt and pepper.

THE CELERY TARTARE — Finely dice the celery root, celery, and scallops. Heat a pan over high and sauté the celery and celery root with a dash of neutral oil for about 20 seconds, until al dente. Remove from the pan and set aside to cool.

Combine the diced celery with the scallops in a bowl. Add the chicken stock, olive oil, salt, and pepper. Mix well.

THE SCALLOPS — Separate the scallops from the roe and the organs (you can clean and refrigerate the roe for later use in a sauce or fumet). Rinse the scallops well under cold running water, then place on a clean towel to dry. Clean the shells.

Add the oil to a pan heated over high, then sear the scallops on each side. Lower the heat to medium, cut the butter into cubes, and add them to the pan. Once the butter is melted, baste the scallops for about 2 minutes on each side.

TO PLATE — Fill each scallop shell with 2 tablespoons of the celery root purée. Add the celery tartare and top with one scallop. Place a slice of lard on each scallop and heat for a few seconds with a kitchen torch (or in the oven under the broiler) to melt. Top each scallop with one teaspoon of chicken stock to finish.

BRASSERIE DES PRÉS

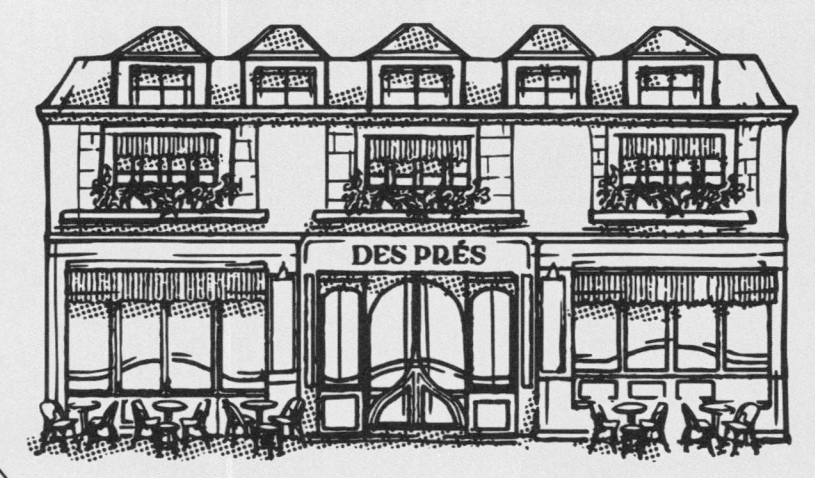

6 Cour du Commerce Saint-André
Paris 06

CUISINE BOURGEOISE

VEGGIE MAINS

VEGGIE MAINS

Gnocchi Parisienne

GNOCCHIS À LA PARISIENNE

PREP TIME 1 HOUR

COOK TIME 4 HOURS

SERVES 2

For the confit egg yolks ½ cup (100 g) sunflower oil · 2 egg yolks **For the gnocchi** coarse salt · 18 ounces (500 g) potatoes · 1 cup (125 g) flour fine sea salt · pepper · nutmeg · 1 egg yolk · 1 whole egg **For the Mornay** 4 teaspoons (20 g) butter · 2 tablespoons plus 2 teaspoons (20 g) flour ⅓ cup plus 2 teaspoons (100 ml) milk · 1 pinch mignonette pepper · salt nutmeg · ¼ cup (30 g) grated young Comté **For the garnish** 2 slices smoked bacon (for the carnivores) · 3 ounces (80 g) button mushrooms salt · 1 ounce (30 g) grated young Comté

THE CONFIT EGG YOLKS —— Preheat the oven to 160°F (70°C). Pour the sunflower oil and egg yolks into a small oven-safe dish; the yolks should be completely submerged. Confit in the oven for 3 hours, then set aside until the eggs have cooled to room temperature in the oil.

THE GNOCCHI —— Preheat the oven to 350°F (180°C). Pour a bed of coarse salt onto a baking sheet. Wash the potatoes and place on the salt unpeeled. Bake for about 40 minutes, until they are very soft. Peel the potatoes while they are still hot, then pass through a food mill. Pour the flour onto your workspace and create a well. Add the fine sea salt, pepper, and nutmeg to the well, then add the egg yolk, whole egg, and mashed potatoes. Knead the mixture until you have a smooth ball. Roll the dough into small logs and cut the gnocchi into the desired size. Transfer the gnocchi to a platter dusted with flour and store in the refrigerator.

THE MORNAY SAUCE —— To make a roux, first melt the butter in a pot. Add the flour, then whisk for several minutes. Pour the milk in gradually while whisking continuously. Season with pepper, salt, and nutmeg. Remove the pot from the heat, add the grated cheese, and whisk until smooth. Set aside.

THE GARNISH —— If you are including the bacon, cut it into small lardons, brown it in a pan, and transfer to a paper towel-lined plate. Clean the mushrooms, then sauté in the same pan with the bacon fat. Season with salt.

TO COOK AND PLATE —— Poach the gnocchi in a pot of salted boiling water; they will rise to the surface once cooked. While the gnocchi are cooking, heat the Mornay sauce in a frying pan with a bit of the gnocchi cooking water. Once cooked, transfer the gnocchi to the pan with the sauce. Add the mushrooms and bacon and stir until everything is evenly covered. The dish can be served as is, or you can sprinkle Comté on top and broil until the cheese is melted and bubbly. Place one confit egg yolk on each place of gnocchi to serve.

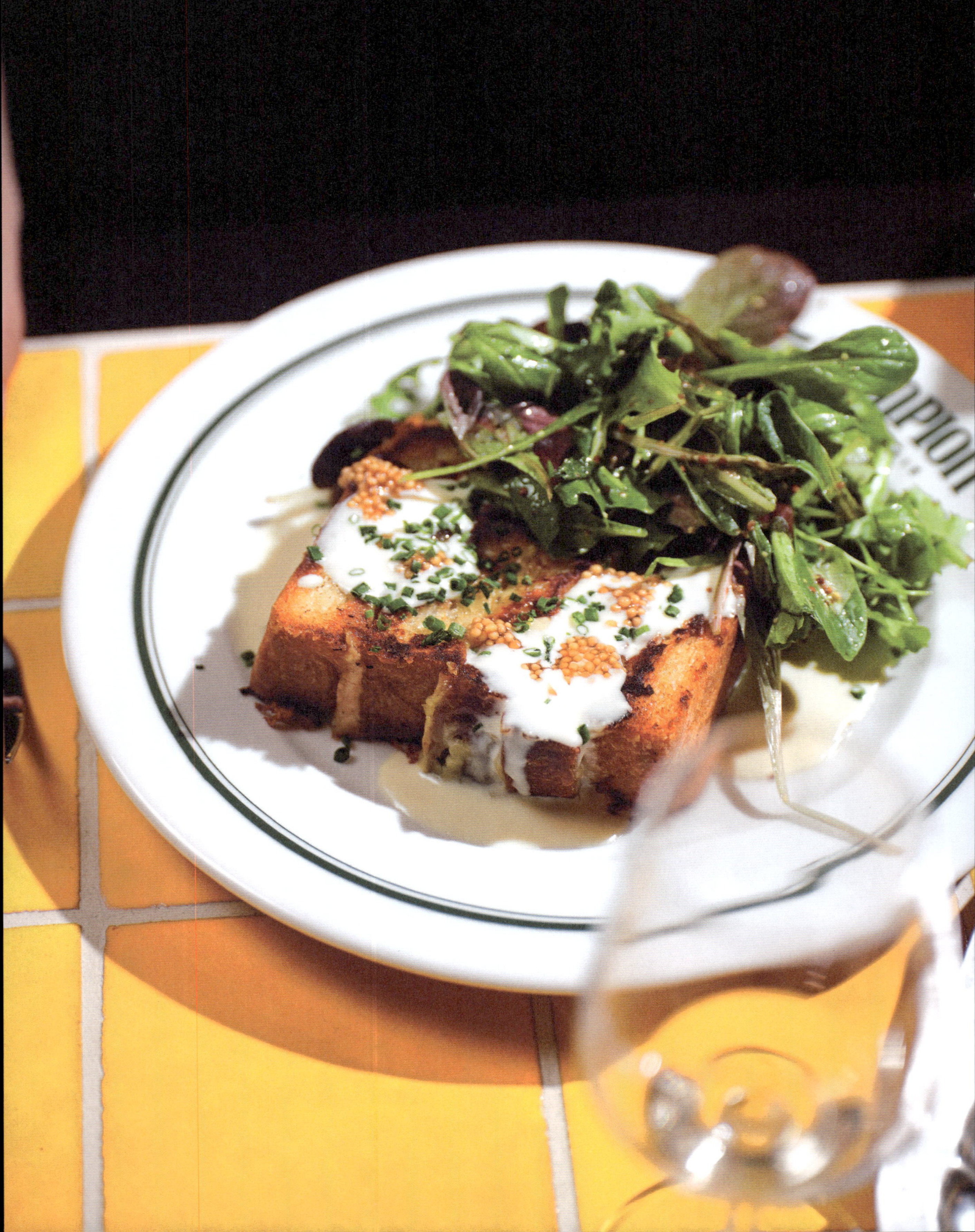

VEGGIE MAINS

Grilled Cheese à la Française

PREP TIME 30 MINUTES **SERVES 4** **COOK TIME** 15 MINUTES

For the onion compote
2 yellow onions
1 large pat butter
1 cup white wine
1 tablespoon white wine vinegar
Pepper

For the sandwiches
¼ cup (50 g) butter + 1 pat for cooking
8 thick slices sandwich bread
Dijon mustard
7 ounces (200 g) young Comté, sliced
5 ounces (150 g) Morbier, thinly sliced
3½ ounces (100 g) cheddar, thinly sliced
¼ red onion

THE ONION COMPOTE —— Slice the onions thinly, sweat in a pan with butter, then add the white wine and vinegar. Season generously with pepper and cook until the liquid has completely reduced and the mixture has taken on a soft, jam-like consistency.

TO ASSEMBLE —— Melt the butter. Using a pastry brush, butter each piece of bread generously on both sides. Spread mustard onto four of the slices of bread and then place a slice of Comté on each. Place another slice of Comté on the other slices, then place a heaping tablespoon of onion compote on top of the cheese. Add two slices of Morbier, two slices of cheddar, and a bit of thinly sliced red onion. Close the four sandwiches.

TO BAKE —— Preheat the oven to 350°F (180°C). Add a pat of butter to a pan and toast the sandwiches on each side, then bake in the oven for 4 minutes. Serve with a fresh green salad.

VEGGIE MAINS

Veggie Quiche

Quiche végé

PREP TIME 20 MINUTES

COOK TIME 1 HOUR

SERVES 8

1 butter pie crust (page 211)

For the filling

1 onion

1 leek

Any leftover vegetables you have

1 pat butter

3½ cups (400 g) grated Comté

For the custard

1 egg yolk

2 eggs

¾ cup plus 4 teaspoons (200 ml) milk

¾ cup plus 4 teaspoons (200 ml) heavy cream

Nutmeg

THE FILLING AND CUSTARD —— Chop the vegetables into fairly small pieces. Sweat the vegetables in butter, then cook over low heat until they take on a soft, jam-like consistency. Transfer to a colander to drain any remaining liquid. Add all the custard ingredients to a bowl and whisk to combine.

TO ASSEMBLE —— Preheat the oven to 350°F (180°C). Grease a tart pan with butter. Roll the dough out onto the pan and press down gently. Pierce the dough with a fork, spread the vegetables evenly on top, then cover with the custard filling. Sprinkle the Comté evenly on top.

TO BAKE —— Bake the quiche for about 40 minutes, until it turns golden brown. Allow to cool before removing from the pan. Serve sliced, with a small salad.

Around THE TABLE

UNDER THE ANCIENT REGIME IN FRANCE, the communal bread oven was lit only once per week. Bread wasn't baked until it had reached the correct temperature, so the villagers of Lorraine used the empty oven to cook their own dishes while the temperature rose. One day, a crust filled with all the ingredients for a quiche was put in the oven. The recipe spread throughout France when inhabitants fled the region during the Franco-Prussian War of 1870, eventually becoming a staple of French cuisine. In 2004, even the French postal service honored its legacy, releasing a "Quiche" stamp as part of its "Regional Portraits" collection.

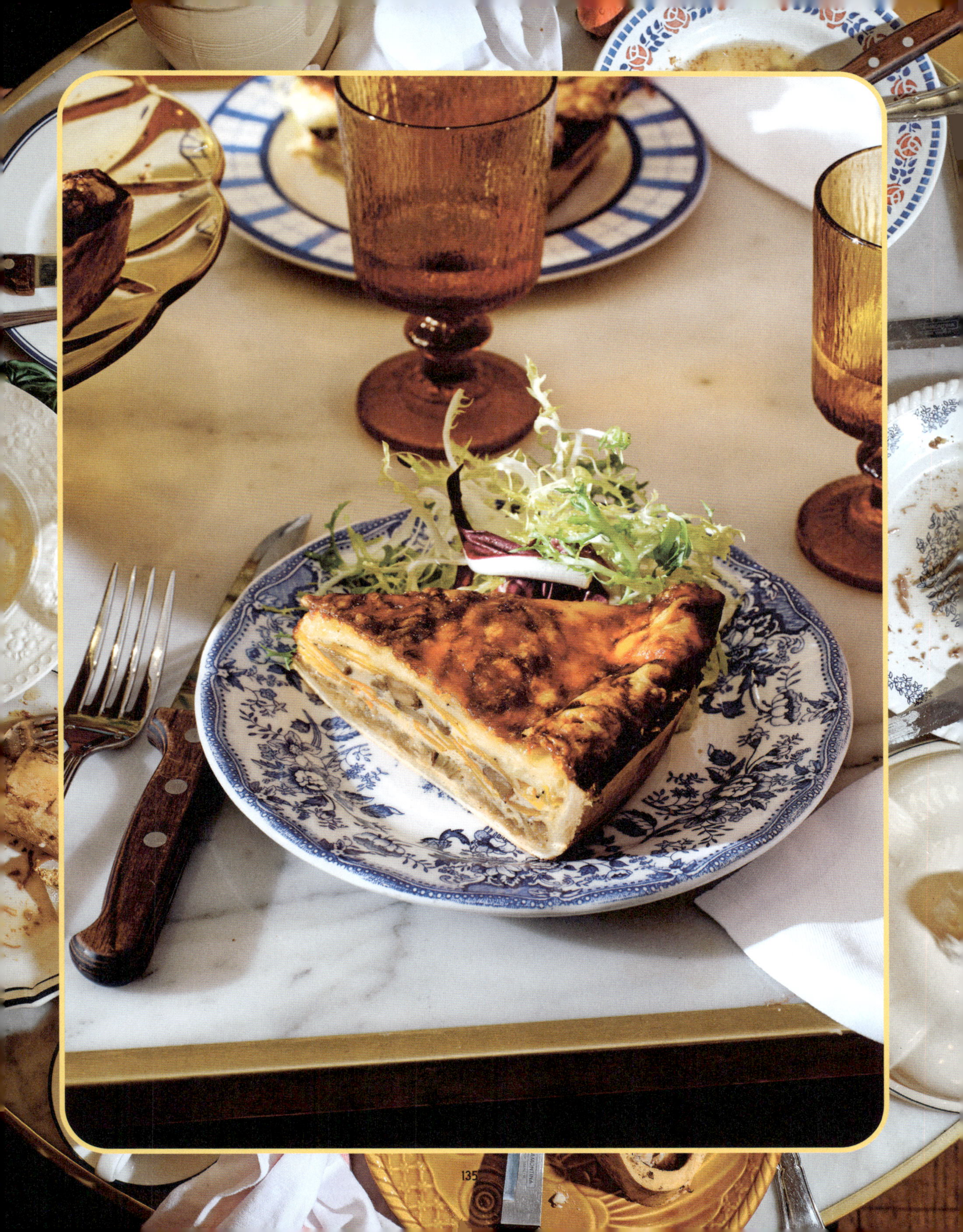

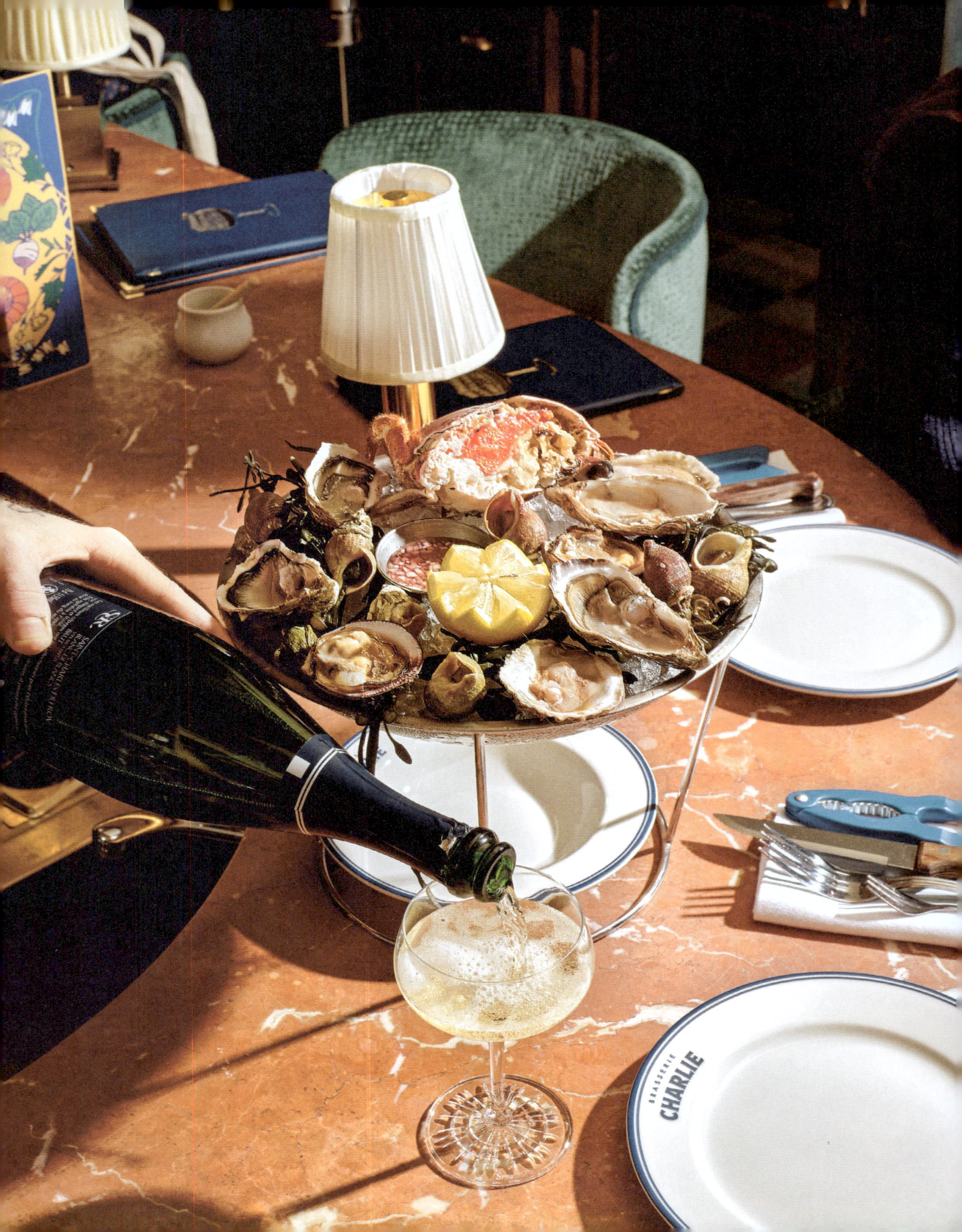
BRASSERIE
CHARLIE

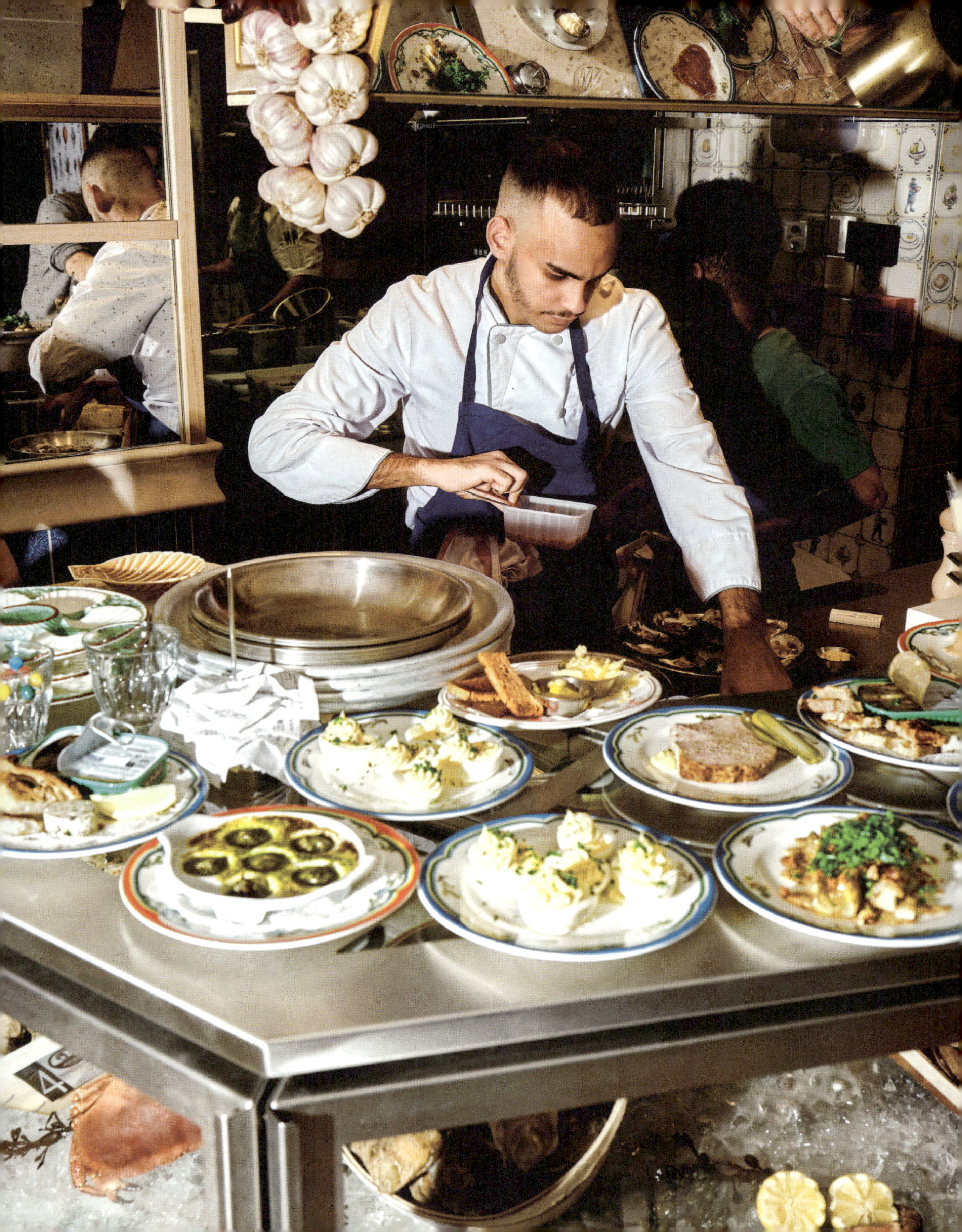

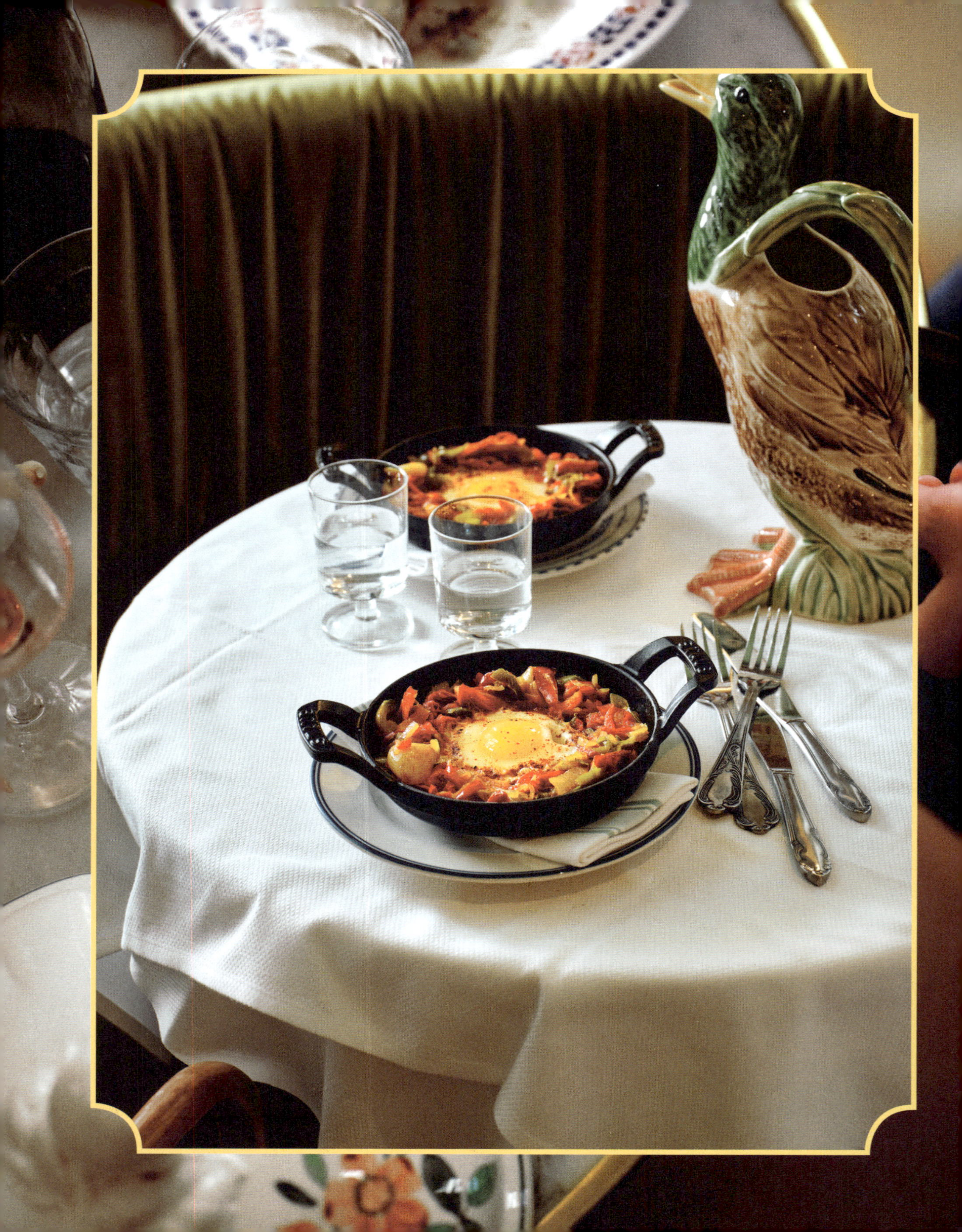

VEGGIE MAINS

Poached Eggs in Piperade

Piperade à l'œuf

PREP TIME
30 MINUTES

COOK TIME
1 HOUR
45 MINUTES

SERVES 2

For the eggs
2 eggs
Espelette pepper

For the vegetables
4 tomatoes
2 red peppers
2 green peppers
1 red onion
1 garlic clove
Olive oil
2 tablespoons (33 g) tomato paste
1 thyme sprig

THE VEGETABLES —— Peel the tomatoes: slice an X into the bottom of each tomato, then blanch for 30 to 60 seconds, until the skin starts to wrinkle. Transfer the tomatoes to an ice bath, then remove the skin and seeds. Cut the peppers into thick strips. Thinly slice the onion and crush the garlic.

TO COOK —— Sweat the onions in a pot with olive oil, then add the tomato paste. Mix in the peppers, tomatoes, garlic, and thyme, then cover the dish and cook for 1 hour 30 minutes, until the vegetables are very soft. You can add a little water to the pot during cooking if necessary.

THE EGGS —— Once the vegetables are cooked, place a pan over medium heat and transfer the vegetables to the pan. Press the back of a spoon into the vegetables to create one well for each guest. Crack 1 egg into each well and cook until the whites are set. Sprinkle Espelette pepper on top.

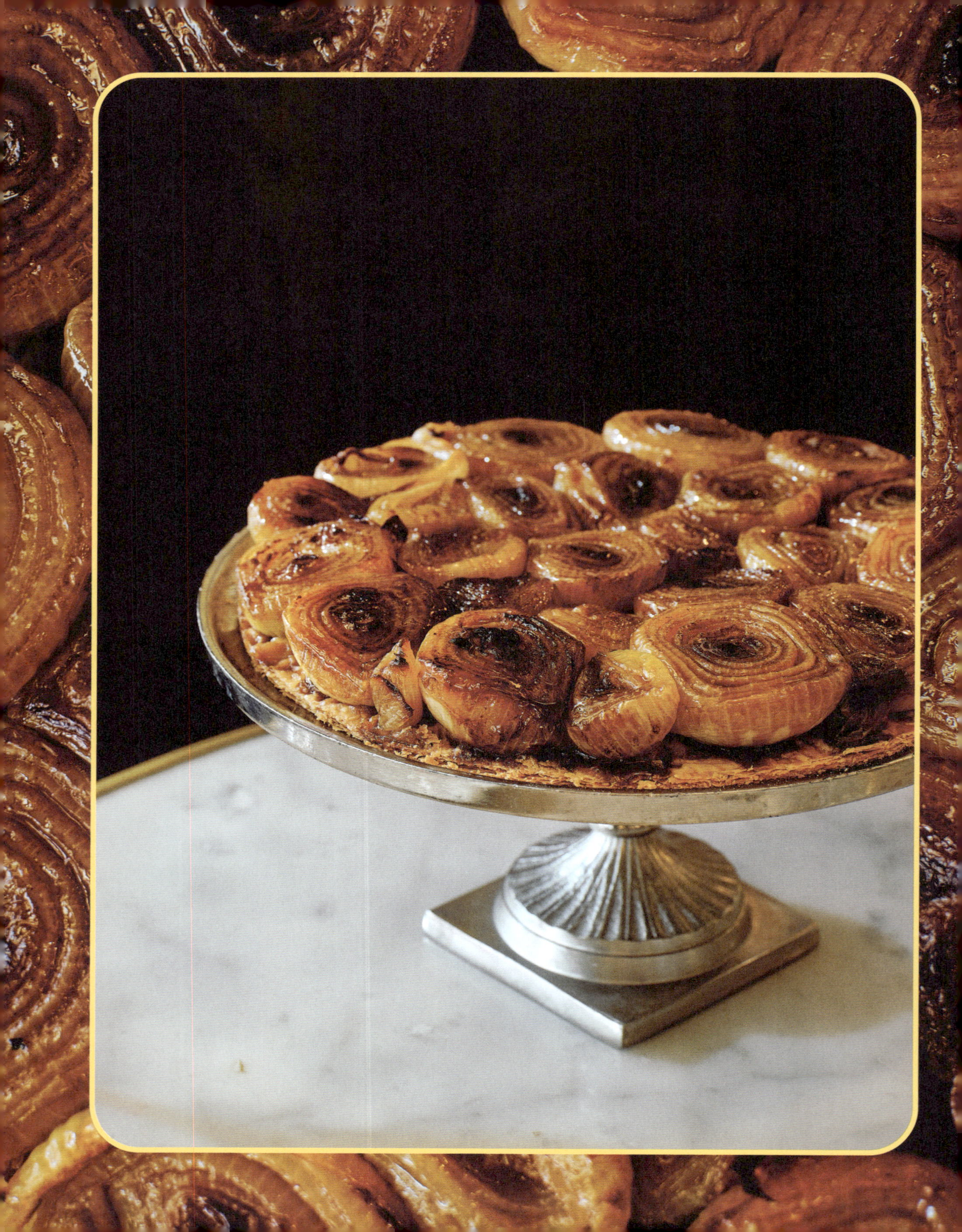

VEGGIE MAINS

Onion Tarte Tatin

Tatin d'oignons

PREP TIME
30 MINUTES

SERVES 4 TO 6

COOK TIME
50 MINUTES

1 butter pie crust (page 211)

10–12 white onions (or sweet onions)

2 tablespoons plus 2 teaspoons (40 ml) vegetable bouillon (page 207)

1 pinch salt

1 thyme sprig

¼ cup (50 g) unsalted butter

5 teaspoons (20 g) brown sugar

1 egg yolk, beaten

Salt and pepper

FOR THE CRUST —— Prepare the dough according to the instructions on page 209.

FOR THE ONIONS —— Peel the onions and cut in half widthwise. Mix the vegetable bouillon, salt, and thyme leaves in a bowl. Heat the butter in a pan over medium until it becomes foamy. Place the onions in the pan with the cut side down and cook for a few minutes. Fill the pan with enough water to cover the onions halfway, then sprinkle the brown sugar on top. Cover and cook for about 20 minutes, then remove the lid and continue cooking for 5 more minutes. The onions will be browned and the liquid will have the appearance and consistency of caramel once cooked.

TO ASSEMBLE AND BAKE —— Preheat the oven to 350°F (180°C). Arrange the onions tightly in a tart pan with the cut side down. Roll out the dough on top of the pan and trim the overhang. Lightly brush the top of the crust with the egg yolk. Bake the tart for about 25 minutes, until it turns golden brown.

TO SERVE —— Allow the tart to cool for a few minutes out of the oven. To remove the tart from the pan, hold a plate or platter (larger than the pan) firmly against the pan, then flip upside down to release.

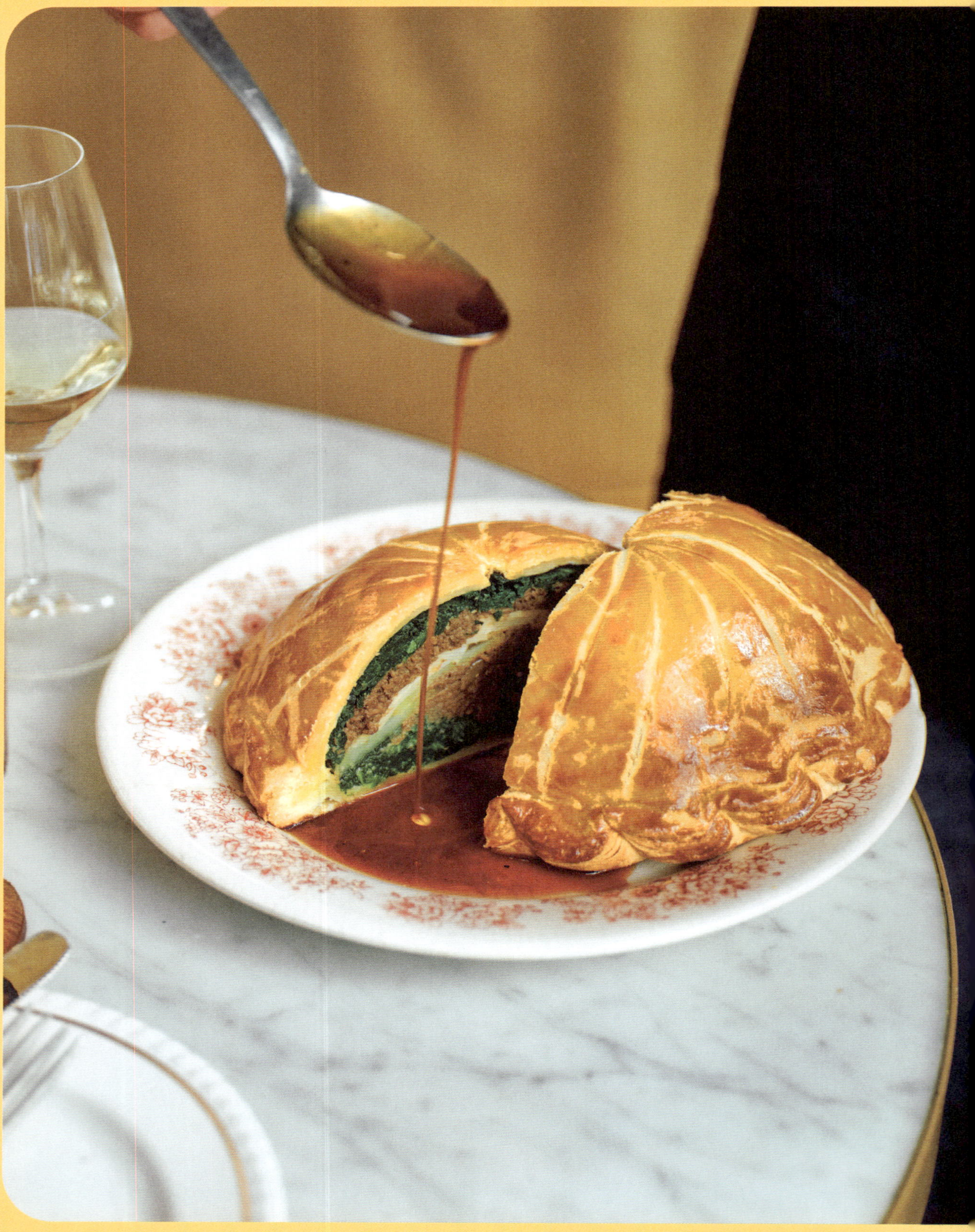

VEGGIE MAINS

Vegetable Torte
Tourte de légumes

PREP TIME 1 HOUR 30 MINUTES

MAKES 1 TORTE OR 4 SERVINGS

COOK TIME 1 HOUR 15 MINUTES
REST TIME: 10 MINUTES

For the vegetables 14 ounces (400 g) spinach · 2¼ pounds (1 kg) button mushrooms · 3 shallots 2 medium potatoes · ¼ celery root · 3 tablespoons olive oil **For the filling** 2 tablespoons (30 g) butter · ¾ cup plus 4 teaspoons tablespoons (200 ml) port · 1¼ cups (300 ml) heavy cream · salt and pepper · 1 bunch parsley, chopped · 1 garlic clove, finely chopped **To assemble** 14 ounces (300 g) puff pastry dough · neutral oil · 1 egg yolk, beaten **For the vegetable jus** 4¼ cups (1 L) vegetable bouillon (page 207)

THE VEGETABLES —— Wash the spinach and remove the stems. Clean the mushrooms and chop into small pieces. Peel and finely chop the shallots. Peel the potatoes and celery root and cut into thin slices. Heat a pan over high and sauté the spinach with oil. Season with salt. Transfer to a colander to drain. Once cooled, spread the spinach on a clean towel.

THE FILLING —— Sauté the mushrooms in a pan with butter. Season with salt. Once they are browned, add the port, cream, and shallots. Reduce the sauce until one-quarter of the liquid remains. Season with salt and pepper and mix in the chopped parsley and garlic clove. Mix well and transfer to the refrigerator to chill.

TO ASSEMBLE —— Lightly grease a bowl that is wider than it is deep, then line the bowl with plastic wrap. Lay half of the spinach leaves inside the bowl so that the surface is evenly covered. Add a layer of mushrooms on top of the spinach, followed by a layer of potatoes, then celery root. Fill the bowl with the rest of the mushrooms, then cover with the remaining spinach leaves. Wrap tightly with plastic. Gently pierce the plastic to remove any extra air. Chill in the refrigerator for 10 minutes. In the meantime, roll the dough out to about ¼-inch (0.5 cm) thickness. Use a cake ring or a plate to cut the dough into 2 circles that are about 1¼ inches (3 cm) larger than the diameter of the filling. Pierce the inner side of each dough circle with a fork. Brush one of the circles with egg. Remove the plastic wrap from the filling and place the filling on top of the dough circle with the egg, then place the other circle on top of the filling to cover. Pinch the edges of the dough evenly to seal and brush the top with egg.

THE VEGETABLE JUS —— Heat the bouillon over high, reduce by three-quarters, and set aside.

TO BAKE —— Preheat the oven to 350°F (180°C) and bake the torte for 30 minutes. Rest for 10 minutes. Serve with the vegetable au jus.

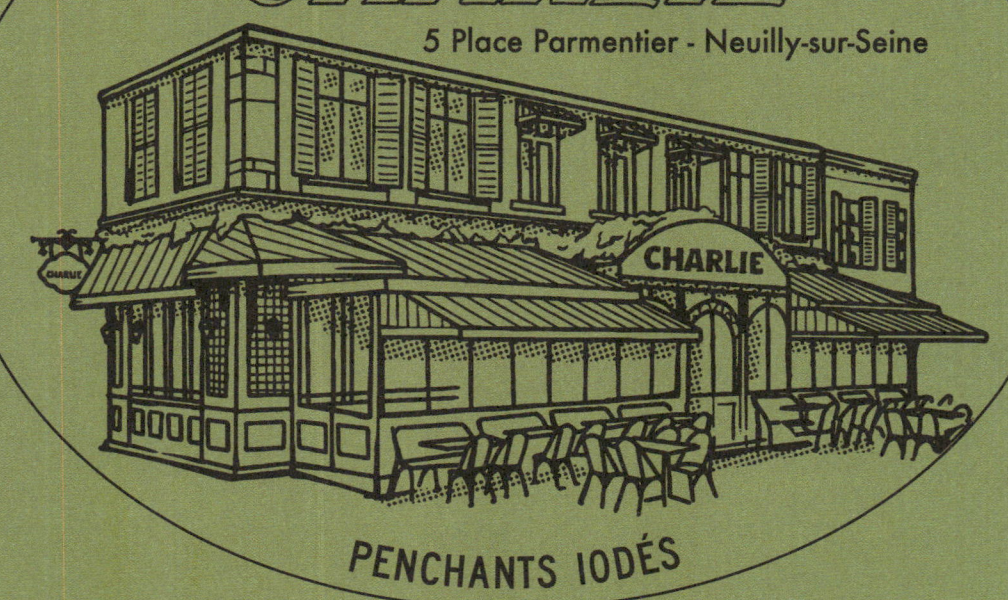

BRASSERIE
CHARLIE
5 Place Parmentier - Neuilly-sur-Seine

PENCHANTS IODÉS

SIDE DISHES

Ratatouille

PREP TIME 30 MINUTES

COOK TIME 45 MINUTES

SERVES 4

5 ½ pounds (2.5 kg) red peppers

3 onions

Olive oil

3 eggplants

3 ripe tomatoes on the vine

½ cup plus 1 tablespoon (150 g) tomato paste

4 garlic cloves, crushed

1 thyme sprig

3 ⅓ pounds (1.5 kg) zucchini

1 teaspoon sea salt

1 teaspoon mignonette pepper

1 teaspoon Espelette pepper

THE RATATOUILLE —— Julienne the peppers. Chop the onions into large pieces. Add both to a pan and sweat with olive oil. While the vegetables cook, cut the eggplants into cubes and sauté with olive oil in a second pan. Add the eggplant to the pan with the peppers and onions, then mix in the tomatoes, tomato paste, crushed garlic, and thyme sprig.

Dice the zucchini. Add the zucchini, salt, mignonette pepper, and Espelette pepper to the pan and simmer over medium heat, stirring frequently. Remove the pan from the heat once the zucchini is fully cooked but slightly al dente and serve.

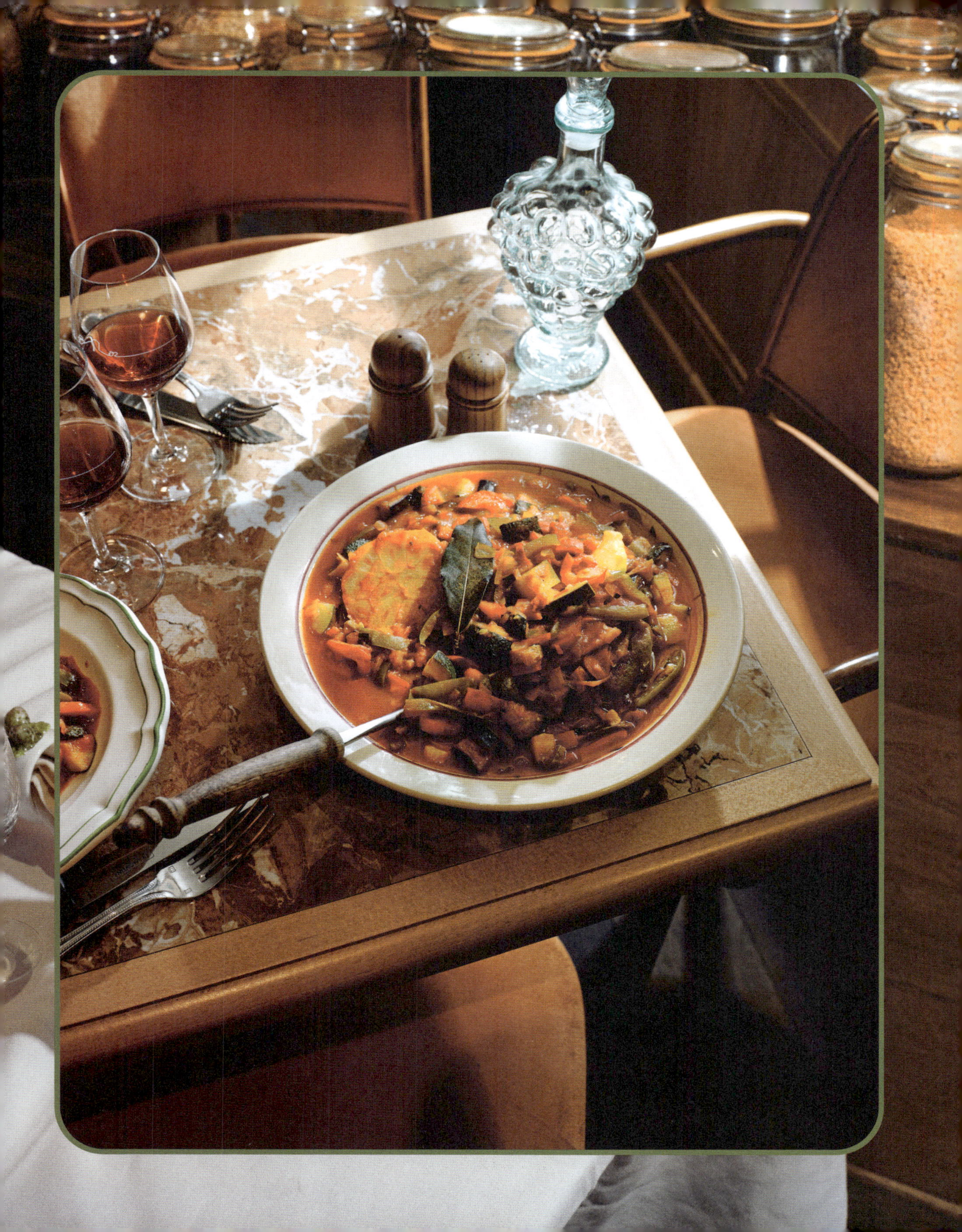

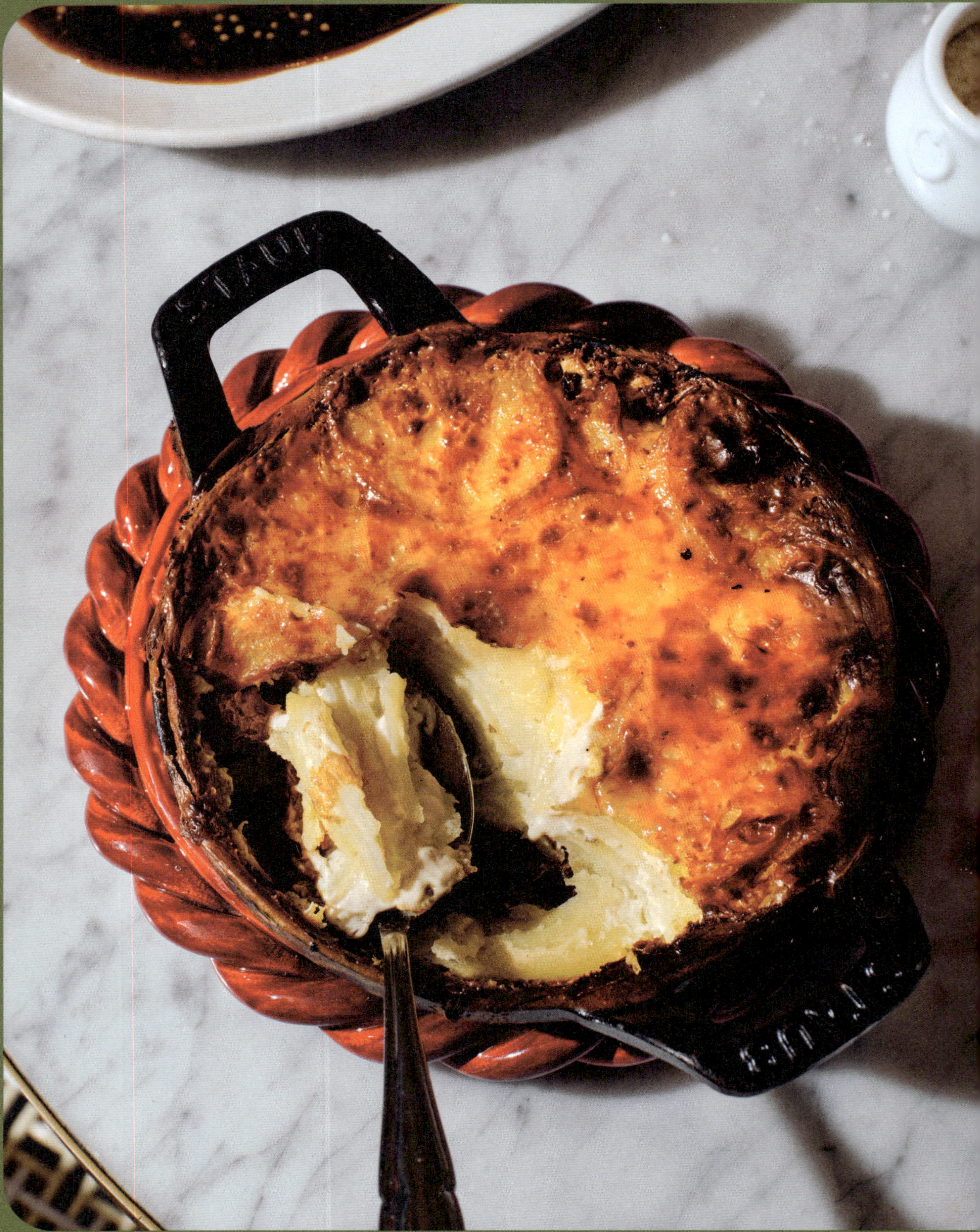

SIDE DISHES

Potatoes au Gratin

Gratin dauphinois

(PREP TIME 30 MINUTES) (COOK TIME 45 MINUTES) (REST TIME 10 MINTUES)

SERVES 6

For the sauce 4¼ cups (1 L) heavy cream · 2 thyme sprigs · 2 garlic cloves, crushed · sea salt · mignonette pepper · nutmeg **For the potatoes** 4½ pounds (2 kg) potatoes · ¼ cup (50 g) butter

THE SAUCE —— Add the cream, thyme, and crushed garlic cloves to a pot and reduce by one-third. Season with salt, pepper, and nutmeg. Preheat the oven to 350°F (180°C).

THE POTATOES —— While the cream is reducing, begin peeling the potatoes. Cut into thin slices about ¼-inch (0.5 cm) thick. Generously butter a gratin dish. Spread a layer of potato slices onto the bottom of the dish, then top with the reduced cream, salt, and pepper. Repeat this operation for the rest of the potatoes. Cut the remaining butter into small cubes and place on top of the gratin.

TO BAKE —— Bake the potatoes for about 45 minutes. Pierce the top with a knife to test for doneness: they should be very soft. Let rest for 10 minutes before serving.

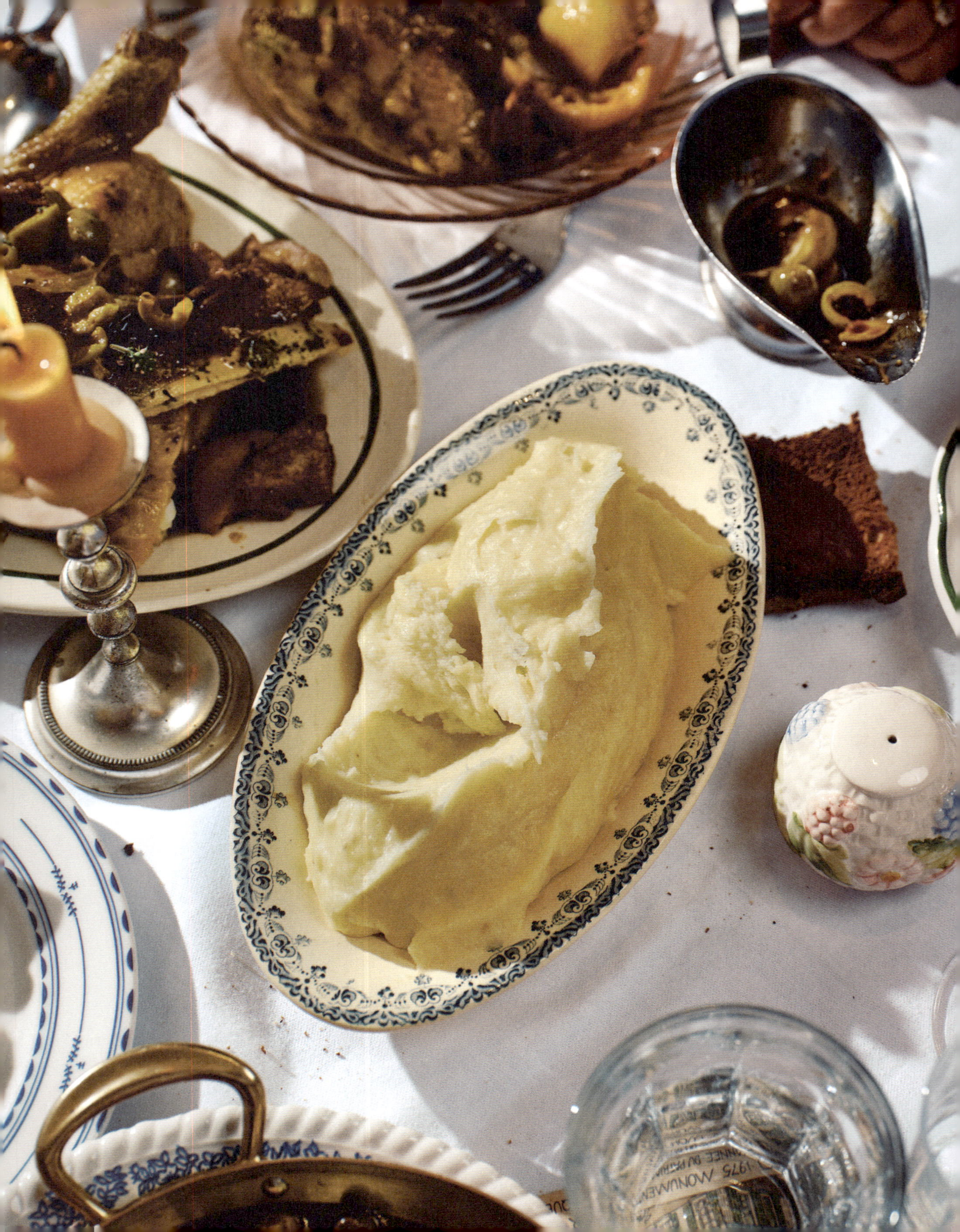

SIDE DISHES

Potato Purée

Purée de pommes de terre

PREP TIME 15 MINUTES

COOK TIME 30 MINUTES

SERVES 6

2¼ pounds (1 kg) starchy potatoes, such as russet or Yukon Gold

1 cup plus 2 teaspoons (250 ml) skim milk

¾ cup plus 2 tablespoons (200 g) salted butter, chilled

Salt and pepper

Nutmeg

THE POTATOES —— Peel the potatoes. Add to a pot of cold water, cover, and bring to a boil. Cook until the potatoes are soft all the way through, then pass through a food mill.

THE PURÉE —— Warm the milk. Cut the butter into cubes. Gradually pour the milk into the potatoes while whisking continuously. Mix in the butter and season with salt, pepper, and nutmeg.

COMICE AGRICOLE
LES CONFITURES
LILET
A BASE DE VIN
APERITIF
KINA LILLET
"TOUT-FRAIS"
VENDU EXCLUSIVEMENT PAR
LA SOCIÉTÉ LAITIÈRE
MAGGI
UNION
Siegel-Pils
Meteor
Carlsberg
Beer
Champigneulles
Jupiler
LE SAVEUR EN PLUS

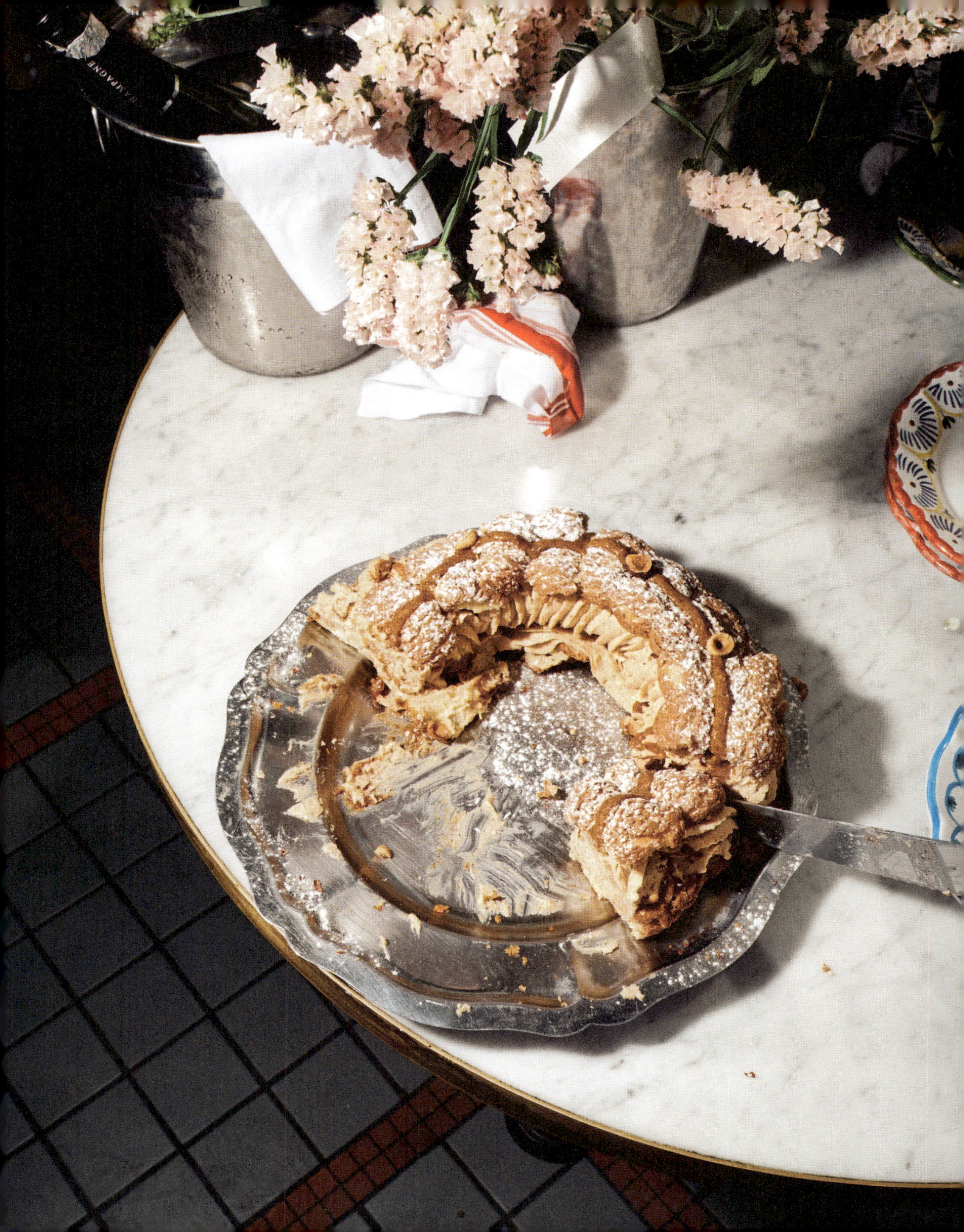

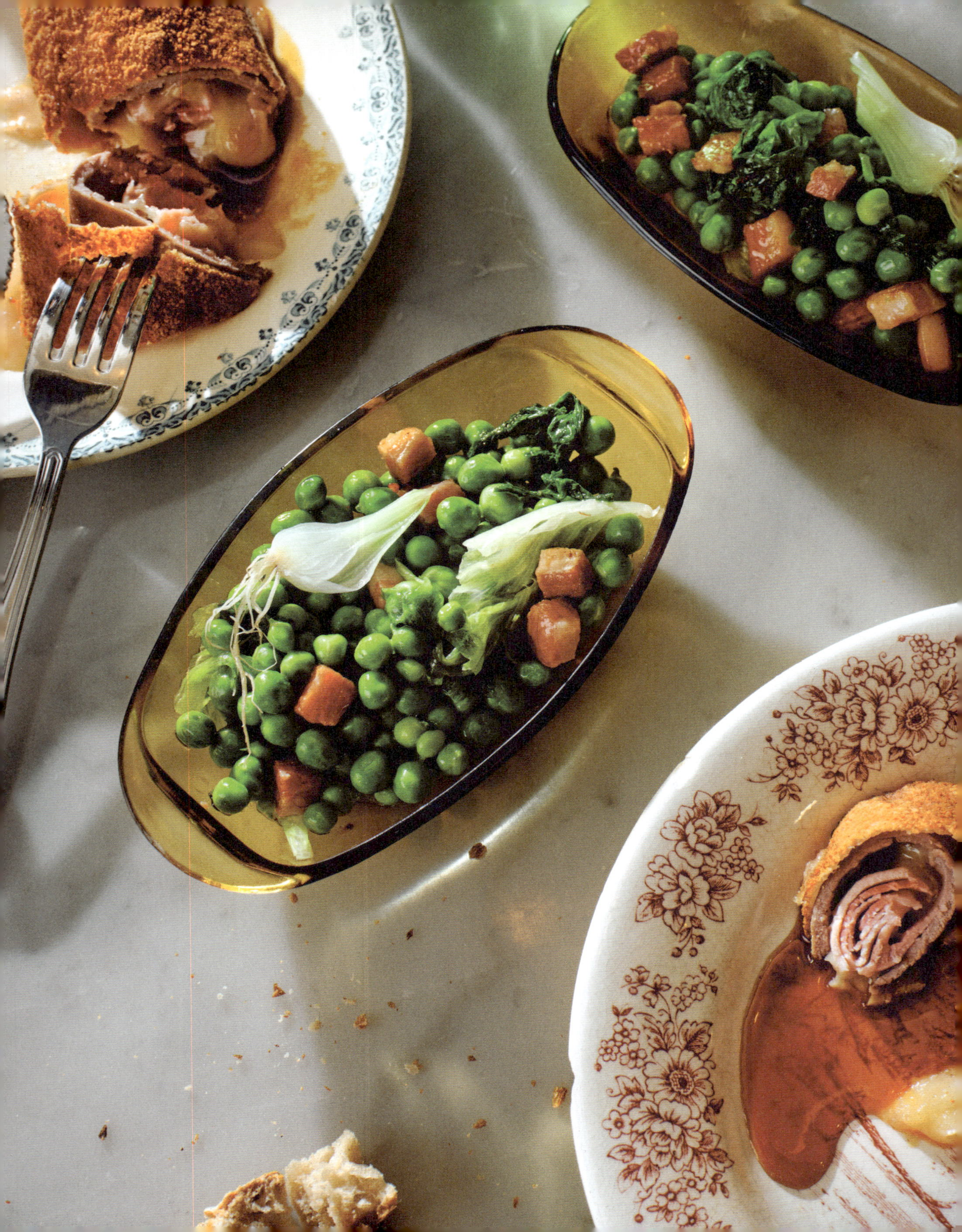

SIDE DISHES

PREP TIME 45 MINUTES

Braised Peas with Spring Onions and Lettuce

COOK TIME 20 MINTUES

Petite Pois à la Française

SERVES 4

4½ pounds (2 kg) French petit pois or shelled sugar snap peas

1 head of lettuce

1 bunch spring onions

3 slices bacon

4 tablespoons plus 2 teaspoons (70 ml) vegetable bouillon (page 207), divided

1 pinch salt

1 pinch sugar

Oil

¼ cup plus 1 teaspoon (60 g) butter

3 chervil sprigs

THE VEGETABLES —— Shell the peas. Roughly chop the lettuce. Remove the greens from the onions and set them aside, then cut the bulbs in half. Cut the bacon slices into lardons.

THE ONIONS —— To glaze the onions, bring 2 tablespoons plus 2 teaspoons (40 ml) of the bouillon to a boil in a saucepan. Add the salt and sugar, then the onions. Cover and cook until the onions are very soft. Remove the lid and cook until the liquid is reduced and the onions are glazed.

THE PEAS —— Generously salt a large pot of water and bring to a boil. Once boiling, add the peas and cook for 4 minutes, until al dente. Transfer to an ice bath to stop cooking, drain, and set aside.

THE LARDONS —— Brown the lardons in a pan over high heat, until they are golden brown. Transfer to a paper towel-lined plate.

TO COOK —— Sear the lettuce quickly in a pan with a dash of oil and a pinch of salt. Add the rest of the bouillon and ¼ cup (50 g) butter. Bring to a boil and cook for 3 minutes. Lower the heat, then add the peas, lardons, and onions. Cook for a few minutes to reheat. To thicken the mixture, add more butter and bouillon. Remove the pot from the heat and mix in the chervil and chopped onion greens.

Around THE TABLE

① PETIT POIS
— *recipe page 155*

French-style petit pois — rather than English-style petit pois, which are cooked in salted boiling water — were one of King Louis XIV's obsessions. At the time, there was even a special market dedicated to the vegetable set up each autumn within Paris' Les Halles marketplace. Petit pois became known as the "King of Les Halles." Back then, they were grown in the suburbs of Paris, specifically in Clamart, which is where the French cooking term "à la Clamart" comes from. Today, "à la Clamart" generally refers to a side of petit pois.

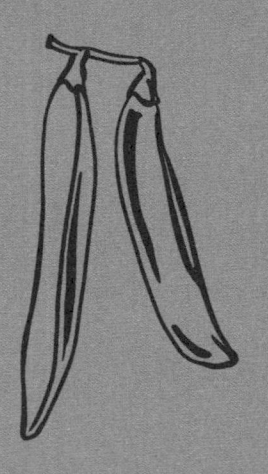

② POTATO PUREE
— *recipe page 151*

There is a goddess of potatoes known as Axomamma in Incan mythology. Although the tuber was worshipped in its native Andes, it was long shunned in France, where it was considered cattle feed and accused of spreading diseases. The potato only began to sneak onto the French dinner table in the 17th century, when pharmacist Antoine Augustin Parmentier notoriously sang the praises of the vegetable. It was not until the end of the 18th century that the potato was formally declared edible by the Paris Faculty of Medicine.

③ LE DORMANT
— *general*

At the time when French table service became popular in the 18th century, *le dormant* referred to the service items that remained on the table in between courses. The legendary salt and pepper duo, the vinegar pot, spice jars... and sometimes even a few pieces of décor, to maintain a certain level of harmony throughout the meal.

④ RATATOUILLE
— *recipe page 146*

Although ratatouille is a close relative of dishes like piperade (a Basque dish of peppers, onions, garlic, and tomatoes), a bohemienne (a Provençal eggplant and tomato casserole) or caponata (a sweet and sour Sicilian dish of fried eggplant and tomatoes), it was not always considered to be the gourmet summer vegetable dish it is today. Simon-Jude Honnorat's 1876 Provencal-French dictionary described "ratatolha" as "a soup for rats." For ages, the word "ratatouille" brought to mind an unappetizing stew of potatoes and boiled meat. In military slang, "rata" referred to a mediocre mixture of beans and potatoes.

⑤ THE KING'S DINNER
— *general*

Nearly every evening at 10 pm, the dinner bell rang for the *"Grand Couvert,"* Louis XIV's public meal. It was an indulgent ceremony that took place in front of his family and courtiers and was held in the royal antechamber, located just past the King's Guard Room. The king would occasionally dine *"au Petit Couvert,"* in other words, either alone or with a small group, and generally in his bedroom.

SIDE DISHES

Braised Gem Lettuces
with Sauce Vierge
Sucrines braisées

PREP TIME 15 MINUTES

COOK TIME 5 MINUTES

SERVES 2

2 large little gem lettuces
½ garlic clove
1 red onion
1 shallot
1 bunch chives
1 red pepper
1 green pepper
1 beefsteak tomato
1 zucchini
½ cup plus 2 tablespoons (150 ml) olive oil
2 tablespoons red wine vinegar
Salt
Espelette pepper
2 cups plus 4 teaspoons (500 ml) vegetable bouillon (recipe page 207)

Cut the lettuces in half and store in the refrigerator.

THE SAUCE VIERGE —— Finely chop the garlic, red onion, shallot, and chives. Deseed and dice the peppers and tomato, and dice the zucchini. Combine these ingredients in a bowl with the olive oil, vinegar, salt, and Espelette pepper.

TO COOK —— Brown the lettuces in a frying pan with a dash of olive oil. Add the vegetable bouillon and cook for 5 minutes. Remove from the pan, drain well, and allow to cool.

TO PLATE —— Arrange the lettuces on a serving platter and cover with the sauce vierge. Transfer the remaining sauce to a gravy boat to serve.

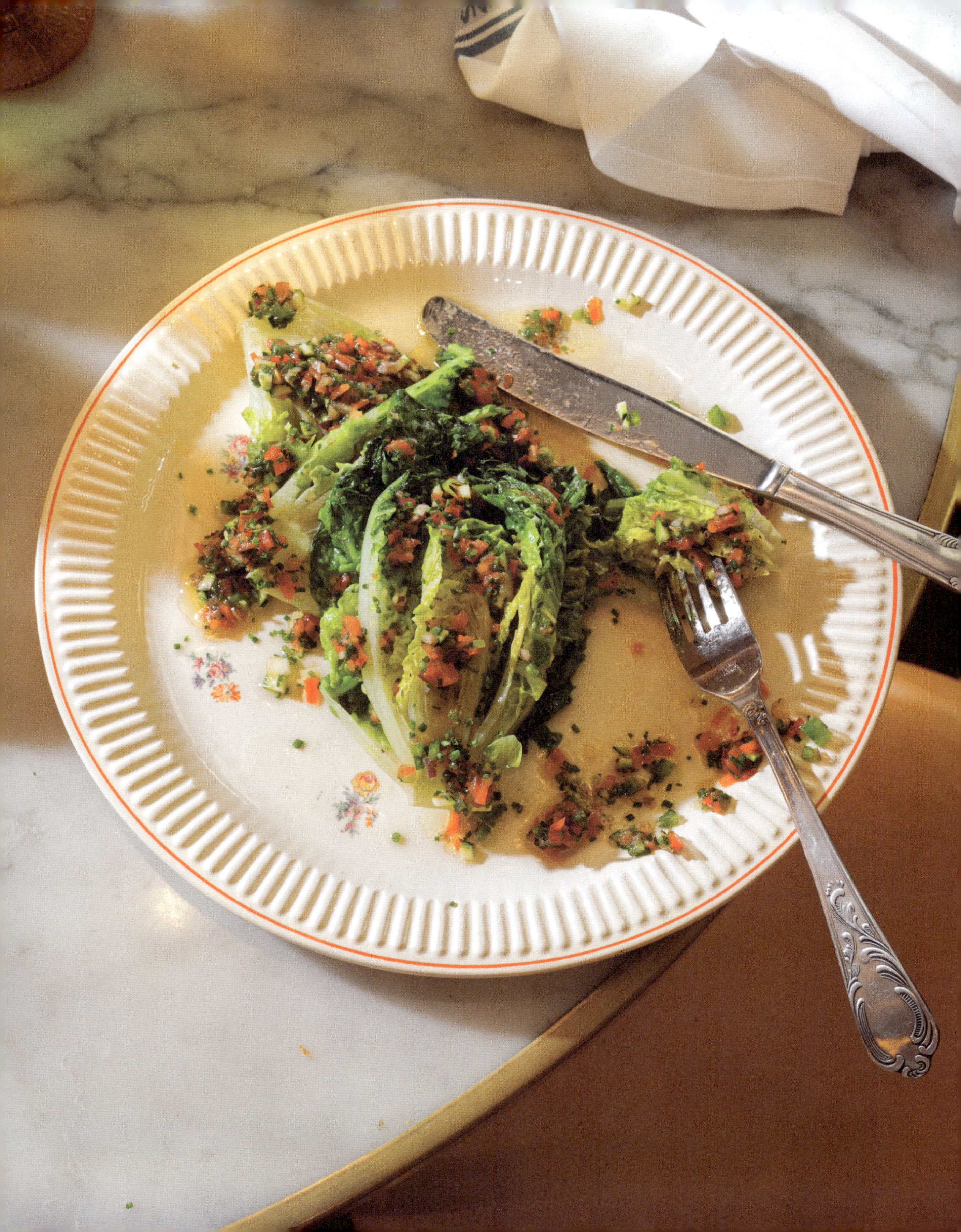

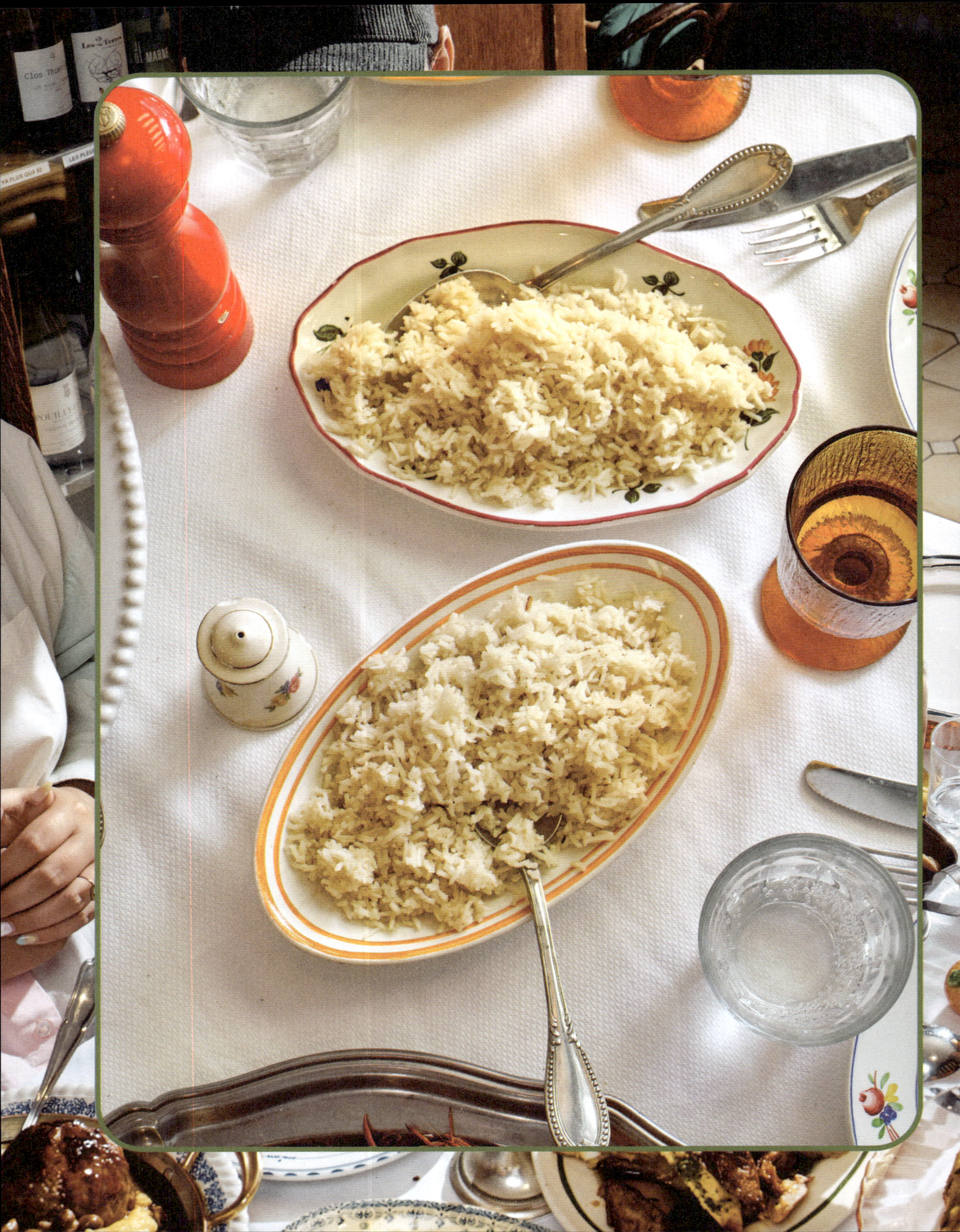

SIDE DISHES

Rice Pilaf

Riz pilaf

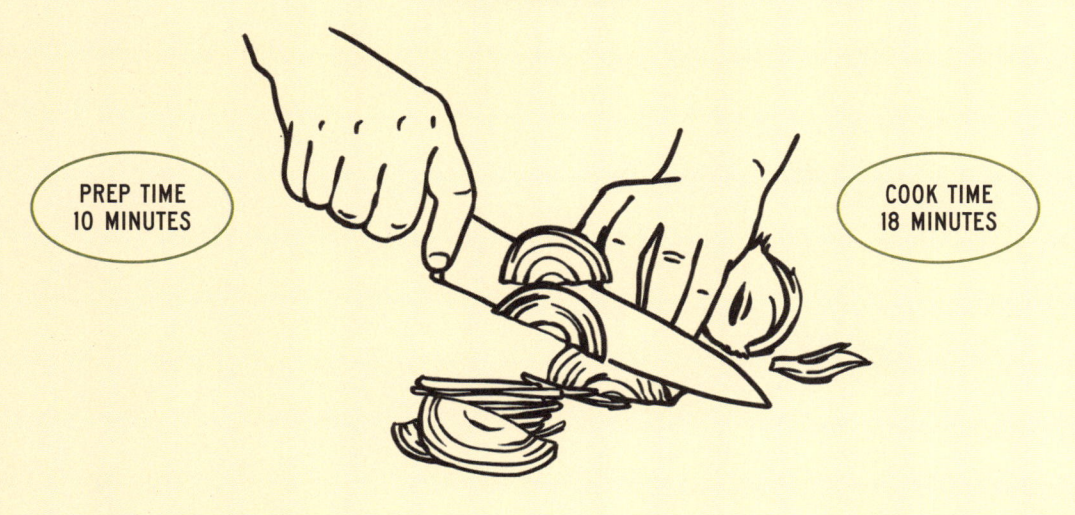

PREP TIME
10 MINUTES

COOK TIME
18 MINUTES

SERVES 4

¼ white onion
1⅔ cups (300 g) rice
¼ cup (50 g) butter
2 cups plus 4 teaspoons (500 ml) vegetable bouillon, white stock (page 207), or water
1 thyme sprig
1 garlic clove
Salt

Chop the onion into very small pieces (the size of a grain of rice). Preheat the oven to 350°F (180°C).

Rinse the rice three times, until the water runs clear. Add the onions to an oven-safe pot and sweat with a little butter over low heat until soft. Add the rice and toast over medium heat until the grains are translucent. Add the bouillon and thyme and bring to a boil. Cover and bake in the oven for 16 to 18 minutes. The rice is cooked when the water has been absorbed and the rice is very tender. Add the butter to the pot. Cut the garlic clove in half, spear it with a fork, and use this to break up the rice. Season with salt to taste.

SIDE DISHES

Spring Vegetables

GARNITURE PRINTANIÈRE

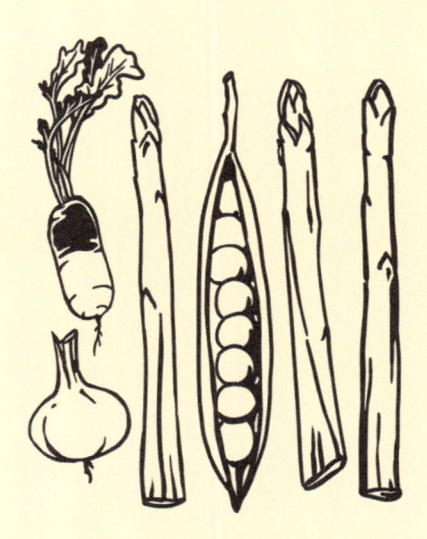

**PREP TIME
45 MINUTES**

**COOK TIME
20 MINUTES**

SERVES 4

2¼ pounds (1 kg) carrots · 4½ pounds (2 kg) petits pois or shelled sugar snap peas · ½ bunch white asparagus · 3 spring onions · ½ bunch red radishes · vegetable bouillon (page 207) · 7 tablespoons (100 g) butter · 2 garlic cloves, crushed · 18 ounces (500 g) young turnips · salt and pepper

THE VEGETABLES —— Wash the vegetables. Peel the carrots and shell the peas. Peel the asparagus and trim the tough ends.

Bring a pot of salted water to a boil and blanch the asparagus for about 10 minutes, depending on their size. Once cooked, transfer to an ice bath, then to a clean towel to dry. Add the peas to the same pot of boiling water and blanch for 3 minutes. Transfer to an ice bath, then drain and set aside. Blanch the carrots in the same water for about 10 minutes, depending on their size. Transfer to an ice bath, then drain and set aside.

Finely chop the onion greens and cut the bulbs into petals. Cut the asparagus and carrots in half or thirds lengthwise. Cut the radishes in half.

TO COOK —— Heat a pot over medium, fill with enough bouillon or water to cover the bottom, and add the butter. Once the butter is melted, add the onions, crushed garlic, and turnips. Cook for several minutes, then add the carrots, radishes, asparagus, and peas. Continue cooking until the liquid is reduced and the vegetables are glazed. Adjust seasoning before serving.

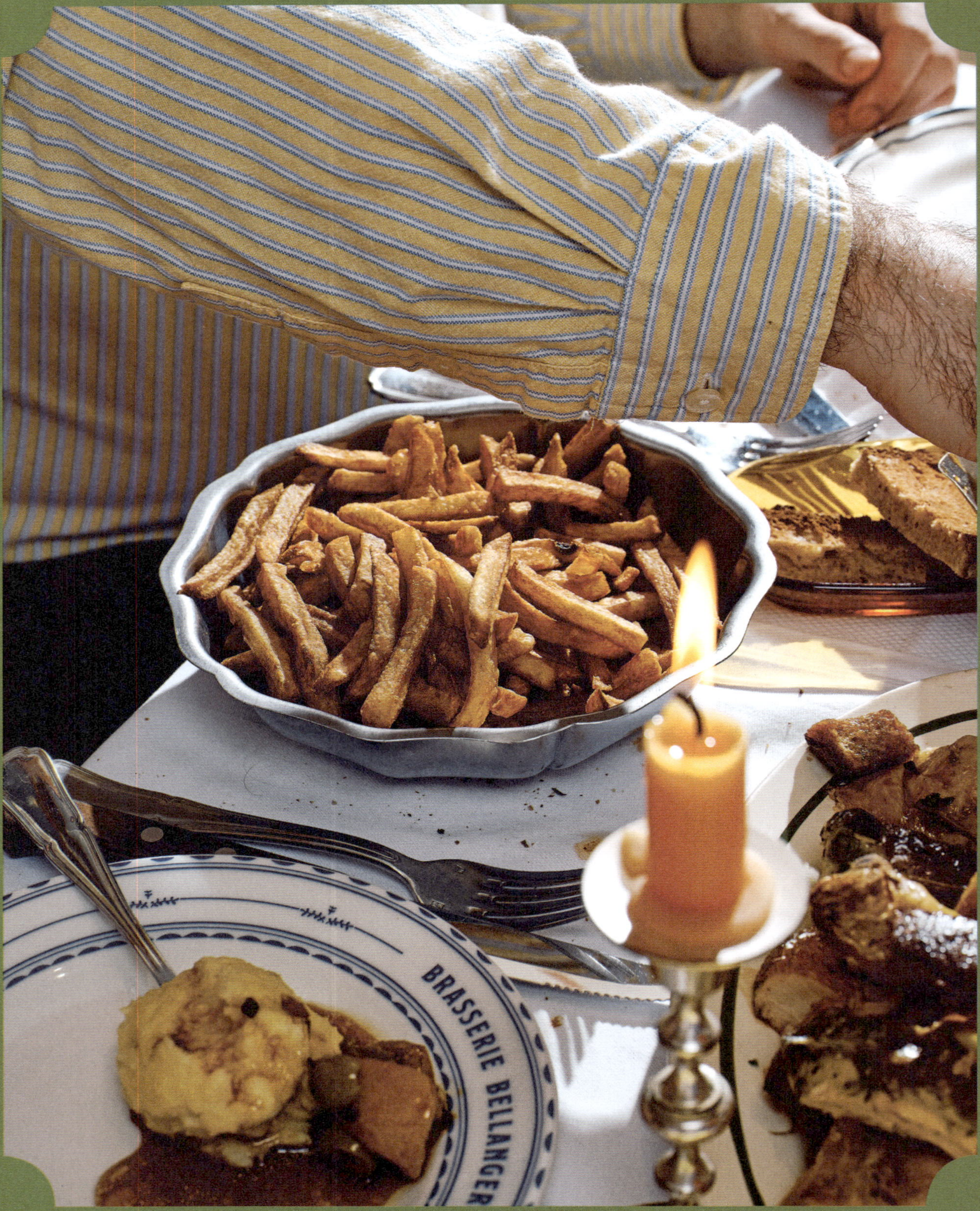
BRASSERIE BELLANGER

SIDE DISHES

French Fries

Frites

PREP TIME
20 MINUTES

COOK TIME
10 MINUTES

SERVES 6

2¼ pounds (1 kg) potatoes

8½ cups (2 L) frying oil (canola or sunflower)

Salt

THE FRIES —— Wash and peel the potatoes (or leave the skin on). Use a French fry cutter or knife to cut the potatoes to your desired thickness. Soak the potatoes in cold water for a few minutes, then transfer to a clean towel to dry.

TO COOK —— The best fries are cooked twice. First, fry the potatoes in a pot of oil heated to 300°F (150°C). To test for doneness, break a fry in half: it will break easily and be yellow in the center once cooked. Let the fries cool completely. Once cooled, fry a second time in oil to 350°F (180°C), until crispy and golden brown. Season with salt to taste.

CAMPION
BRASSERIE

32 rue Lepelletier - Lille

INSPIRÉE DE L'ESTAMINET

DESSERTS

DESSERTS

Île Flottante

PREP TIME
30 MINUTES

INFUSION TIME
1 HOUR

COOK TIME
30 MINUTES

SERVES 4 TO 6

For the salted caramel ¾ cup plus 4¼ teaspoons (200 g) heavy cream ¾ cup plus 4 teaspoons (160 g) sugar · 4¼ teaspoons (20 g) butter · 1 teaspoon (2 g) sea salt **For the crème anglaise** 1¼ cups (300 ml) milk 1 vanilla bean · 3 egg yolks · ¼ cup plus ½ teaspoon (50 g) sugar **For the snow eggs** 5 egg whites · ⅓ cup plus 4 teaspoons (80 g) sugar · 1 teaspoon (2 g) fine salt **To assemble** 2¾ ounces (80 g) toasted sliced almonds

THE SALTED CARAMEL — Pour the cream into a saucepan and bring to a boil, then set aside. Heat a second saucepan over high, add the sugar to the dry pan, and caramelize until it turns golden brown. Next, add the hot cream to the sugar to deglaze the pan. Add the butter and cook for about 5 minutes. Remove the pot from the heat and add the salt. Allow to cool.

THE CRÈME ANGLAISE — Scrape the seeds from the vanilla bean. Add the vanilla seeds and the milk to a pot, bring to a boil, and infuse for 1 hour. Reheat the infusion. In the meantime, quickly whisk together the egg yolks and sugar. Pour this mixture into the hot infused milk, whisking continuously until blended. Cook for a few minutes over medium heat. Refrigerate.

THE SNOW EGGS — Preheat the oven to 200°F (90°C). Beat the egg whites until they become foamy. Add the sugar and salt gradually, then continue beating until stiff peaks form. Use two soup spoons to form the egg whites into dumplings, then place the dumplings on a baking sheet covered with parchment paper. Pour water into a second baking sheet to create a water bath. Place the water bath on the bottom rack of the oven and the baking sheet with the snow eggs on the rack above and bake for 10 minutes at 200 (90°C).

TO ASSEMBLE — Pour a little crème anglaise onto deep plates for serving. Remove the snow eggs from the pan and place one on each plate. Top with a drizzle of caramel and a few toasted sliced almonds.

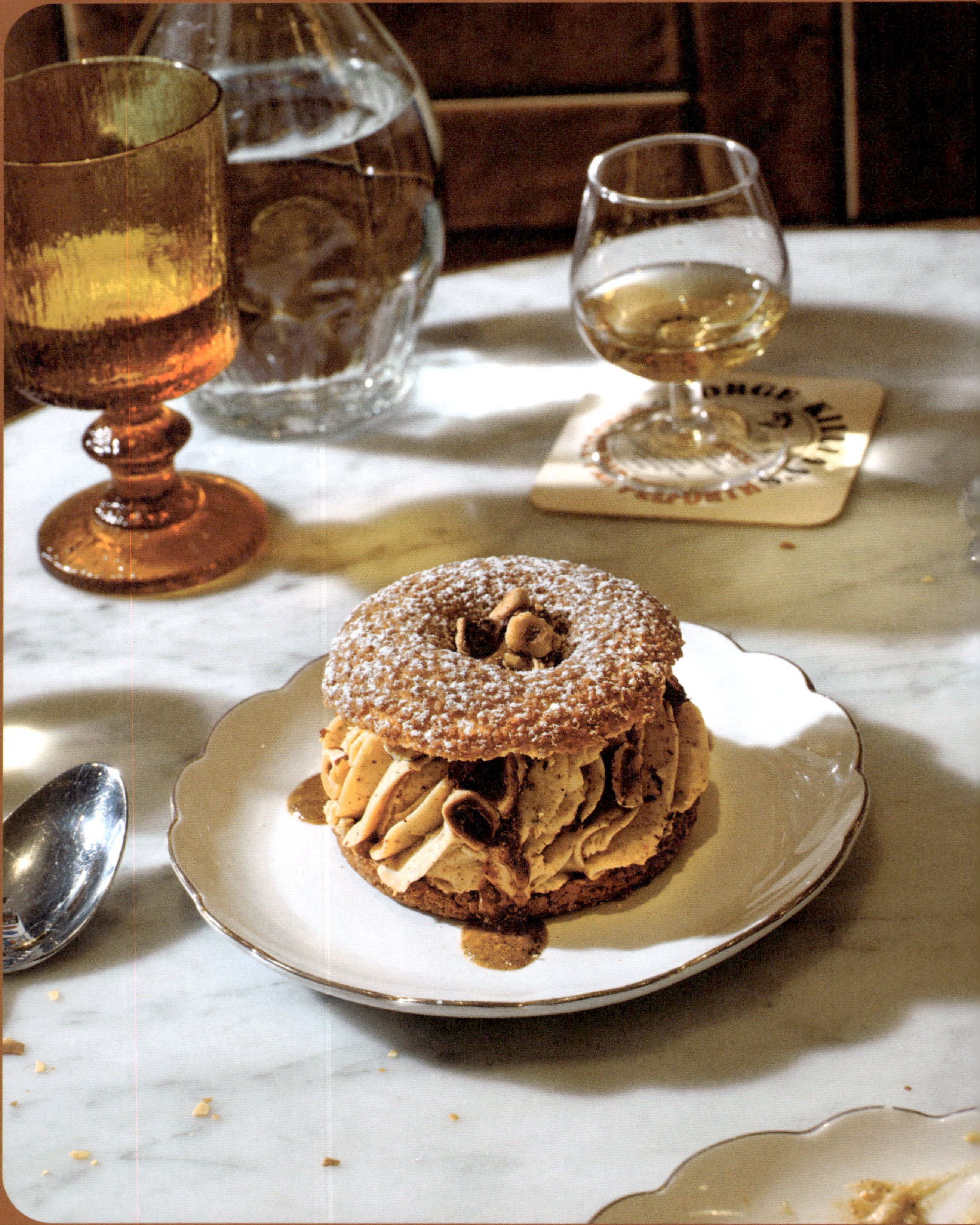

DESSERTS

Paris-Brest

PREP TIME
1 HOUR

COOK TIME
40 MINUTES

REST TIME
1 HOUR
(FOR THE CRAQUELIN)

SERVES 6

For the craquelin 1/3 cup (75 g) butter · 1/4 cup plus 2 tablespoons plus 1 teaspoon (75 g) brown sugar · 1 tablespoon (5 g) cocoa powder · 1/3 cup (75 g) flour **For the choux pastry** 1/3 cup plus 1 teaspoon (80 g) butter · 1/3 cup plus 4 teaspoons (100 ml) water · 1/3 cup plus 4 teaspoons (100 ml) milk · 2 teaspoons (4 g) salt · 1 teaspoon (4 g) sugar · 4 eggs **For the mousseline cream** 1½ cups (360 ml) milk · 2 egg yolks · 3 tablespoons plus 1 teaspoon (40 g) sugar · 1/4 cup plus 2 tablespoons plus 1 teaspoon (30 g) cornstarch · 2/3 cup (150 g) softened butter · 3/4 cup (180 g) praline paste · 3/4 cup plus 4 1/4 teaspoons (200 g) heavy cream **To plate** 8 teaspoons (20 g) powdered sugar · 1/2 cup plus 2 tablespoons (150 g) praline paste · 1 ounce (30 g) toasted hazelnuts, crushed

THE CRAQUELIN TOPPING —— Beat butter and brown sugar together in the bowl of an electric mixer fitted with the paddle. Add the cacao, then the flour, and mix until you have a firm ball. Place the ball between two sheets of parchment paper and roll out to the thickness of a coin. Refrigerate for 1 hour. Use a cookie cutter to cut six 4-inch (10 cm) circles.

THE CHOUX PASTRY —— Cut the butter into cubes, then add the water, milk, salt, sugar, and butter to a saucepan and bring to a boil. Pour all the flour into the saucepan and whisk until no lumps remain. Cook the dough over medium heat, stirring frequently, until it becomes homogenous. Remove the pan from the heat and allow to cool slightly, then incorporate the eggs one at a time. Set aside to cool. Preheat the oven to 325°F (160°C). On a baking sheet covered with parchment paper, pipe six 4-inch (10 cm) rings of choux. Place one circle of craquelin on top of each choux before baking. Bake for 25 minutes without opening the oven.

THE MOUSSELINE CREAM —— Prepare the pastry cream: bring the milk to a simmer in a saucepan. Mix the egg yolks, sugar, and cornstarch together in a bowl. Pour half of the simmering milk into the bowl and stir until combined. Pour this mixture into the pan with the simmering milk and cook, stirring continuously. The pastry cream is ready once the mixture begins to bubble. Transfer to a bowl and chill in the refrigerator. Whisk the chilled pastry cream to loosen it. Add the softened butter, then the praline paste. Separately, whip the cream with a hand mixer until it thickens. Fold the whipped cream into the pastry cream gently, so that it doesn't collapse. Transfer to a piping bag and refrigerate.

TO PLATE —— Place a dollop of mousseline cream on each plate to stabilize the pastries. Cut each choux in half widthwise. Place the bottom half of each choux pastry on the dollop of mousseline cream. Dust the top halves with powdered sugar. Pipe the mousseline onto each pastry base in a circular pattern. Cover with praline paste and crushed hazelnuts, then top with the other half of the pastry.

DESSERTS

Pear and Almond Tart

Tarte Bourdaloue

PREP TIME 30 MINUTES

COOK TIME 2 HOURS 30 MINUTES

SERVES 6 TO 8

For the poached pears

1 vanilla bean

4 Conference or Bosc pears

4¼ cups (1 L) water

1⅓ cups (250 g) sugar

2 capfuls rum

For the almond cream

⅓ cup plus 1 teaspoon (80 g) butter, softened

⅓ plus 4 teaspoons (80 g) caster sugar

⅔ cup plus 2 teaspoons (80 g) almond flour

2 eggs

1 capful rum

To assemble

1 butter pie crust (page 211)

1 pat butter (to grease the pan)

4 tablespoons toasted sliced almonds

THE POACHED PEARS —— Dry the vanilla bean in the oven for 1 hour at 200°F (90°C). Grind into a powder. Peel the pears, then cut in half and remove the core. Add the water to a pot with the sugar and vanilla and bring to a boil. Place the pear halves in the syrup and cook at a low boil for about 15 minutes. The pears are cooked when they can be easily pierced all the way through with knife. Add the rum to the pot and let everything cool.

THE ALMOND CREAM —— In an electric mixer, beat together the butter and sugar. Mix in the almond flour, eggs, and rum. Set aside.

TO ASSEMBLE —— Preheat the oven to 325°F (160°C). Roll the dough out onto a buttered tart pan. Pierce the base of the dough with a fork. Spread the almond cream on top. Cut the pears into thin slices and arrange in the shape of a rose window on top of the cream. Sprinkle with sliced almonds and bake for 40 minutes.

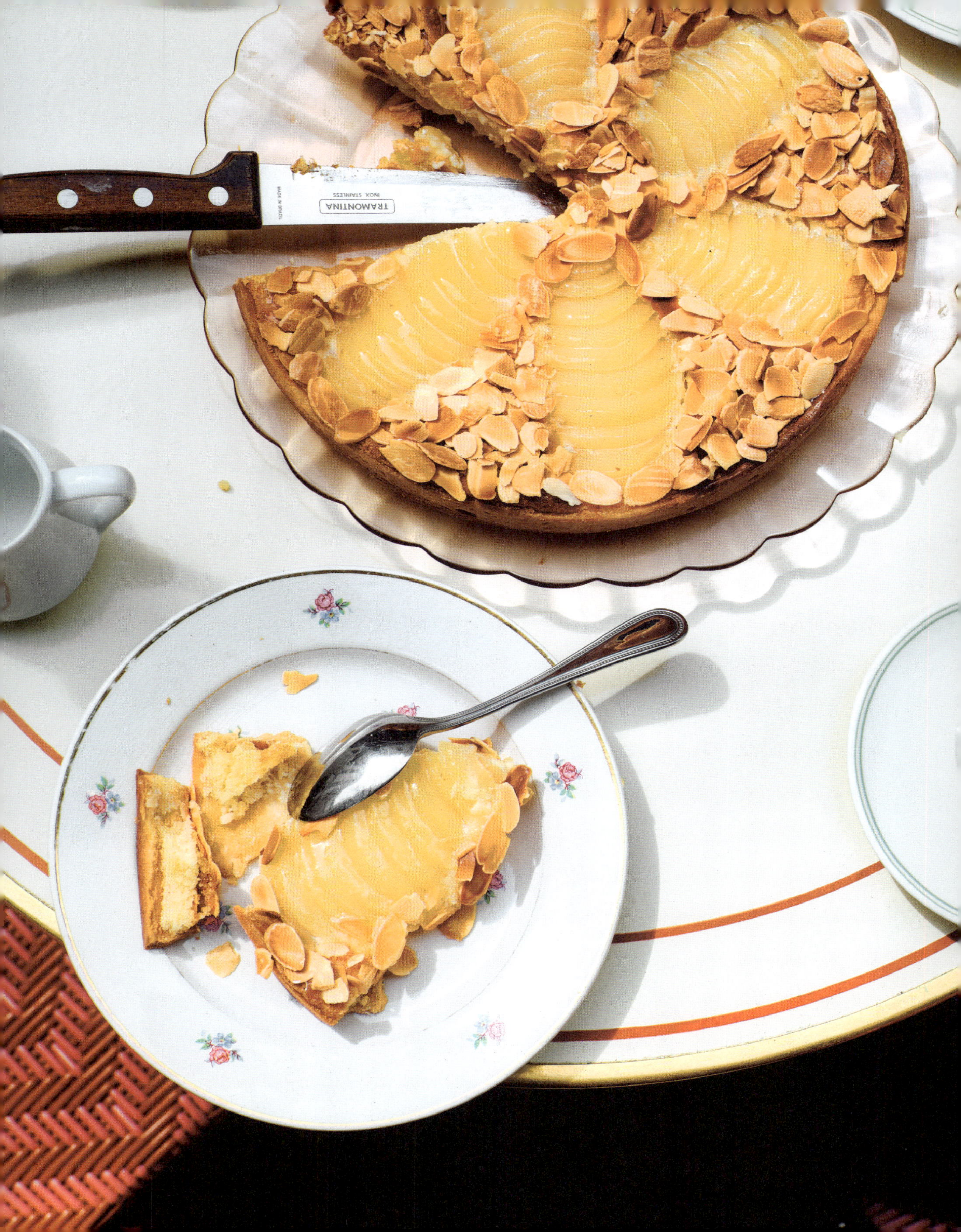
TRAMONTINA

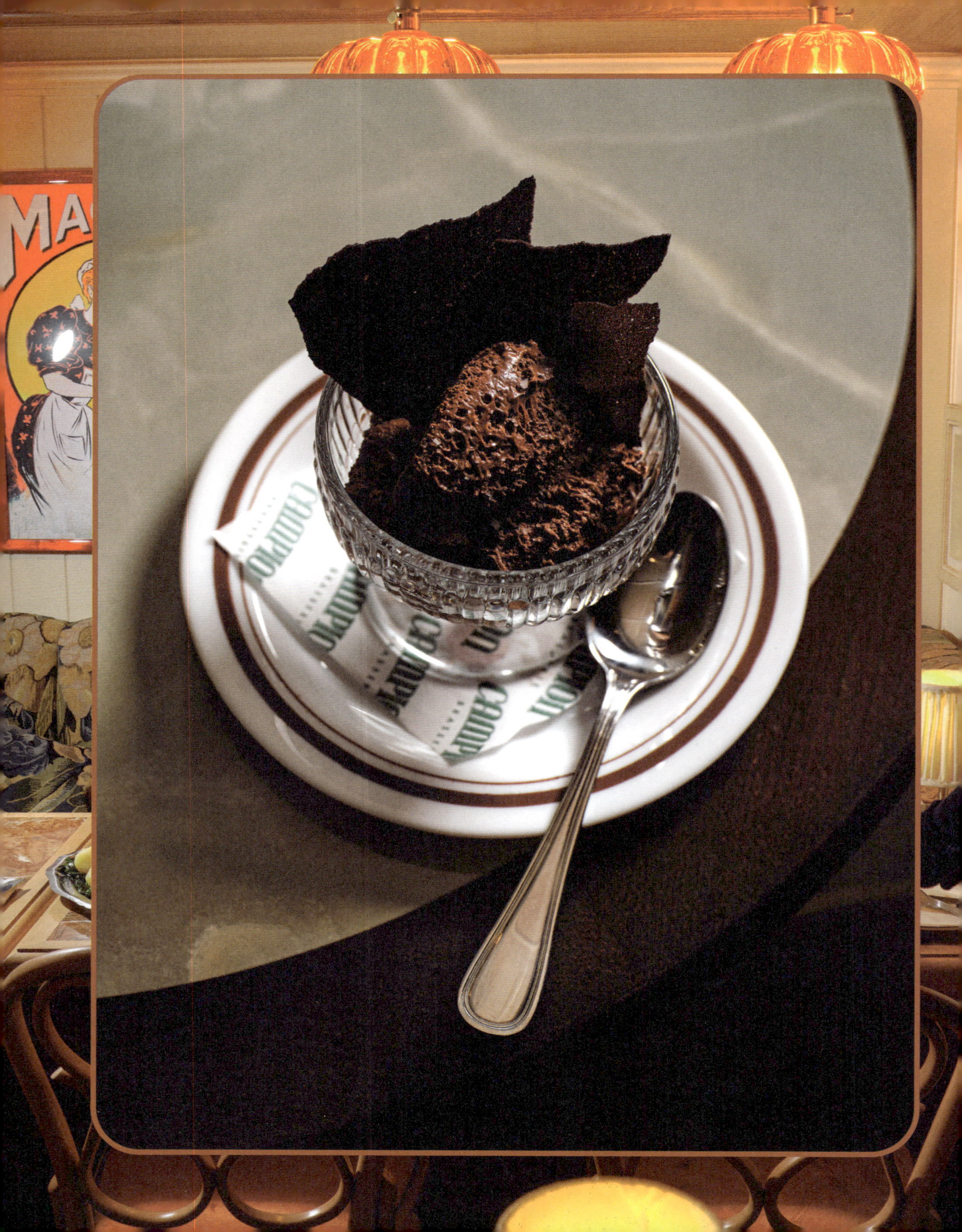

Chocolate Mousse

Mousse au chocolat

**PREP TIME
10 MINUTES**

**COOK TIME
3 MINUTES**

REST TIME: 3 HOURS

SERVES 6 TO 8

⅓ cup plus 4 teaspoons (100 ml) milk

¾ cup plus 3 tablespoons (220 ml) heavy cream

12 ounces (350 g) dark chocolate

10 egg whites

3 tablespoons (50 g) brown sugar

THE CHOCOLATE GANACHE —— Bring the milk and cream to a boil in a saucepan. Break the chocolate into pieces and transfer to a bowl. Remove the pan from the heat and pour the milk and cream on top of the chocolate. Stir with a spatula until the mixture becomes smooth.

THE EGG WHITES —— Beat the eggs in the bowl of an electric mixer until stiff peaks form. Gradually mix in the brown sugar.

TO MAKE —— In a mixing bowl, gently fold the egg whites into the chocolate ganache. Chill in the refrigerator for at least 3 hours before serving.

DESSERTS

Lemon Meringue Tart

TARTE AU CITRON MERINGUÉE

PREP TIME
40 MINUTES

COOK TIME
40 MINUTES

REST TIME
45 MINUTES

SERVES 8

For the lemon curd ½ cup plus 1 tablespoon (140 g) lemon juice · ¾ cup plus 1 ½ teaspoons (150 g) sugar · 3 eggs · 2 tablespoons plus 1 teaspoon (18 g) cornstarch · ½ cup plus 2 tablespoons (140 g) unsalted butter **For the Swiss meringue** 4 egg whites · 1 ¼ cups (240 g) sugar **To assemble** 1 pat butter (to grease the pan) · 1 shortcrust pastry (page 211)

THE LEMON CURD — Warm the lemon juice in a pot with half of the sugar. In the meantime, whisk the eggs and the rest of the sugar in a bowl, then whisk in the cornstarch. Whisk the warm lemon juice into the bowl, then pour the mixture back into the pot. Cook just until the mixture begins to boil while whisking continuously. Remove from the heat and cover in plastic wrap. Allow to cool for 15 minutes, then chop the butter into small pieces, add to the mixture, and incorporate using an immersion blender, until the texture is very smooth. Wrap the lemon curd in plastic and allow to cool once more before finishing the tart.

THE SWISS MERINGUE — You will need a cooking thermometer. Prepare a water bath. Pour the egg whites and sugar into a heat-resistant bowl and place the bowl in the water bath. Begin to whisk the egg whites until the temperature reaches 125.6°F (52°C), then whip the egg whites off the heat until they set.

TO ASSEMBLE AND BAKE — Grease a tart pan with butter, then roll out the dough on top of the pan and press down gently. Pierce the base of the dough with a fork and refrigerate for at least 30 minutes before baking. Preheat the oven to 350°F (180°C). Bake the crust for about 30 minutes. Allow to cool before removing from the pan. Spread a thick layer of lemon curd on the crust and top with the meringue. Brown the meringue with a kitchen torch before serving.

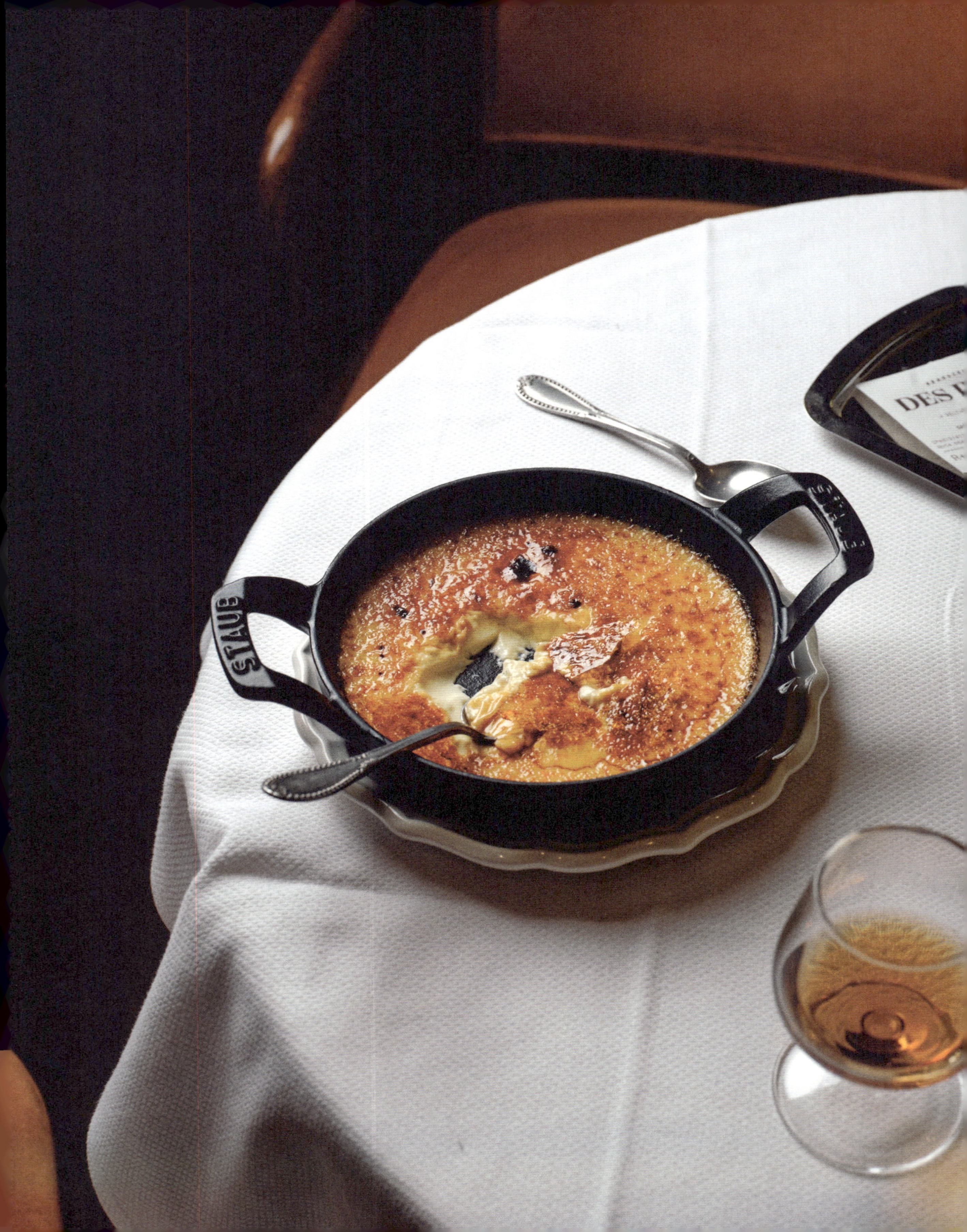
STAUB
DES

DESSERTS

Crème Brûlée

**PREP TIME
10 MINUTES**

**COOK TIME
50 MINUTES**

REST TIME: 5 HOURS

SEVRVES 6

1 vanilla bean
1 cup (240 ml) milk
7 egg yolks
⅓ cup plus 4 teaspoons (80 g) superfine sugar
2¾ cups (660 ml) heavy cream
6 tablespoons brown sugar

THE MILK —— Slice the vanilla bean in half and scrape out the seeds. Pour the milk into a pot and bring to a boil. Remove the pot from the heat and add the vanilla. Infuse for at least 1 hour for an intense vanilla flavor.

THE CUSTARD —— Whisk the egg yolks and caster sugar together in a bowl. Whisk in the cream, then divide evenly between 6 crème brûlée ramekins.

TO BAKE —— Preheat the oven to 325°F (160°C). Arrange the ramekins on an oven-safe baking dish and fill the dish halfway with boiling water. Bake 35 to 40 minutes. The centers should be slightly wobbly out of the oven. Chill the ramekins for at least 4 hours before serving.

TO PLATE —— Sprinkle brown sugar on top of each crème brûlée and use a kitchen torch to caramelize the sugar into a thick crust.

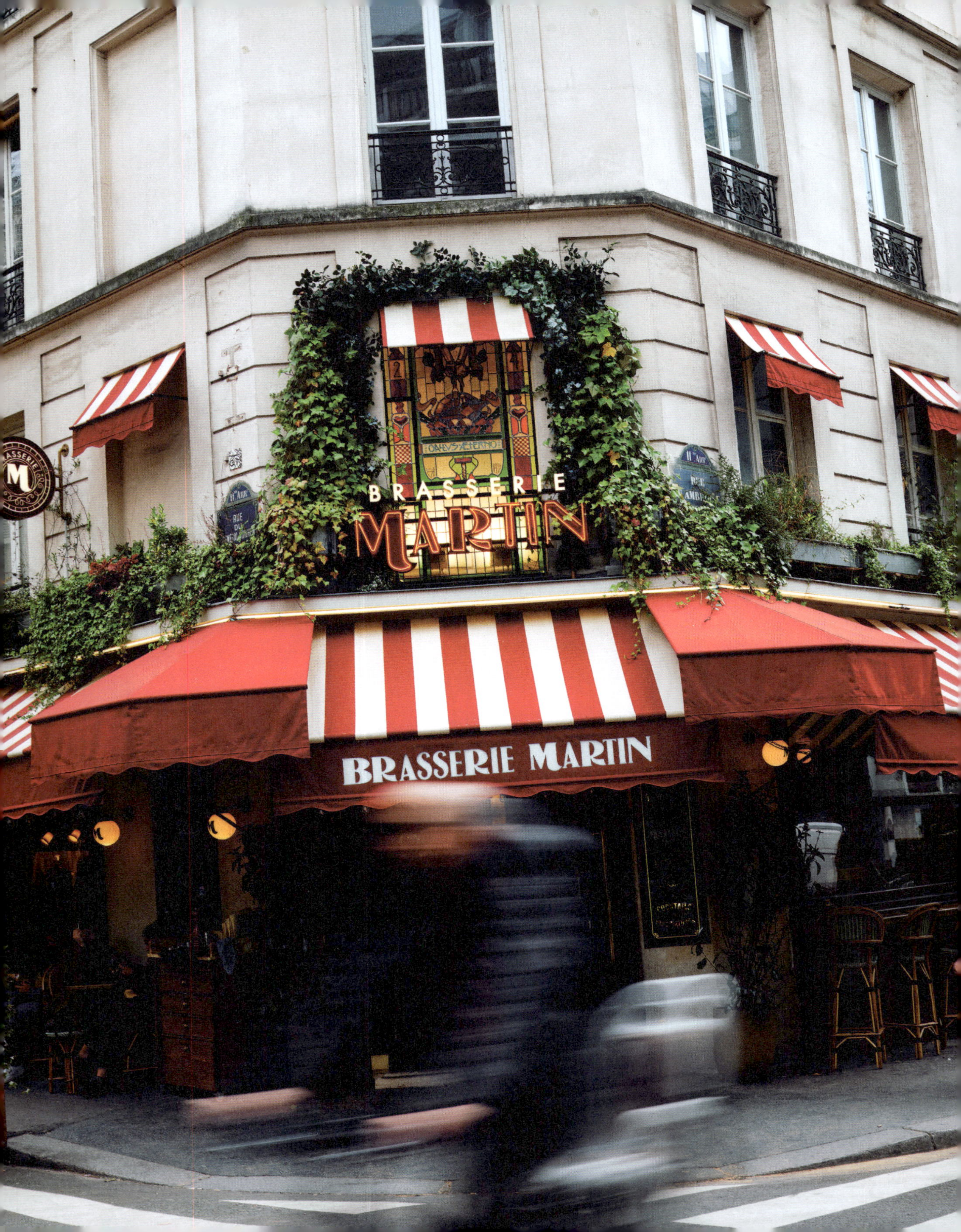
BRASSERIE
MARTIN
BRASSERIE MARTIN

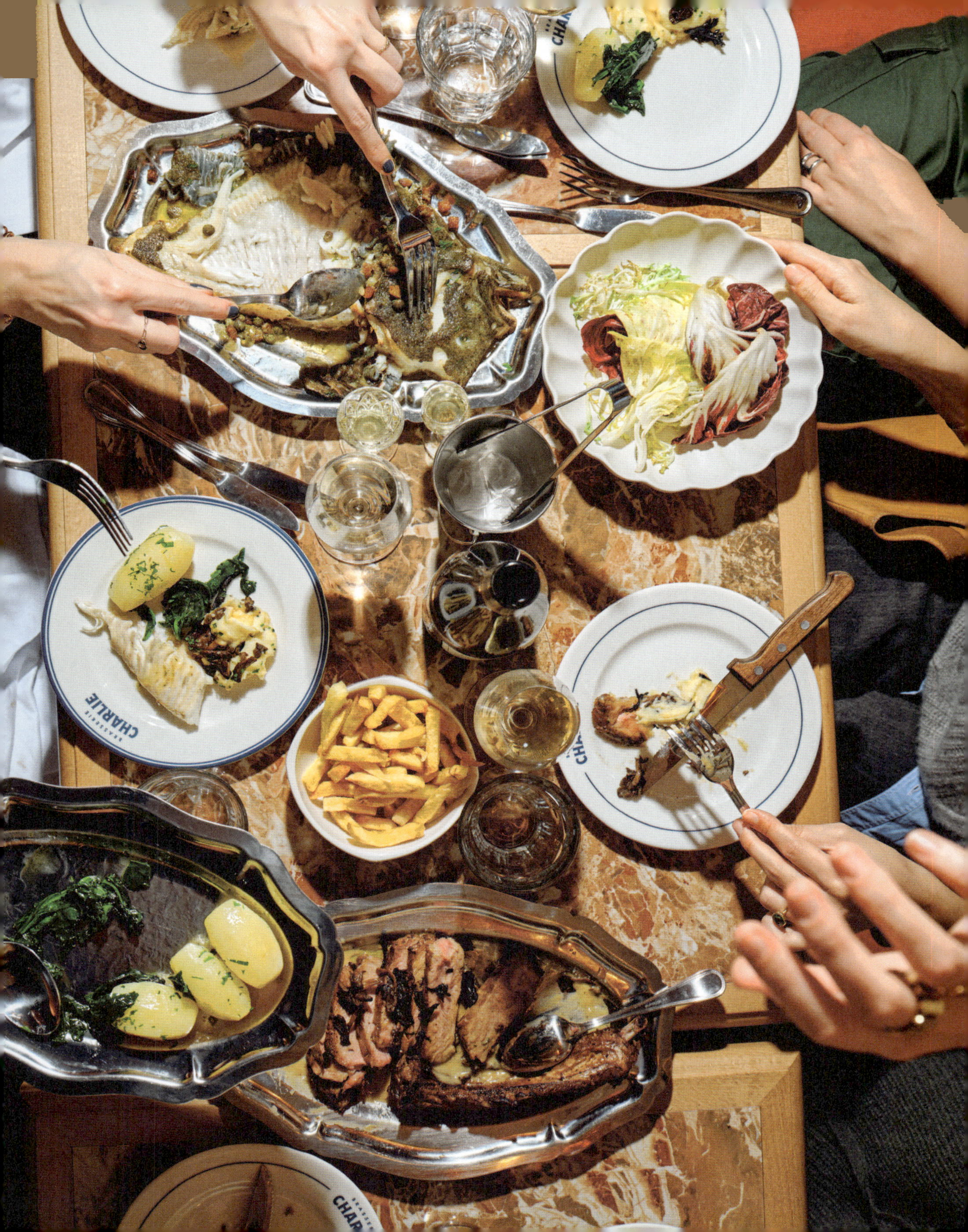
BRASSERIE
CHARLIE

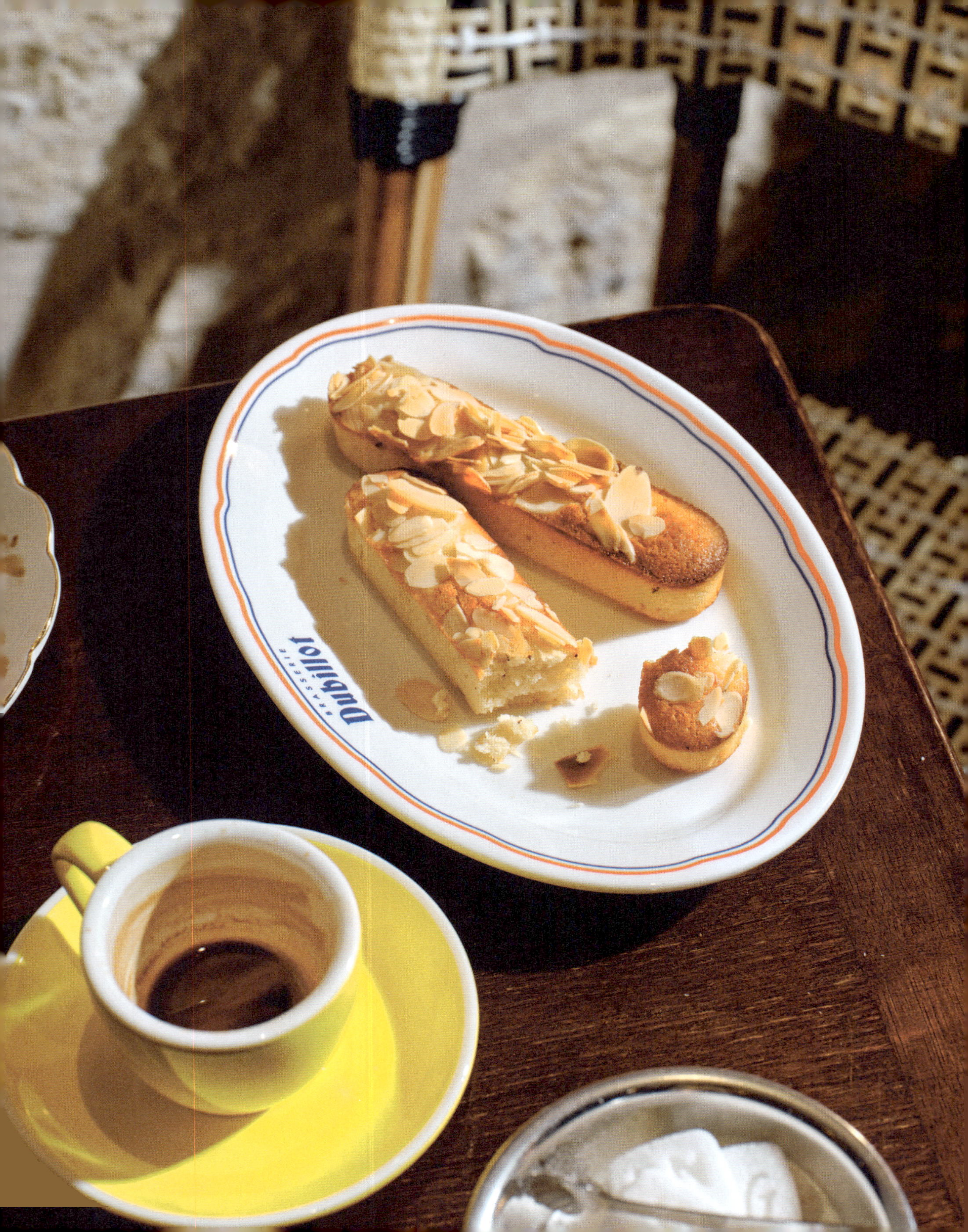
BRASSERIE
Dubillot

DESSERTS

Financiers

PREP TIME 10 MINUTES

MAKES ABOUT 20 FINANCIERS

COOK TIME 12 MINUTES

1 cup (225 g) unsalted butter, plus more for greasing the pan

3 ⅓ cups (400 g) powdered sugar

1 ¾ cups plus 2 teaspoons (200 g) almond flour

1 cup plus 5 teaspoons (130 g) flour

10 egg whites

1 teaspoon (5 g) sea salt

½ capful bitter almond extract

THE BATTER —— Preheat the oven to 340°F (170°C). Cut the butter into small cubes. Heat the butter in a pot until browned. Let cool. Mix all the ingredients in a bowl in the order they are listed, finishing with the browned butter. Grease a mini cupcake pan with butter and fill each cup with batter.

TO BAKE —— Bake the financiers for about 12 minutes. Insert the tip of a knife into one to test for doneness: it should come out clean. Allow to cool, then remove from the pan.

Around THE TABLE

THE FINANCIER was invented in the 17th century in a convent in Nancy by the talented nuns of the Order of the Visitation of Holy Mary. The cakes were soon forgotten, though, due to a rather sinister reason. At the time, cases of poisoning were alarmingly common. The scent of cyanide was eerily similar to that of bitter almonds, and the cakes inevitably fell out of style. The financier reappeared in 1865 in Pierre Lacam's pastry grimoire *Le Nouveau Pâtisssier-Glacier*. But it wasn't until the late 19th century that pastry chef Paul Lasne came up with a golden idea to revive the pastry. Baking the cakes into the shape of a small gold bar, he paid tribute to his clients—the bustling traders at the Paris Stock Exchange.

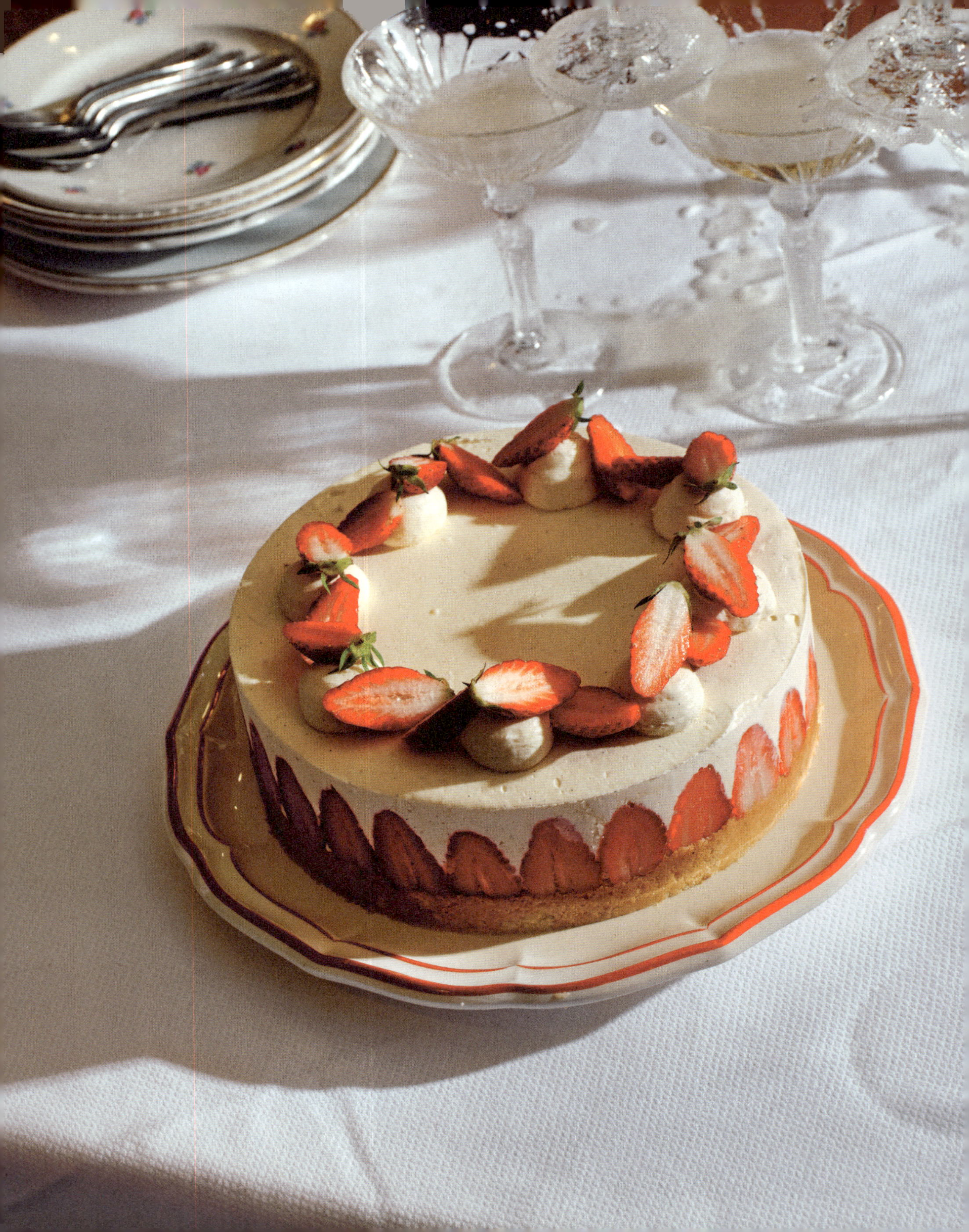

DESSERTS

Fraisier Cake

PREP TIME 1 HOUR 30 MINUTES

COOK TIME 40 MINUTES

REST TIME: 10 HOURS

SERVES 4 TO 6

For the sponge cake 5 egg whites · ⅓ cup plus 2 tablespoons (90 g) sugar · 4 egg yolks · ½ cup plus 2 teaspoons (65 g) flour, sifted **For the strawberry marmalade** 18 ounces (500 g) strawberries · 4 teaspoons (20 ml) water · 1½ cups plus 1 tablespoon (300 g) sugar · 4 teaspoons (20 ml) lemon juice **For the syrup** ¾ cup plus 4 teaspoons (200 ml) water · ⅜ cup plus 1 tablespoon (75 g) vanilla sugar · 2 teaspoons (10 ml) dark rum **For the diplomat cream** *pastry cream:* 1 vanilla bean · 1 cup (230 ml) whole milk · 2 tablespoons (28 g) unsalted butter · 3 egg yolks · 3 tablespoons plus 1 teaspoon (40 g) sugar · 4½ teaspoons (12 g) cornstarch, sifted · *whipped cream:* ¾ cup plus 3 tablespoons (220 ml) heavy cream · ½ cup plus 2 tablespoons (140 g) mascarpone · ¼ cup (30 g) powdered sugar **To assemble** 18 ounces (500 g) strawberries

THE SPONGE CAKE —— Preheat the oven to 365°F (185°C). Beat the egg whites in the bowl of an electric mixer. When they become foamy, add the sugar gradually and beat until stiff peaks form. Fold in the egg yolks one at a time, working quickly but gently to avoid deflating the egg whites. Gently fold in the flour. Grease a 12-inch (30 cm) cake ring and place it on top of a baking sheet covered with parchment paper. Pour the batter into the cake ring and bake for 14 minutes. Once cooked, place the cake on a cooling rack and use a knife to remove it from the ring. Allow to cool.

THE STRAWBERRY MARMALADE —— Hull and halve the strawberries then add them to a pot with the water and cook over low heat, stirring frequently, until they soften and the sauce thickens. Add the sugar and continue stirring frequently for about 20 minutes. Remove the pot from the heat and stir in the lemon juice. Allow to cool.

THE SYRUP —— Add the water and vanilla sugar to a pot and bring to a boil. Remove from the heat and allow to cool, then stir in the rum.

THE DIPLOMAT CREAM —— To prepare the pastry cream, scrape the vanilla seeds from the bean, then add with the milk and butter to a pot and bring to a simmer. Add the egg yolks and sugar to a bowl and whisk to combine, then incorporate the cornstarch.

Once the milk-vanilla-butter mixture reaches a simmer, slowly pour it into the egg-sugar-cornstarch mixture while whisking vigorously to combine. Continue whisking over medium heat. Add the mixture back to the pot, then continue whisking for 1 minute after the mixture begins to boil. Transfer the pastry cream to a bowl and cover with plastic wrap directly in contact with the surface of the cream. Chill the pastry cream in the refrigerator for at least 4 hours before use. To make the whipped cream, combine the cream, mascarpone, and powdered sugar in a bowl and whisk until soft peaks form. Beat the pastry cream for 2 to 3 minutes, until shiny. Gently fold the whipped cream into the pastry cream one-third at a time so that the cream doesn't collapse. Refrigerate.

TO ASSEMBLE —— Line a cake ring that is 8 inches (20 cm) in diameter and 1½–2 inches (4–5 cm) high with parchment paper. Cut the cake in half widthwise. Place one half in the cake ring. Use a pastry brush to spread a generous layer of syrup on the cake. Cut a portion of the strawberries in half and arrange them around the perimeter of the circle. Top with diplomat cream. Dice the strawberries (save a few for decoration) and mix into the marmalade. Spread a layer of the strawberry mixture on top of the pastry cream, then cover with another layer of cream. Place the second cake round on top and cover completely with cream. Use a spatula to smooth the cream. Chill in the refrigerator for at least 6 hours before serving. Before serving, arrange the remaining strawberries on top for decoration.

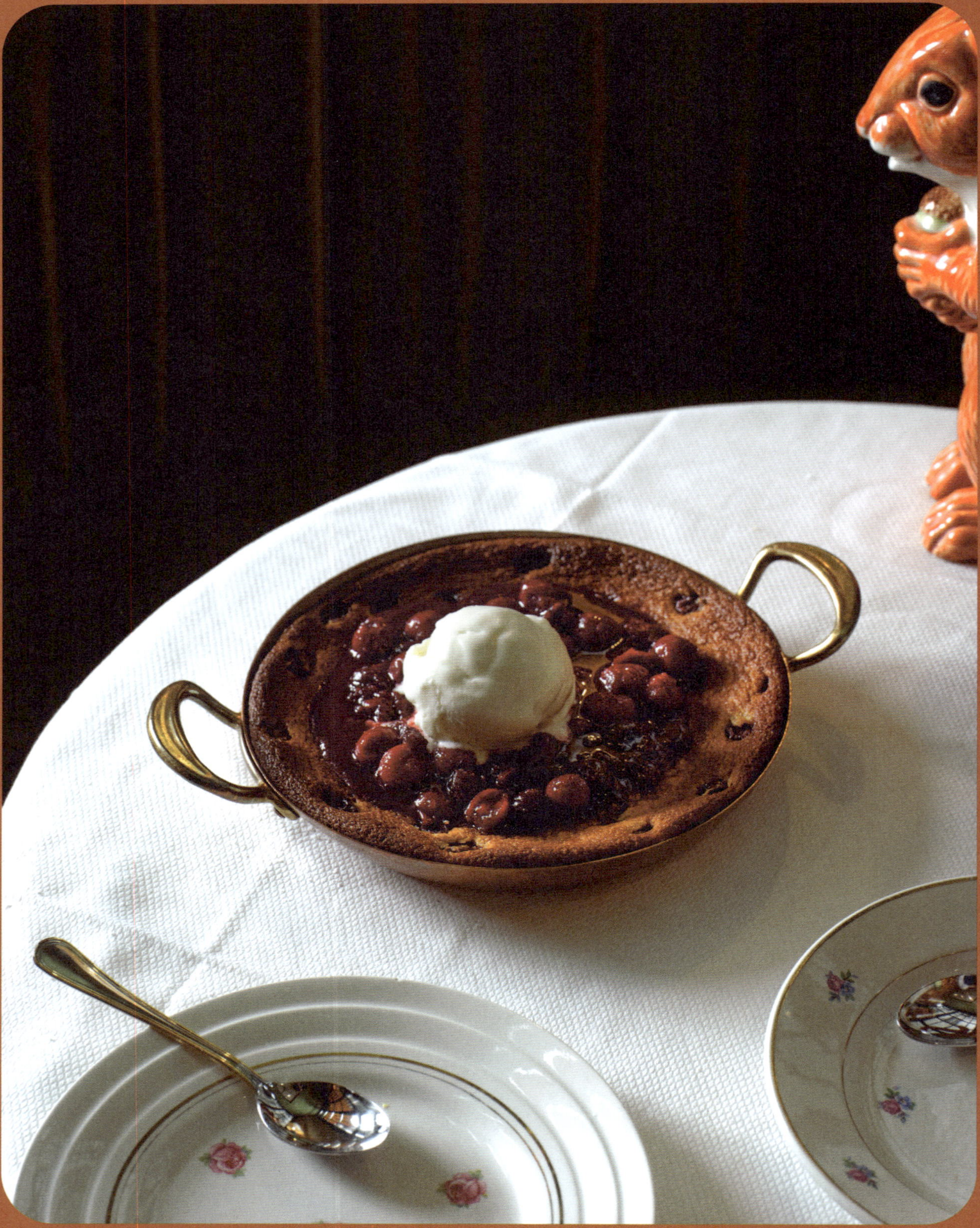

Cherry Clafoutis

Clafoutis aux cerises

PREP TIME
15 MINUTES

COOK TIME
40 MINUTES

REST TIME: 15 MINUTES

SERVES 4 TO 6

Butter, for greasing the pan

¼ cup plus 2 teaspoons (35 g) flour

5 ½ teaspoons (15 g) cornstarch

3 ounces (85 g) whole eggs

⅓ cup plus 4 teaspoons (80 g) brown sugar

¼ cup (55 g) crème fraîche

5 ½ ounces (150 g) cherries

1 frozen yogurt scoop per person

Grease a clafoutis pan with butter. Preheat the oven to 325°F (160°C).

THE BATTER —— Sift the flour and cornstarch. Combine the eggs and brown sugar in a bowl and mix well. Add the crème fraîche and stir to combine. Finally, mix in the flour and cornstarch. Pour the batter into the pan.

TO BAKE —— Pit and halve the cherries, then spread evenly on top of the batter. Bake for 40 minutes. Let rest for 15 minutes, then serve warm with a scoop of frozen yogurt.

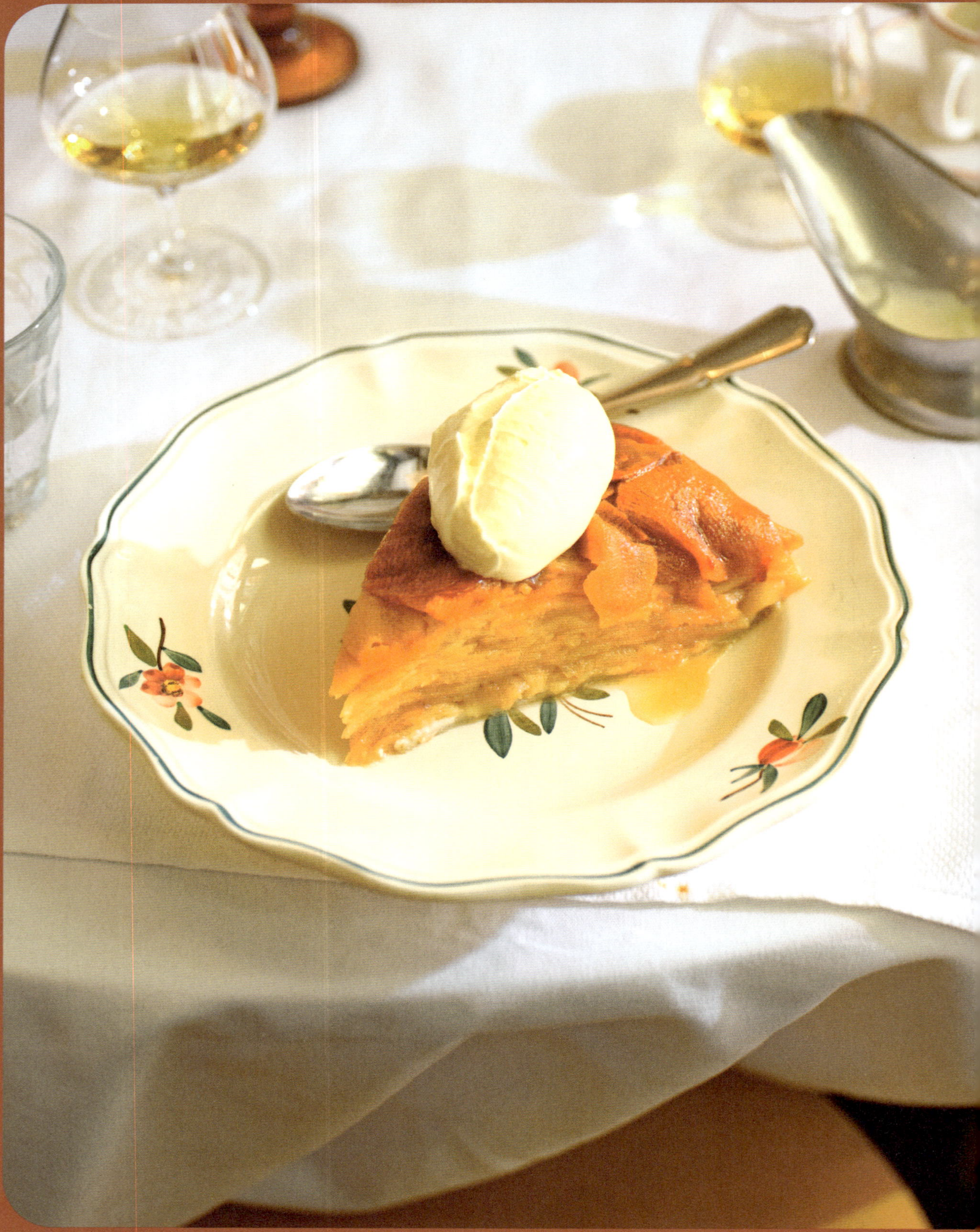

DESSERTS

Tarte Tatin

PREP TIME 30 MINUTES **COOK TIME 30 MINUTES** **REST TIME 30 MINUTES**

SERVES 4 TO 6

For the caramel 1 cup plus 2 teaspoons (200 g) sugar · ¼ cup (60 ml) water 4 teaspoons (20 ml) lemon juice **For the apples** 6 apples · 2 tablespoons plus 1½ teaspoons (30 g) vanilla sugar · 1 teaspoon (2 g) cinnamon **To assemble** 1 butter pie crust (page 211) or store-bought puff pastry

THE CARAMEL —— Add all the caramel ingredients to a pot and heat over low, stirring continuously, until it turns golden brown. Cover a baking sheet with parchment paper and place a tart ring on top. Pour the caramel into the tart ring and let cool to room temperature.

THE APPLES —— Peel the apples, cut in half, and remove the cores. Use a mandolin to cut each half into thin slices. Transfer to mixing bowl, sprinkle with vanilla sugar and cinnamon, then stir to combine.

TO ASSEMBLE AND BAKE —— Preheat the oven to 400°F (200°C). Completely cover the top of the caramel with apple slices, then layer the rest evenly on top. Roll the dough out on top of the apples and pierce the top with a fork. Put the tart in the oven, then lower the temperature to 350°F (180°C) and bake for about 25 minutes. Let rest for 30 minutes at room temperature before inverting onto your serving dish. Serve with a scoop of ice cream.

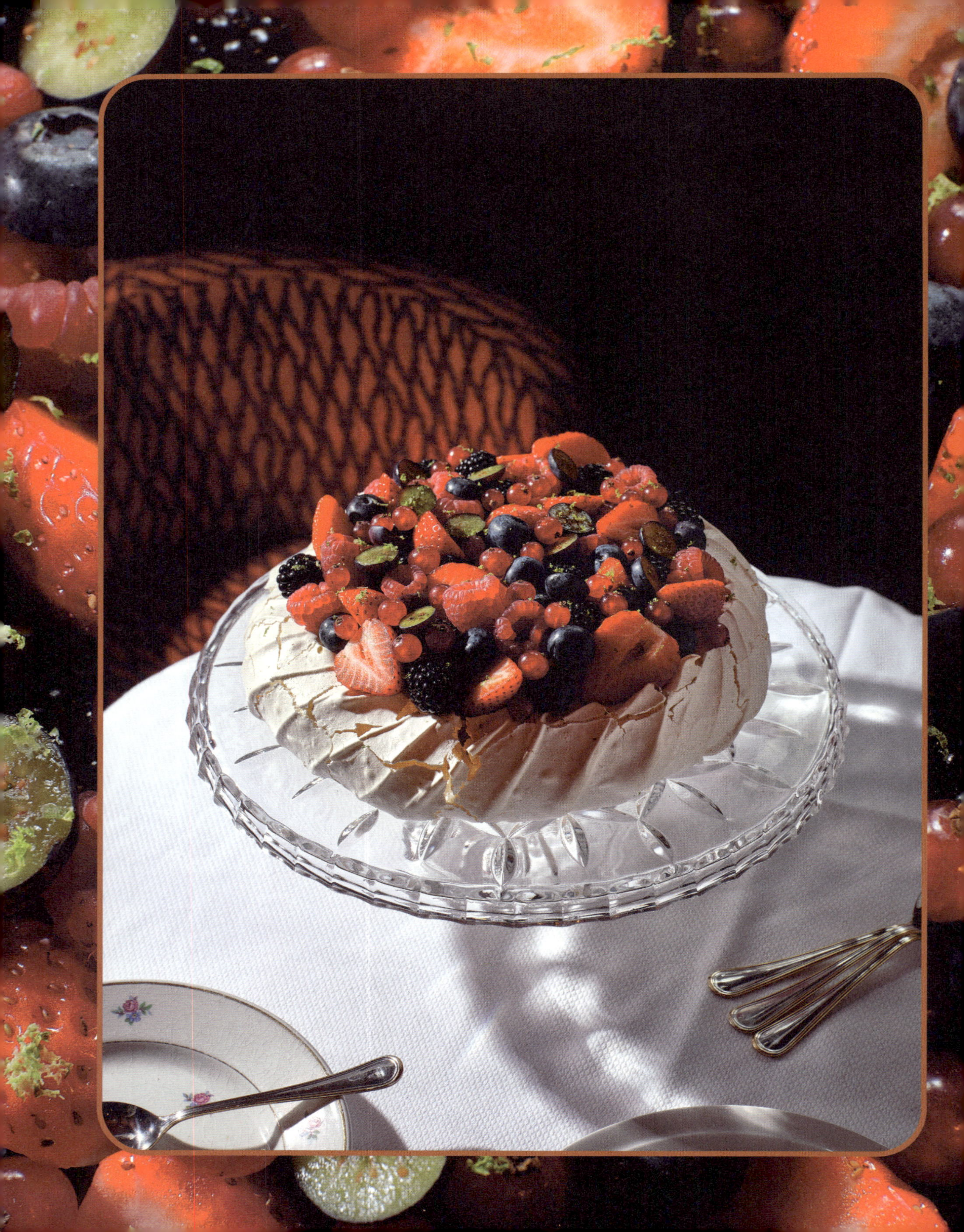

Berry Pavlova

Pavlova aux baies

PREP TIME 45 MINUTES

COOK TIME 2 HOURS

REST TIME: 6 HOURS

SERVES 4 TO 6

For the meringue

¾ cup (90 g) powdered sugar, sifted

5 egg whites

¾ cup plus 1 ½ teaspoons (150 g) superfine sugar

For the berry compote

18 ounces (500 g) mixed red fruits

4 teaspoons (20 g) water

1 ½ cups plus 1 tablespoon (300 g) sugar

4 teaspoons (20 g) lemon juice

For the vanilla whipped cream

Seeds from 1 vanilla bean

¾ cup (90 g) powdered sugar

¾ cup plus 2 tablespoons (200 g) mascarpone

1 ½ cups (350 g) heavy cream

To assemble

12 ounces (350 g) berries

Zest of 1 lime (optional)

Mint leaves (optional)

THE MERINGUE —— Preheat the oven to 200°F (90°C). Beat the egg whites with a hand mixer, gradually adding the superfine sugar. Once stiff peaks form, beat in the powdered sugar. Place a tart ring on a lined baking sheet. Gently scoop the meringue into the tart ring and form a well in the center. Bake about 1 hour 30 minutes, until it looks dry.

THE BERRY COMPOTE —— Rinse the fruit. Add to a pot with the water and cook over low heat until the fruit takes on a soft, jam-like consistency and the liquid has thickened. Add the sugar, stirring continuously. Cook at a low boil for about 20 minutes. Remove from the heat and add the lemon juice. Transfer to a bowl and set aside until cool.

THE VANILLA WHIPPED CREAM —— Bring the cream to a boil with the vanilla seeds and powdered sugar. Remove from the heat, mix in the mascarpone, and transfer to a bowl. Chill in the refrigerator for at least 6 hours. Whip the chilled cream until it's fluffy.

TO ASSEMBLE —— Place the meringue on a serving platter and top it with a thin layer of whipped cream. Add the compote and a handful of the berries, then top with another layer of whipped cream and finish with the rest of the fruit. Garnish with lime zest or mint leaves.

Around
THE TABLE

② FRAISIER
— *recipe page 184*

Auguste Escoffier and Pierre Lacam may have paved the way, but it was Gaston Lenôtre who crafted the ultimate hit of the 1960s: the *fraisier*. This iconic pastry is made with vanilla mousseline and strawberries (Brittany's prized *red gold*) sandwiched between two layers of sponge cake. At the time, Lenôtre had a different name in mind: *Bagatelle*, a nod to the elegant garden of Paris' Bois de Boulogne Park.

① PARIS-BREST
— *recipe page 171*

The Paris-Brest gets its name from an epic long-distance cycling race between Paris and Brest. The race's founder Pierre Giffard wanted to commemorate the event and pay tribute to the athletes, so he asked pastry chef Louis Durand, who owned a renowned pastry shop in Maisons-Lafitte to create a special cake. The unique pastry is inspired by the shape of a bicycle wheel.

③ TARTE TATIN
— *recipe page 189*

The story behind this dish is one worth knowing. *Tarte Tatin*, the famous upside-down tart, is often credited to either absent-mindedness or clumsiness. Another theory that the Tatin sisters, who managed their family's esteemed hunting lodge in the Loir-et-Cher, stumbled upon an old regional specialty in an old cookbook and gave it a new twist. Regardless of its true origins, one fact remains: the owner of Maxim's in Paris was so enchanted by it that he added it to his menu with the name "The Tatin Sisters' Tart" as a tribute.

⑤ PAVLOVA
— *recipe page 191*

Pavlova owes its name to the legendary Russian ballerina Anna Pavlova. Created in her honor during her tour of Oceania in the 1920s, the dessert's origins remain a point of rivalry between Australia and New Zealand. Among the different stories, the most enchanting is that of a Wellington chef who was so mesmerized by the dancer's tutu and grace that he created a dessert as light and airy as her dance.

④ BOUTE-HORS
— *general*

In the Middle Ages, no grand feast was complete without the traditional *boute-hors*. This ritual followed the *issue de table*, which was a course similar to a modern dessert, featuring fruits and pastries. Once the table was cleared, guests often moved to another room to enjoy the boute-hors as a digestif. This final course included sugar-coated almonds and candied fruits paired with Hypocras, a sweetened and spiced red wine.

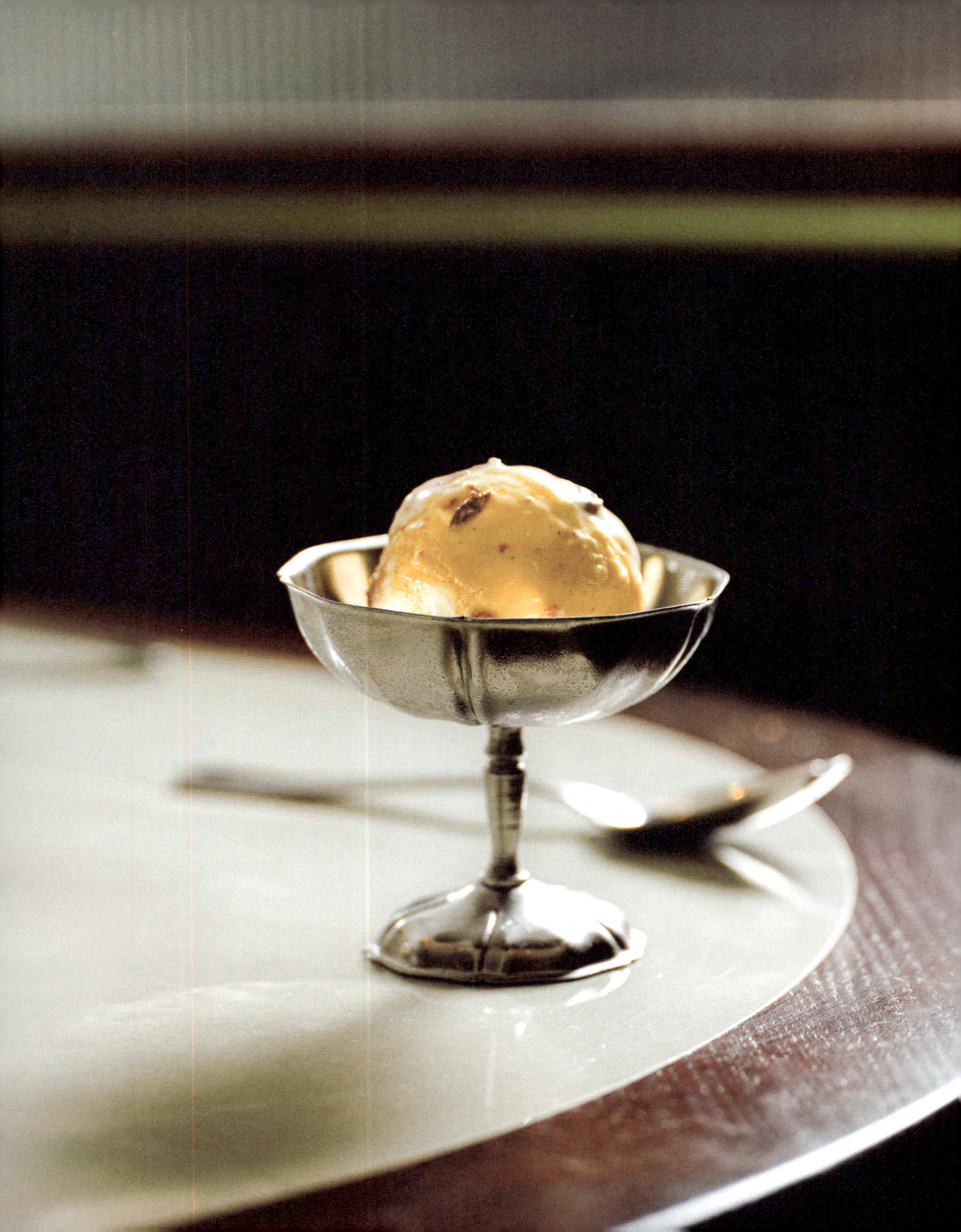

DESSERTS

Rum Raisin Ice Cream

Parfait glacé rhum-raisins

**PREP TIME
15 MINUTES**
SOAK: 24 HOURS

SERVES 4

**COOK TIME
2 MINUTES**
FREEZE: OVERNIGHT

1 ounce (30 g) raisins

2 tablespoons (30 ml) light rum

½ vanilla bean

6 egg yolks

1 tablespoon (15 g) water

5 tablespoons (60 g) sugar

¾ cup plus 2 teaspoons (190 ml) heavy cream

THE RAISINS —— Soak the raisins in the rum for 24 hours before use.

THE CUSTARD —— Scrape the seeds from the vanilla bean. Beat the egg yolks and vanilla seeds in a bowl. Combine the water and sugar in a saucepan and bring to a low boil. Slowly pour this syrup into the eggs with the mixer still running. Continue mixing until the custard has completely cooled. Set aside.

TO ASSEMBLE —— Whip the cream, then fold the whipped cream into the custard. Drain the raisins and mix into the cream-custard mixture. Chill in the freezer overnight before serving.

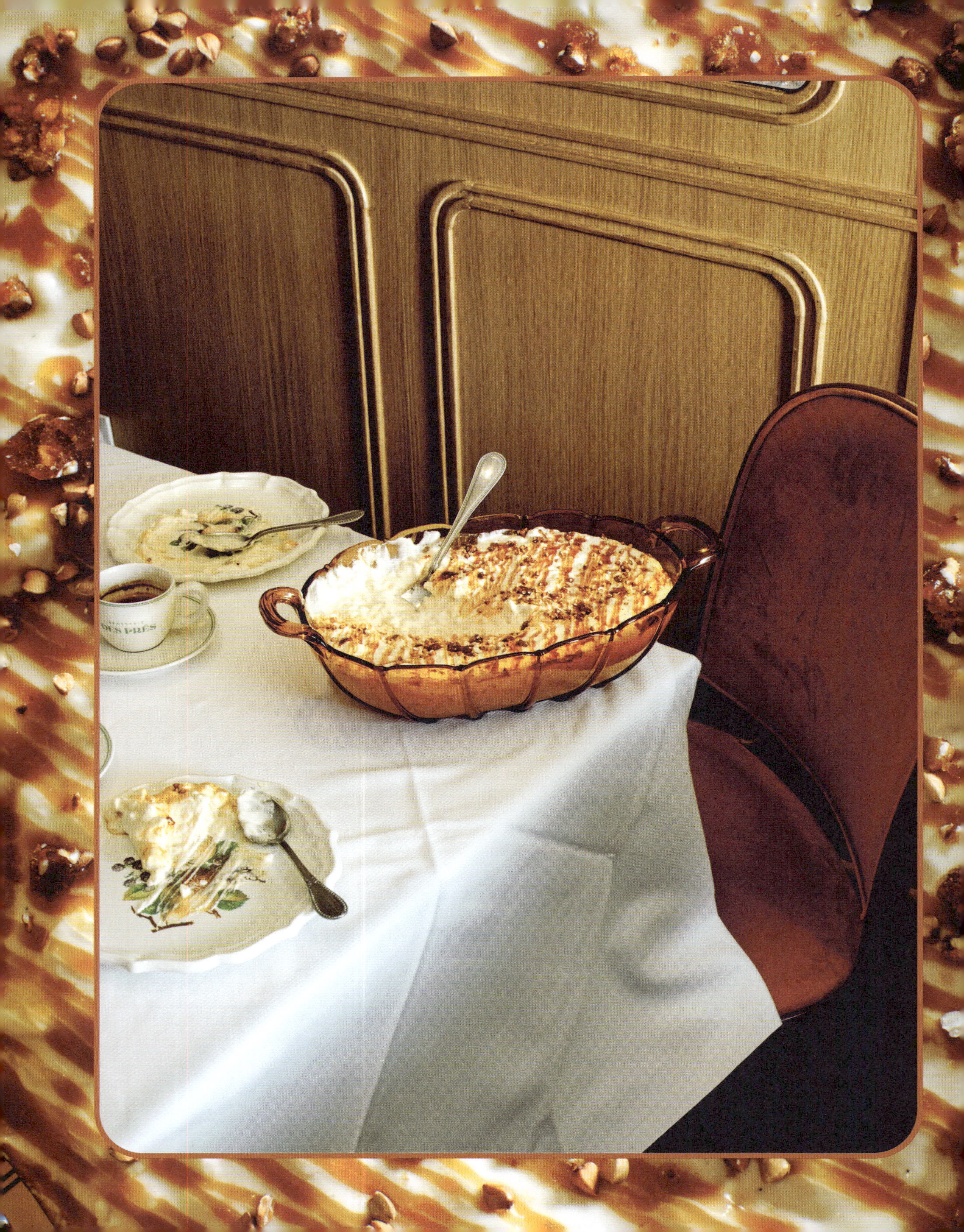
DES PRÉS

DESSERTS

Rice Pudding
Riz au lait

PREP TIME 15 MINUTES

COOK TIME 30 MINUTES

SERVES 4

For the salted caramel

¾ cup plus 4¼ teaspoons (200 g) heavy cream

¾ cup plus 4 teaspoons (160 g) sugar

4¼ teaspoons (20 g) butter

1 teaspoon (2 g) sea salt

For the rice pudding

¾ cup (140 g) short-grain rice

1 vanilla bean

¾ cup plus 4 teaspoons (200 ml) heavy cream

2½ cups (600 ml) whole milk

½ cup plus 1 teaspoon (100 g) sugar

For the whipped cream

¾ cup plus 4 teaspoons (200 ml) heavy cream

¼ cup (30 g) powdered sugar

THE SALTED CARAMEL — Add the cream to a saucepan, bring to a boil, then set aside. Caramelize the sugar in a dry pan over high heat until it turns golden brown. Pour the hot cream into the pan. Stir in the butter and cook for about 5 minutes. Remove from the heat and add the sea salt. Allow to cool.

THE RICE PUDDING — Rinse the rice until the water runs clear, then repeat.

Scrape the vanilla seeds out of the bean. Add the cream, milk, and vanilla seeds to a pot and bring to a boil. Reduce the heat to low and add the rice. Cook for about 20 minutes, stirring frequently. Remove from the heat, add the sugar, and stir gently until it has completely dissolved. Return the pot to the heat for 1 minute. Transfer the rice pudding to a bowl and allow to cool.

THE WHIPPED CREAM — In a mixing bowl, whip the cream and powdered sugar until fluffy. Gently fold the whipped cream into the rice pudding in thirds. The mixture will become creamy.

TO PLATE — Scoop the rice pudding onto a serving platter and top with the salted caramel.

DESSERTS

Crème Caramel

| PREP TIME 15 MINUTES | COOK TIME 40 MINUTES | REST TIME OVERNIGHT |

SERVES 4 TO 6

For the caramel 1 cup plus 2 tablespoons plus 1 teaspoon (220 g) sugar 4 teaspoons (20 ml) water · 1 teaspoon (5 ml) lemon juice **For the cream** 4 whole eggs · 1 egg yolk · 1 teaspoon vanilla extract · 5 tablespoons (60 g) sugar · 2¼ cups (550 ml) whole milk · ⅓ cup plus 4 teaspoons (100 ml) heavy cream

THE CARAMEL — Mix all the ingredients in a saucepan and cook over medium, stirring continuously, until the mixture turns golden brown. Pour directly into the pan. Allow to cool.

THE CREAM — Add the whole eggs, egg yolk, vanilla extract, and sugar to a bowl and whisk vigorously. Whisk in the milk and cream. Pour the mixture into the pan, on top of the cooled caramel.

TO BAKE — Preheat the oven to 375°F (190°C). Place the pan in an oven-safe dish and fill halfway with boiling water. Cover everything with aluminum foil. Put the dish in the oven, lower the heat to 325°F (160°C), and bake for 35 minutes. The cream should be set. Carefully remove the dish from the oven and chill in the refrigerator overnight. Remove the crème caramel from the pan and serve.

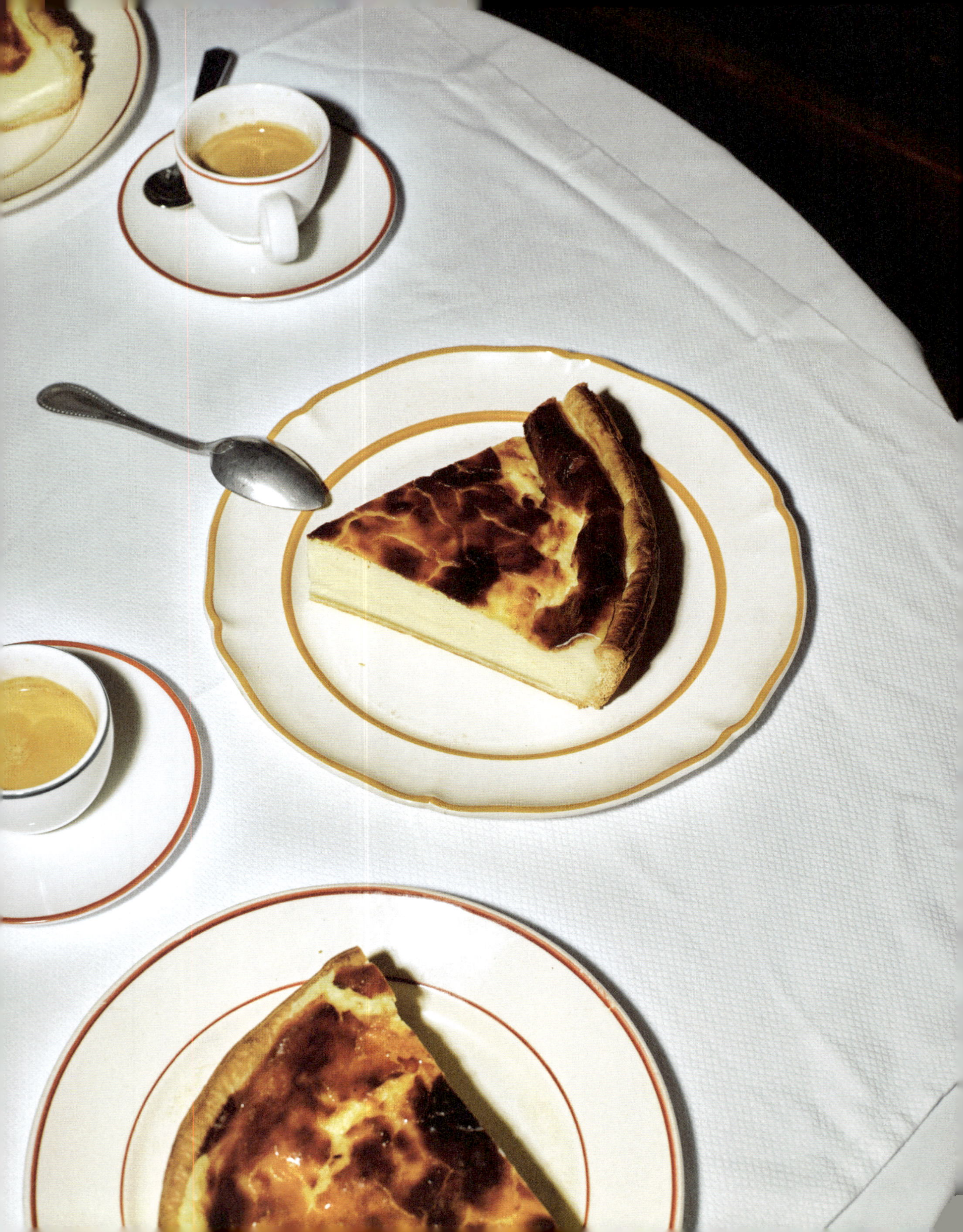

DESSERTS

Flan Parisien

PREP TIME 20 MINUTES

SERVES 4 TO 6

COOK TIME 50 MINUTES

REST TIME: OVERNIGHT

1 butter pie crust
1 vanilla bean
1 ⅔ cups (400 g) milk
⅓ cup plus 4 teaspoons (150 g) heavy cream
2 whole eggs
2 egg yolks
⅔ cup (130 g) sugar
5 tablespoons (40 g) cornstarch

THE DOUGH —— Unroll the pie crust into the pie pan and chill in the refrigerator.

THE CUSTARD —— Scrape the seeds from the vanilla bean. Heat the milk, cream, and vanilla seeds in a saucepan until it begins to simmer. Whisk the whole eggs, egg yolks, and sugar together in a bowl, then whisk in the cornstarch. Preheat the oven to 350°F (180°C). Whisk the milk mixture into the egg mixture vigorously, return the custard to the pot and bring to a boil. Once boiling, continue cooking for 1 minute, stirring continuously.

TO BAKE —— Pour the custard evenly onto the pie crust. Transfer to the oven, lower the temperature to 325°F (160°C), and bake for 40 minutes.

TO PLATE —— Once the tart is cooked, let it cool, then chill in the refrigerator. A custard tart is best prepared a day in advance. Pull the tart from the refrigerator 30 minutes before serving it and remove from the pie pan.

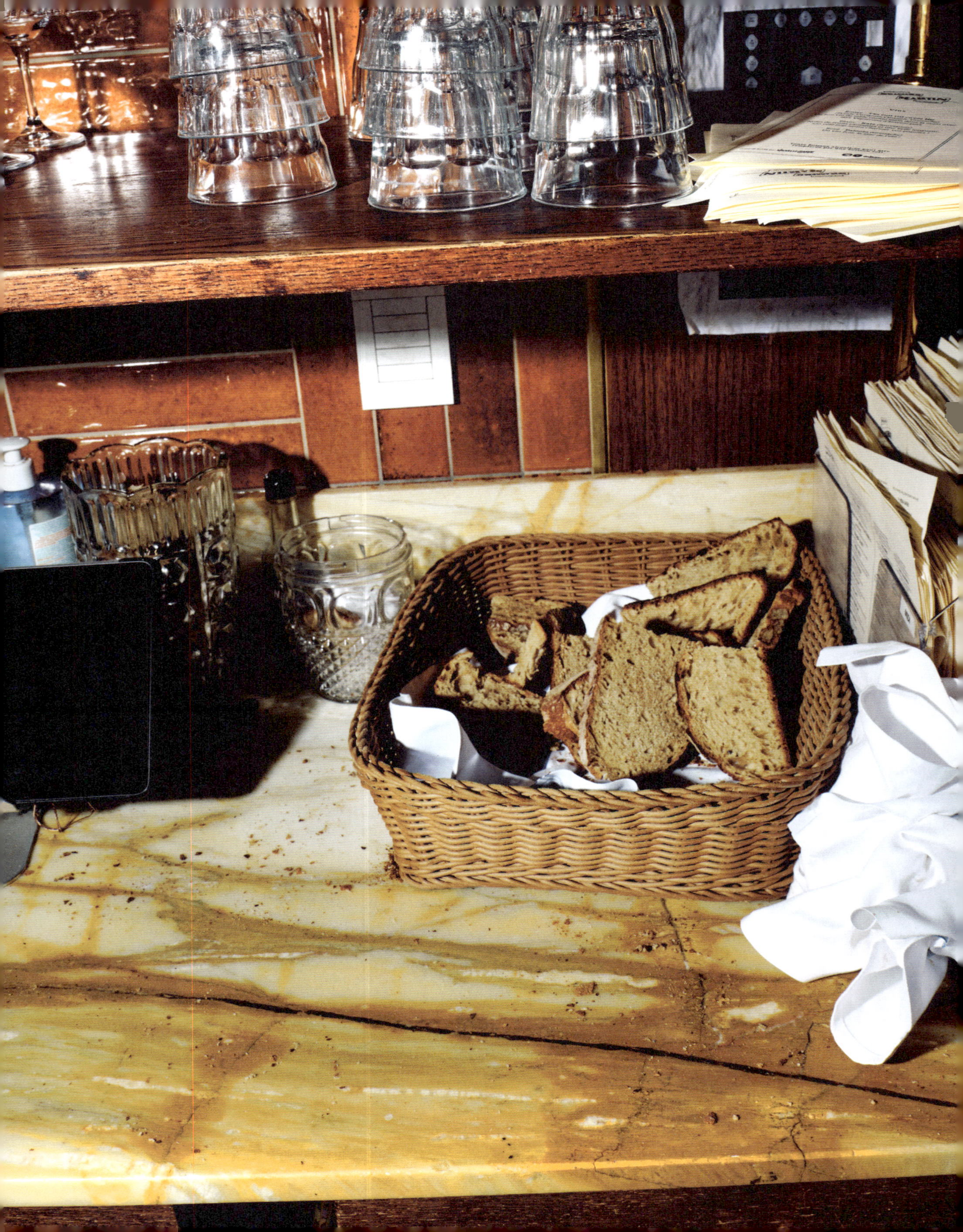

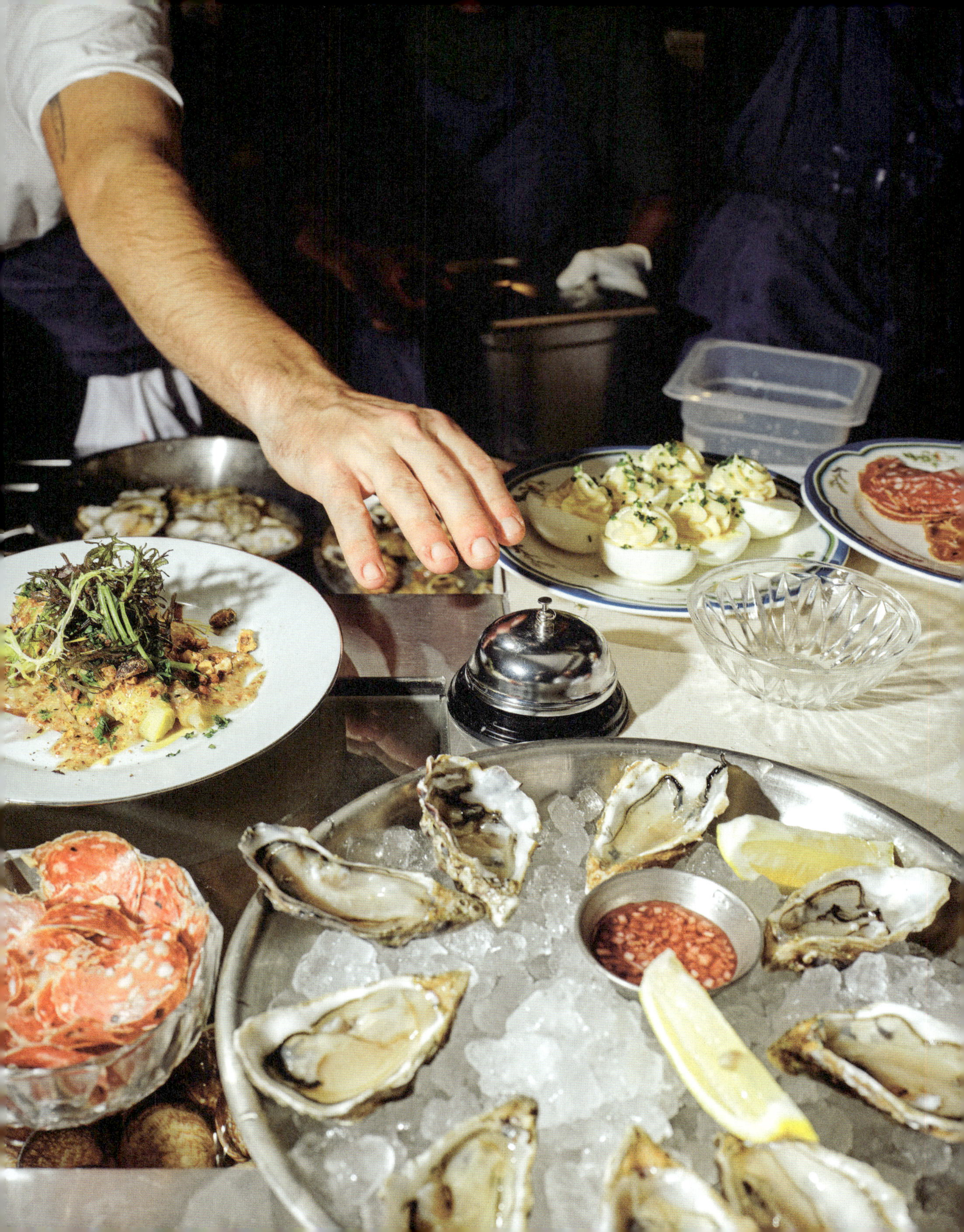

INSPIRÉE DU BOUCHON 68 rue Mercière
Lyon 02

BRASSERIE
DES DEUX RIVES

BASE RECIPES

Basic Stocks

MAKES 8½ CUPS (2 L) OF STOCK / ½ CUP (100 ML) OF AU JUS

PREP AND COOK TIME ABOUT 4 HOURS

Brown Stock

4½ POUNDS (2 KG) BONES (CHICKEN WINGS, BONES, MEAT TRIMMINGS, ETC.) · ½ CUP WHITE WINE
ALL THE LEFTOVER VEGETABLES IN THE REFRIGERATOR · 2 ONIONS · 1 HEAD OF GARLIC · SALT · 1 BOUQUET GARNI

Preheat the oven to 425° F (220°C). Spread the bones evenly across a rimmed baking dish. Bake for 40 minutes, flipping halfway. Remove the bones from the dish once they are golden brown. Add the wine to deglaze. Transfer this sauce to a bowl and set aside.

Wash and roughly chop the vegetables and peel and chop the onion and garlic cloves. Add the vegetables to a large pot and sweat with a pinch of salt, then add the roasted bones and sauce. Cover with water, add the bouquet garni, and bring to a boil. Cook for about 3 hours at a low boil, skimming away any foam that rises to the top. Strain the stock and adjust the seasoning if necessary. The stock can be stored in an airtight container in the refrigerator for several days or frozen.

Au Jus

4½ POUNDS (2 KG) BONES (CHICKEN WINGS, BONES, MEAT TRIMMINGS, ETC.) · ½ CUP WHITE WINE · ALL THE LEFTOVER VEGETABLES IN THE REFRIGERATOR · 2 ONIONS
1 HEAD OF GARLIC · 1 BOUQUET GARNI · SALT

An au jus is made simply by slowly reducing brown stock in a large pot to intensify the flavors. The au jus is ready when the consistency is thick enough to coat the back of a spoon.

Tip: Dip a soup spoon into the reduction and run your finger across the back side: if a clear line remains and the sauce doesn't run, the au jus is ready. It freezes very well; try freezing it in an ice cube tray for convenient portioning.

White Stock

4½ POUNDS (2 KG) BONES (CHICKEN WINGS, BONES, MEAT TRIMMINGS, ETC.) · ½ CUP WHITE WINE · ALL THE LEFTOVER VEGETABLES IN THE REFRIGERATOR · 2 ONIONS · 1 HEAD OF GARLIC · 1 BOUQUET GARNI · SALT

A white stock is similar to a brown stock, but the bones are first blanched rather than roasted. To blanch the bones, add them to a large pot of cold water and bring to a boil. Cook for about 5 minutes, skimming away any foam that rises to the top. Remove the bones from the pot.

Continue with the recipe for brown stock, beginning with the step of cleaning the vegetables.

Vegetable Bouillon

MAKES 8½ CUPS (2 L)

PREP AND COOK TIME 1 HOUR 30 MINUTES

2 CARROTS · 2 ONIONS · 1 LEEK · ALL THE LEFTOVER VEGETABLES IN THE REFRIGERATOR AS WELL AS THE SCRAPS · 1 SHALLOT · SALT · 1 CUP WHITE WINE 1 GARLIC CLOVE · 1 BOUQUET GARNI

Wash and peel the vegetables, then chop into large pieces. Add the vegetables to a large pot and sweat with a pinch of salt. Add the white wine and reduce by half. Fill the pot with enough water to cover the vegetables, add the garlic and the bouquet garni, and bring to a boil. Reduce the heat and cook at a low boil for about 1 hour, skimming away any foam that rises to the top. Strain the bouillon and adjust seasoning if necessary. Store in an airtight container in the refrigerator or freeze.

For a more deeply colored bouillon, sear two onion halves and add these to the pot with the vegetables. Bouillon can be used in many ways—for example, as a poaching liquid, to concentrate the flavors of soups, or to glaze vegetables.

Fish Fumet

PREP AND COOK TIME 1 HOUR 30 MINUTES

MAKES 4¼ CUPS (1 L)

REST TIME 30 MINUTES

1 ONION · 2 CARROTS · 1 CELERY RIB ALL THE LEFTOVER VEGETABLES IN THE REFRIGERATOR 2¼ POUNDS (1 KG) FISH BONES AND MEAT SCRAPS SALT · 1 CUP WHITE WINE · ½ CUP WHITE VERMOUTH 1 BOUQUET GARNI

Wash and peel the vegetables, then cut into large pieces. Separate the fish bones from the meat and soak them in a bowl of ice water for 30 minutes to remove any impurities.

Sweat the vegetables in a large pot with a pinch of salt, then add the bones and scraps. Add the white wine and vermouth. Reduce until almost all the liquid has evaporated, then fill with water to cover the vegetables. Add the bouquet garni and bring to a boil. Simmer for 1 hour, skimming away any foam that rises to the top. Strain the fumet and store in an airtight container in the refrigerator or freeze.

Fish fumet can be used in many ways—for example, to poach fish, as a base for sauces like Nantua, Normande, and bonne femme, or to add flavor to soups.

Sauces

SERVES 4

PREP TIME 25 MINTUES

Sabayon

4 EGG YOLKS · 5 TEASPOONS (25 ML) WATER · 1 PINCH SALT

Combine the egg yolks, water, and salt in a saucepan and whisk vigorously over low heat. The sabayon should increase in volume and become foamy. Remove the pot from the heat occasionally throughout cooking so that the mixture does not get too hot: you should be able to hold your hand against the pot without getting burned.

Béarnaise

2 TABLESPOONS (30 G) RED WINE VINEGAR · 2 TABLESPOONS (30 G) WHITE WINE · 1 TARRAGON SPRIG · 2 SHALLOTS · 1 PINCH MIGNONETTE PEPPER · SEVERAL CHERVIL LEAVES
SABAYON INGREDIENTS (AT LEFT)
1 CUP PLUS 2 TABLESPOONS (250 G) BUTTER

Heat a saucepan over low and pour the vinegar and wine into the pan. Strip the leaves from the tarragon sprig, set them aside, and add the stem to the pan. Finely chop the shallots and add to the pan with the mignonette pepper. Reduce until one-quarter of the liquid remains.

In the meantime, chop a few of the tarragon and chervil leaves. Once the liquid has reduced, add the sabayon ingredients (at left) to the pan and whisk until the mixture increases in volume.

Melt the butter in a second pan over low heat. Skim off the foam. Slowly pour the melted butter into the first pot, whisking continuously. Be careful not to add the solids (the white residue in the melted butter). The texture should be smooth and even. Adjust seasoning, if necessary. Add the chopped herbs to finish.

Mayonnaise

MAKES 1 SMALL POT — **PREP TIME 5 MINUTES**

ENOUGH FOR 3 DAYS

1 EGG YOLK · 1 TEASPOON DIJON MUSTARD · 1 PINCH SEA SALT
1¼ CUPS (300 G) NEUTRAL OIL
1 TEASPOON RED WINE VINEGAR · PEPPER

Add the egg yolk, mustard, and salt to a bowl and whisk until smooth. Whisk a drizzle of oil into the mixture, until the desired consistency has been achieved.

Once the mayonnaise is emulsified, whisk in the vinegar and adjust the seasoning as necessary. For a spicy mayo, add diced sweet peppers, a dash of lemon juice, ground pepper (like cayenne, Espelette, or paprika), and a bit of pickle juice.

Vinaigrette

MAKES 1 SMALL JAR — **PREP TIME 5 MINUTES**

ENOUGH FOR 1 WEEK

½ CUP (120 G) WHOLE-GRAIN MUSTARD
2 TABLESPOONS (30 G) RED WINE VINEGAR
1 CUP (250 ML) SUNFLOWER OIL
SALT AND PEPPER

Mix the mustard and vinegar together in a large bowl. Pour in a drizzle of oil while whisking continuously, until the mixture is emulsified. Season with salt and pepper.

Try substituting different types of mustard, oil, and vinegar to vary the flavors of this base recipe.

Hollandaise

SABAYON INGREDIENTS (PAGE 208)
1 CUP (250 G) BUTTER · JUICE OF 1 LEMON
SALT AND PEPPER

Prepare a sabayon sauce. Melt the butter in a saucepan over low heat. Skim off the foam. Slowly pour the butter into the sabayon while whisking continuously; be careful not to add the whey (the white residue in the melted butter). Add the lemon juice and whisk until the texture is smooth. Adjust seasoning if necessary.

Herbed Oil

MAKES ¾ CUP (200 ML)

10 MINUTES + 2 HOURS REST TIME

2 BUNCHES FRESH HERBS (YOUR CHOICE) + GREEN TOPS FROM VEGETABLES (LEEK TOPS, CELERY LEAVES, CARROT GREENS, ETC.) · ¾ CUP (200 ML) NEUTRAL OIL · 1 PINCH SALT

Bring a pot of salted water to a boil. Submerge the herbs and green vegetable tops in the water for 30 seconds, then shock in an ice bath to maintain their vibrant green color. Remove the herbs from the ice bath and squeeze out as much excess water as possible. Transfer to a blender with the oil and salt and process at medium speed for 4 minutes.

Transfer the oil to a bowl and set aside to infuse for a minimum of 2 hours. Use a cheesecloth to strain the solids from the oil. Transfer the oil to an airtight container and store in a cool, dark place.

Pickled Vegetables

MAKES ONE 32-OUNCE (1L) JAR

PREP TIME 30 MINUTES

1½ POUNDS (750 G) SEASONAL VEGETABLES · 1 CUP (300 ML) WATER · ⅔ CUP (200 ML) VINEGAR (CIDER, RICE, WINE, ETC.) · 5 TEASPOONS (30 G) SALT · ⅓ CUP (100 G) SUGAR · A FEW BAY LEAVES · 1 GARLIC CLOVE · SPICES OF YOUR CHOICE (FENNEL SEEDS, PEPPER, MUSTARD SEEDS, ETC.)

The 3-2-1 method is a tried-and-true ratio for perfect pickles: 3 parts water, 2 parts vinegar, and 1 part sugar. Salt is optional, if you prefer more sour flavors. Wash the vegetables well and cut into the desired shape.

Add the water and vinegar to a pot and bring to a boil. Add the salt and sugar and whisk until dissolved. Add the aromatics and boil for 1 to 2 minutes. Place the vegetables in a sterilized container and pour the boiling liquid on top. Seal the container and turn it upside down. Pickled vegetables will keep for several weeks.

Pastry

MAKES 1 CRUST | **PREP TIME 10 MINUTES** | **REST TIME 30 MINUTES**

Butter Pie Crust

1 2/3 CUPS (200 G) FLOUR · 2 TEASPOONS SUGAR
1 PINCH SALT · 8 TEASPOONS (40 ML) WATER · 1 EGG YOLK
7 TABLESPOONS (100 G) BUTTER, SOFTENED

Pour the flour onto your workspace and create a well. Combine the sugar and salt in the well, then add the water and egg yolk. Use your fingers to crumble the softened butter into the well last. Fold the flour over this mixture and quickly begin to knead the dough until the texture becomes smooth and does not stick to your work surface. Roll the dough into a ball and chill in the refrigerator for at least 30 minutes before using it.

Shortcrust Pastry

1 2/3 CUPS (200 G) FLOUR · 1/2 CUP (100 G) SUGAR · 8 TEASPOONS (40 ML) WATER
1 EGG YOLK · 7 TABLESPOONS (100 G) BUTTER, SOFTENED

Follow the steps for the butter crust recipe, but omit the salt and increase the sugar to 1/2 cup (100 g).

Choux Pastry

SERVES 4 | **PREP TIME 45 MINUTES**

1/3 CUP PLUS 4 TEASPOONS (100 ML) MILK
1/3 CUP PLUS 4 TEASPOONS (100 ML) WATER
7 TABLESPOONS (100 G) BUTTER SALT · 1 CUP
(125 G) FLOUR · 4 EGGS

Add the milk, water, butter, and salt to a pot. Bring to a boil, then remove from the heat and add the flour. Use a rigid spatula to vigorously stir the mixture until the texture becomes smooth. Return the pot to the heat and cook the mixture over low until the dough pulls away from the sides of the pot.

Remove the pot from the heat and mix in the eggs one at a time, stirring until the consistency is smooth. Pour the dough into a piping bag and pipe and bake as desired.

BRASSERIE

BARBOTIN

21 Cours Honoré
d'Estienne d'Orves
Marseille 01

BRASSERIE ENSOLEILLÉE

APPENDIX

RECIPE INDEX

STARTERS

Sausage in Brioche	28
Chilled Tomato Soup	31
Haricots Verts with Gribiche	32
French Onion Soup	35
Country Terrine	36
Frisée and Lardon Salad	40
Stuffed Clams	43
Celery Root Remoulade	44
Poached Eggs in Red Wine	46
Foie Gras	49
Mackerel Escabèche	50
Asparagus with Mousseline Sauce	54
Leeks with Vinaigrette	56
Eggs with Mayo	59
Shrimp Croquettes	61
Stuffed Mushrooms	62
Octopus and Tomato Pie	67

MEATS

Steak with Peppercorn Sauce	70
Endive and Ham Gratin	73
Stuffed Cabbage	75
Beef Stew	76
Cassoulet	79
Roast Chicken with Lemon Confit	82
Croque-Monsieur	84
Braised Chicken with Morels and Vin Jaune	87
Beef and Beer Stew	89
Braised Rabbit in Mustard Sauce	90
Braised Lamb Shoulder with White Bean Ragout	95
Veal Stew	96
Veal Axoa	99
Stuffed Veal	100
Cordon Bleu	102

FISH

Monkfish Stew	106
Braised Chicken with Crawfish	109
Salade Niçoise	111
Salt-Baked Sea Bass	114
Bouillabaisse	116
Skate Wing with Grenobloise Sauce	120
Mussels with Poulette Sauce	123
Sole Meunière	125
Scallops with Celery Root Purée	126

VEGGIE MAINS

Gnocchi Parisienne	130
Grilled Cheese à la Française	133
Veggie Quiche	134
Poached Eggs in Piperade	139
Onion Tarte Tatin	141
Vegetable Torte	143

SIDE DISHES

Ratatouille	146
Potatoes au Gratin	149
Potato Purée	151
Braised Peas with Spring Onions and Lettuce	155
Braised Gem Lettuces with Sauce Vierge	158
Rice Pilaf	161
Spring Vegetables	162
Frites	165

DESSERTS

Île Flottante	168
Paris-Brest	171
Pear and Almond Tart	172
Chocolate Mousse	175
Lemon Meringue Tart	176
Crème Brûlée	179
Financiers	183
Fraisier Cake	185
Cherry Clafoutis	187
Tarte Tatin	189
Berry Pavlova	191
Rum Raisin Ice Cream	195
Rice Pudding	197
Crème Caramel	198
Flan Parisien	201

BASE RECIPES

Brown Stock	206
Au Jus	206
White Stock	206
Vegetable Bouillon	207
Fish Fumet	207
Sabayon	208
Béarnaise	208
Mayonnaise	209
Vinaigrette	209
Hollandaise	209
Herbed Oil	210
Pickled Vegetables	210
Butter Pie Crust	211
Shortcrust Pastry	211
Choux Pastry	211

INDEX

ALMOND
Financiers 183
Île Flottante 168
Pear and Almond Tart 172

ANCHOVY
Salade Niçoise 111

APPLE
Tarte Tatin 189

ARTICHOKE
Salade Niçoise 111

ASPARAGUS
Asparagus with
Mousseline Sauce 54
Spring Vegetables 162

BACON
Cassoulet 79

BASE RECIPES
Au Jus 206
Béarnaise 208
Brown Stock 206
Butter Pie Crust 211
Choux Pastry 211
Fish Fumet 207
Herbed Oil 210
Hollandaise 209
Mayonnaise 209
Pickled Vegetables 210
Sabayon 208
Shortcrust Pastry 211
Vegetable Bouillon 207
Vinaigrette 209
White Stock 206

BECHAMEL
Endive and Ham Gratin 73

BEEF
Beef and Beer Stew 89
Beef Stew 76
Steak with
Peppercorn Sauce 70

BELL PEPPER
Chilled Tomato Soup 31
Poached Eggs in Piperade 139
Ratatouille 146

BERRIES
Berry Pavlova 191

BREAD
Chilled Tomato Soup 31
French Onion Soup 35
Leeks with Vinaigrette 56

BREADCRUMBS
Cassoulet 79
Cordon Bleu 102
Shrimp Croquettes 61
Stuffed Clams 43
Stuffed Mushrooms 62

BROWN SUGAR
Beef and Beer Stew 89

BUTTER
Asparagus with
Mousseline Sauce 54
Roast Chicken with
Lemon Confit 82
Stuffed Clams 43

BUTTER PIE CRUST
Flan Parisien 201
Onion Tarte Tatin 141
Pear and Almond Tart 172
Tarte Tatin 189
Veggie Quiche 134

BUTTON MUSHROOMS
Gnocchi Parisienne 130
Poached Eggs in Red Wine 46
Stuffed Cabbage 75
Stuffed Mushrooms 62
Stuffed Veal 100
Veal Stew 96
Vegetable Torte 43

CARROT
Beef Stew 76
Bouillabaisse 116
Braised Chicken
with Crawfish 109
Braised Lamb Shoulder
with White Bean Ragout 95
Mackerel Escabèche 50
Spring Vegetables 162
Veal Stew 96

CELERY ROOT
Celery Root Remoulade 44
Scallops with
Celery Root Purée 126
Vegetable Torte 143

CHEDDAR
Grilled Cheese
à la Française 133

CHERRY
Cherry Clafoutis 187

CHERRY TOMATO
Salade Niçoise 111

CHERVIL
Roast Chicken with
Lemon Confit 82

CHICKEN
Braised Chicken
with Crawfish 109
Braised Chicken with
Morels and Vin Jaune 87
Roast Chicken with
Lemon Confit 82

CHILI PEPPERS
Braised Gem Lettuces
with Sauce Vierge 158
Veal Axoa 99

CHOCOLATE
Chocolate Mousse 175

CINNAMON
Tarte Tatin   189

CLAMS
Stuffed Clams   43

COGNAC
Foie Gras   49
Monkfish Stew   106
Steak with
Peppercorn Sauce   70

COMTÉ
Cordon Bleu   102
Croque-Monsieur   84
Endive and Ham Gratin   73
French Onion Soup   35
Gnocchi Parisienne   130
Grilled Cheese
à la Française   133
Shrimp Croquettes   61
Veggie Quiche   134

CONFIT DUCK THIGHS
Cassoulet   79

CORNICHON
Haricots Verts
with Gribiche   32

CRAWFISH
Braised Chicken
with Crawfish   109

CREAM
Asparagus with
Mousseline Sauce   54
Berry Pavlova   191
Braised Rabbit
in Mustard Sauce   90
Chocolate Mousse   175
Crème Brûlée   179
Crème Caramel   198
Flan Parisien   201
Fraisier Cake   185
Île Flottante   168
Potatoes au Gratin   149
Rice Pudding   197

Roast Chicken with
Lemon Confit   87
Rum Raisin Ice Cream   195
Steak with
Peppercorn Sauce   70
Stuffed Mushrooms   62
Veal Stew   96
Veggie Quiche   134

CUCUMBER
Salade Niçoise   111

DIJON MUSTARD
Braised Rabbit
in Mustard Sauce   90

EGG
Berry Pavlova   191
Cherry Clafoutis   187
Chocolate Mousse   175
Crème Brûlée   179
Crème Caramel   198
Eggs with Mayo   59
Financiers   183
Flan Parisien   201
Fraisier Cake   185
Frisée and Lardon Salad   40
Gnocchi Parisienne   130
Haricots Verts
with Gribiche   32
Île Flottante   168
Lemon Meringue Tart   176
Paris-Brest   171
Poached Eggs in Piperade   139
Poached Eggs in Red Wine   46
Rum Raisin Ice Cream   195
Salade Niçoise   111
Veggie Quiche   134

EGGPLANT
Ratatouille   146

ENDIVE
Endive and Ham Gratin   73

FAVA BEANS
Salade Niçoise   111

FOIE GRAS
Foie Gras   49

FRISÉE
Frisée and Lardon Salad   40

GEM LETTUCE
Braised Gem Lettuces
with Sauce Vierge   158

GOAT CHEESE
Haricots Verts
with Gribiche   32

GREEN CABBAGE
Beef Stew   76
Stuffed Cabbage   75

GROUND SAUSAGE
Stuffed Cabbage   75
Stuffed Mushrooms   62

HAM
Cordon Bleu   102
Croque-Monsieur   84
Endive and Ham Gratin   73

HAZELNUT
Leeks with Vinaigrette   56
Paris-Brest   171

HARICOTS VERTS
Haricots Verts
with Gribiche   32
Salade Niçoise   111

LAMB
Braised Lamb Shoulder
with White Bean Ragout   95

LEEK
Bouillabaisse   116
Leeks with Vinaigrette   56
Veggie Quiche   134

LEMON
Lemon Meringue Tart	176
Roast Chicken with Lemon Confit	82

LETTUCE
Braised Peas with Spring Onions and Lettuce	155
Salade Niçoise	111

MACKEREL
Mackerel Escabèche	50

MARROW BONES
Beef Stew	76

MASCARPONE
Berry Pavlova	191
Fraisier Cake	185

MAYONNAISE
Celery Root Remoulade	44
Eggs with Mayo	59

MILK
Crème Caramel	198
Flan Parisien	201
Île Flottante	168
Paris-Brest	171
Rice Pudding	197

MONKFISH
Bouillabaisse	116
Monkfish Stew	106

MORBIER
Grilled Cheese à la Française	133

MOREL MUSHROOMS
Braised Chicken with Morels and Vin Jaune	87

MORNAY SAUCE
Croque-Monsieur	84
Gnocchi Parisienne	130

MUSSELS
Mussels with Poulette Sauce	123

OCTOPUS
Octopus and Tomato Pie	67

OLIVES
Roast Chicken with Lemon Confit	82
Salade Niçoise	111

ONION
Country Terrine	36
French Onion Soup	35
Grilled Cheese à la Française	133
Onion Tarte Tatin	141
Veggie Quiche	134

PAIMPOL BEANS
Braised Lamb Shoulder with White Bean Ragout	95

PARSLEY
Stuffed Clams	43
Roast Chicken with Lemon Confit	82

PEAR
Pear and Almond Tart	172

PEAS
Spring Vegetables	162
Braised Peas with Spring Onions and Lettuce	155

PEPPERCORN
Steak with Peppercorn Sauce	70

PIGS FEET
Stuffed Mushrooms	62

PORK
Country Terrine	36

PORT
Foie Gras	49

POTATO
Beef Stew	76
French Fries	165
Gnocchi Parisienne	130
Mackerel Escabèche	50
Potato Purée	151
Potatoes au Gratin	149
Skate Wing with Grenobloise Sauce	120
Vegetable Torte	143

PRALINE PASTE
Paris-Brest	171

PROSCUITTO
Stuffed Cabbage	75

PUFF PASTRY
Vegetable Torte	143

RABBIT
Braised Rabbit in Mustard Sauce	90

RADISH
Salade Niçoise	111
Spring Vegetables	162

RAISINS
Rum Raisin Ice Cream	195

RICE
Rice Pudding	197
Rice Pilaf	161

ROCK FISH
Bouillabaisse	116

ROUGET BARBET
Bouillabaisse	116

RUM
Rum Raisin Ice Cream   195

SANDWICH BREAD (PAIN DE MIE)
Croque-Monsieur   84
Grilled Cheese à la Française   133

SAUCISSON (GARLIC)
Cassoulet   79

SAUCISSON (PISATCHIO)
Sausage in Brioche   28

SAUSAGE (MORTEAU)
Celery Root Remoulade   44

SAUSAGE (TOULOUSE)
Cassoulet   79

SCALLOPS
Scallops with Celery Root Purée   126

SEA BASS
Salt-Baked Sea Bass   114

SEA BREAM
Bouillabaisse   116

SHIITAKE MUSHROOMS
Stuffed Veal   100

SHORTCRUST PASTRY
Lemon Meringue Tart   176

SHRIMP
Shrimp Croquettes   61

SKATE WING
Skate Wing with Grenobloise Sauce   120

SMOKED BACON
Braised Peas with Spring Onions and Lettuce   155
Frisée and Lardon Salad   40
Gnocchi Parisienne   130
Poached Eggs in Red Wine   46
Stuffed Cabbage   75

SOLE
Sole Meunière   125

SPINACH
Vegetable Torte   143

SPRING ONION
Braised Peas with Spring Onions and Lettuce   155
Spring Vegetables   162

STRAWBERRY
Fraisier Cake   185

TARBAIS BEANS
Cassoulet   79

TOMATO
Bouillabaisse   116
Braised Gem Lettuces with Sauce Vierge   158
Chilled Tomato Soup   31
Monkfish Stew   106
Octopus and Tomato Pie   67
Poached Eggs in Piperade   139
Ratatouille   146
Veal Axoa   99

TURNIPS
Beef Stew   76
Spring Vegetables   162

VANILLA
Crème Brûlée   179
Flan Parisien   201
Fraisier Cake   185
Île Flottante   168
Pear and Almond Tart   172

Rice Pudding   197
Rum Raisin Ice Cream   195

VEAL
Cordon Bleu   102
Stuffed Veal   100
Veal Axoa   99
Veal Stew   96

VEAL STOCK
French Onion Soup   35

VIN JAUNE
Braised Chicken with Morels and Vin Jaune   87

WINE, RED
Poached Eggs in Red Wine   46

WINE, WHITE
Country Terrine   36
Mackerel Escabèche   50
Monkfish Stew   106
Mussels with Poulette Sauce   123
Braised Chicken with Crawfish   109

YEAST
Octopus and Tomato Pie   67
Poached Eggs in Red Wine   46
Sausage in Brioche   28

ZUCHINNI
Braised Gem Lettuces with Sauce Vierge   158
Ratatouille   146

Acknowledgments

A heartfelt thank-you to our executive chefs, Thibaut Darteyre and Baptiste Zwygart, for their immense talent, their fierce passion for French cuisine, and their dedication to creating and cooking our dishes.

To our pastry chef, Victoria Arosteguy, for her stunning desserts; to Théophile Hauser-Peretti, Antoine Casel, Raphaël Campion, Gaëlle Dieraert, and Céleste Martin for their invaluable assistance, and to all our cooks who expertly man the stoves of La Nouvelle Garde brasseries. Thank you for your dedication.

To our front-of-house staff on the floor, who welcome both new customers and our most loyal regulars every day with enthusiasm, warmth, and friendship.

To Lucie Turenne, whose brilliant design skills brought these stunning illustrations to life.

To Faustine Bohanne for her impeccable taste and remarkable talent in sourcing the finest tableware.

To Pierre Lucet-Penato and Garlone Bardel for your boundless energy, wisdom, and attention to detail.

A special thanks to the Marabout teams, the guardians of culture and knowledge, for continuing to tell stories—and most of all, for believing in this one.

Last but not least, to Victor and Charly, who believed in our fantastic vision to restore the brasserie and without whom the project would not have come to life. Thank you for your courage and unwavering determination, which made the Nouvelle Garde adventure possible.

And to all of you who have supported us with your kind words and insatiable appetite for our brasseries. We hope this book inspires you to cook, to savor, and to share.

Lou Le Bloas from La Nouvelle Garde

First published in 2024 by Marabout – Hachette Livre

This edition published in 2025 by Hardie Grant North America, an imprint of Hardie Grant Publishing.

All rights reserved. No part of this book may be reproduced in any form without written permission from the publisher.

Library of Congress Cataloging-in-Publication Data is available upon request.

Hardie Grant North America
2912 Telegraph Ave
Berkeley, CA 94705
hardiegrant.com

ISBN: 9781964786346
ebook ISBN: 9781964786353

Printed in China by Toppan
FIRST EDITION

Text: Lou Le Bloas of Nouvelle Garde

Recipe text: Thibaut Darteyre and Baptiste Zwygart of Nouvelle Garde

Layout: Studio Recto Verso

Illustrations: Lucie Turenne of Nouvelle Garde

Cover design: Toni Tajima

Translation: Maggie Smith

Typesetting: Hadley Hendrix

Hardie Grant
NORTH AMERICA